God against the Revolution

AMERICAN POLITICAL THOUGHT
Wilson Carey McWilliams and Lance Banning
Founding Editors

God against the Revolution

The Loyalist
Clergy's Case
against the
American
Revolution

Gregg L. Frazer

University Press of Kansas

Published by the University Press of Kansas (Lawrence, Kansas 66045), which was organized by the Kansas Board of Regents and is operated and funded by Emporia State University, Fort Hays State University, Kansas State University, Pittsburg State University, the University of Kansas, and Wichita State University

© 2018 by the University Press of Kansas
All rights reserved

Library of Congress Cataloging-in-Publication Data

Names: Frazer, Gregg L., author.
Title: God against the revolution : the loyalist clergy's case against the American Revolution / Gregg L. Frazer.
Description: Lawrence, Kansas : University Press of Kansas, [2018] | Series: American political thought | Includes bibliographical references and index.
Identifiers: LCCN 2018027415
ISBN 9780700626960 (cloth : alk. paper)
ISBN 9780700630585 (paperback)
ISBN 9780700626977 (ebook)
Subjects: LCSH: American loyalists. | United States—History—Revolution, 1775–1783—Religious aspects—Christianity. | United States—Politics and government—1775–1783.
Classification: LCC E277 .F885 2018 | DDC 973.3/1—dc23.
LC record available at https://lccn.loc.gov/2018027415.

British Library Cataloguing-in-Publication Data is available.

10 9 8 7 6 5 4 3 2

The paper used in this publication is acid free and meets the minimum requirements of the American National Standard for Permanence of Paper for Printed Library Materials z39.48–1992.

To my wonderful wife Leanne,

for her selfless love and steadfast support

CONTENTS

Acknowledgments   ix

1. The Context for the Loyalist Argument   1
2. Biblical Arguments   36
3. Theoretical Arguments from the Nature of Government   78
4. Legal Arguments   99
5. Rational Arguments Regarding the American Situation   127
6. Rational Arguments Based on Colonial Actions   172

Epilogue   227

Notes   235

Bibliography   255

Index   261

ACKNOWLEDGMENTS

I am grateful for the interest, encouragement, and input of faculty colleagues at The Master's University. Special appreciation goes to Esther Chua, Clyde Greer, Kurt Hild, and Grant Horner for willingly answering questions of style and word choice and to Abner Chou for being a sounding board. I am indebted to John Stead for a timely sabbatical, during which a principal part of the book was written. I also wish to thank the amazing Grace Kamffer for a number of seemingly impossible-to-find interlibrary loan acquisitions.

Thanks are due to Christians in Political Science and the Conference on Faith and History for opportunities to present parts of this book at conferences that produced feedback from political theory and history colleagues at other institutions. Thanks as well to Fred Woodward for seeing the potential of this work and enthusiastically supporting it from the beginning.

Finally, I greatly appreciate the encouragement and support given by family and friends.

God against the Revolution

1 The Context for the Loyalist Argument

> If government was God's ordinance to man, little more need be said. Disagreement with government became rebellion against authority and, in turn, *opposition to God.*
>
> —Lawrence Leder

> Much does it concern those who direct these tribunals to remember, that though they may destroy those persons who maintain the truth, yet can they not finally destroy truth itself: in attempting it, they may find, to their cost, that they *fight against God.*
>
> —Jonathan Boucher

"No taxation without representation!" "Give me liberty or give me death!" "Rulers have no authority from God to do mischief." The slogans and the basic arguments of those Americans who rebelled against the British government in 1776 are familiar not only to scholars but also to generations of schoolchildren. Whether the leaders of the American Revolution were heroes who fought for their rights and liberty or ambitious men seeking social and economic promotion, their aversion to paying taxes and their desire to govern themselves are well known. College courses and political think tanks analyze, celebrate, and disseminate their ideas. Their ideas form the basis for accepted American political truth and for basic American principles that are transmitted to the rest of the world. This is largely true because they won. The voices and ideas of the losers—of those who remained loyal to England during the American Revolution—are virtually unknown. They were also Americans who loved the land in which they lived and desired what was best for it. They were as well (or better) educated as the rebel spokesmen and appealed to strong legal, theoretical, rational, and biblical arguments. The best, most effective of them were clergymen. If one wants to properly understand the historical and philosophical context of the American Revolution, one must know and grapple with their arguments. This is a study of the arguments against the American Revolution made by Loyalist ministers.

Several of the Loyalist clergymen are generally considered to be the best spokesmen for their cause, and their sermons and pamphlets are particularly valuable because they cover the full range of Loyalist argument. Although a few lawyers and politicians made notable but limited contributions, public advocates for Loyalism were "relatively scarce" aside from churchmen. This was "the age of the sermon, which was the discourse from which most men imbibed their beliefs." The preacher was a public figure, a "natural leader," and "a learned man" who was often as well versed in the writings of modern political theorists and law as in the writings of prominent churchmen.[1] The role of Patriot pastors in promoting and recruiting for the Revolution is well documented, along with analysis of the content of their message.[2] Less known to scholars and to the public is the influence and content of the sermons and pamphlets published by Loyalist ministers. Perhaps the greatest testament to their effectiveness is the tremendous campaign by the Patriots to silence them, to prevent publication of their materials, and to destroy all copies of any materials that managed to make it to publication. This study seeks to fill the knowledge gap regarding the content of those writings.

Loyalist pamphlets often contained propaganda and polemics, but no more so than their Patriot counterparts. Loyalist sermons occasionally included Bible verses out of context and made applications from only loosely relevant passages, but they did that far less than did Patriot sermons. Loyalist pamphlets and sermons primarily appealed to history, law, and the Bible; Patriot pamphlets and sermons primarily appealed to theory, fear, and John Locke. Readers of the sermons and pamphlets from both would see common themes and subjects addressed, but from very different perspectives. The two sides have traditionally been labeled Whigs and Tories.

Whigs versus Tories

Donald Chidsey notes that both "'Tory' and 'Whig' were originally pejorative and borrowed without acknowledgment from the English." Both terms had connotations of criminality in their etymologies. For reasons no one seems to know, during the time of conflict with Great Britain, Americans began using "Whig" for liberal and "Tory" for conservative.[3] It is critical at the outset to make it clear that neither American Whiggism nor American Toryism was the same as its English counterpart. The names were appropriated and some ideas and characteristics borrowed, but there is no equivalence between the groups from opposite sides of the Atlantic. Throughout this study, references to Whig or Tory are references to the American brands.

Contrary to popular belief and to popular history, there were no particular social, economic, or religious groups that were entirely Whigs or entirely Tories. Looking at it from the other angle, a Whig or a Tory might be from any part of the country, might be from any social or economic class, and might hold to any religious persuasion. Scholars have noted that "the average loyalist might come from any walk of life" and that "Loyalists, like their Patriot counterparts, came from all ranks of society." Maya Jasanoff suggests that "a host of factors" were involved in choosing sides, "including core values and beliefs, self-interest, local circumstance, and personal relationships." She puts the emphasis on "employers, occupations, profits, land, faith, family, and friendships." In discussing the diversity of loyalism, Jasanoff notes that more than 700 people signed the little-known Loyalist "Declaration of Dependence" and that a majority of them were "ordinary people" such as "tavern-keepers and carpenters, farmers."[4]

It is also important to understand at the outset that large numbers of Americans—perhaps as many as one third—were neither Whigs nor Tories but wanted to remain noncommittal, neutral, and simply left alone. Indeed, "in the more sparsely settled parts of the middle and southern colonies much of the population was inclined to acquiesce to whatever regime could maintain order and security." So "the British and patriots were competing for the allegiance and respect of a sizable, uncommitted segment of the population which was loyalist, neutral, inoffensive, or disaffected, depending on an observer's immediate perspective." Key representatives of each side discounted this neutral group, however. Loyalist minister Jonathan Boucher proclaimed that "it is a certain fact, of the truth of which I at least am thoroughly convinced, that nine out of ten of the people of America, properly so called, were adverse to the revolt." On the other side, Whig John Adams declared that "nine-tenths of the people" were "high whigs" in political thought, if not in support for the revolt.[5] Hyperbole abounded on both sides when it came to claims of support.

Contrary to early histories and assumptions, the Whigs were not exclusively "common men" and the Tories were not distinctively wealthy aristocrats. Scholarship has revealed that "loyalists, like patriots, were drawn from all classes.... It was not a conflict in which one side was predominantly upper class and the other predominantly lower class." Patrick Griffin concludes: "Loyalists included the recently arrived and the descendants of the oldest American families. They came from every colony and every social position and occupation and lived on the frontier and in cities." Four of the richest men in the colonies were Whigs; and Virginia, which, along with New York, had the most large property holdings, had the smallest percentage of Tories. Less than 2 percent of the signers of Loyalist petitions in New York were officeholders. Signers were "not united by birth, profession, or class"; they "included apothecaries, farmers, shopkeepers, artisans, tavern owners, and cartmen. A substantial portion of the signers were those of middling stature, people who won no special favors and achieved no prominence under British military government." The records of the Parliamentary commission on compensation for Tories financially hurt by the Revolution show that about 49 percent of claimants were farmers, 10 percent artisans, 19 percent merchants and shopkeepers, 10 percent officeholders, and only 9 percent professional men. These numbers reflect a cross section of the population, not elites. Ruma Chopra effectively summarizes the traditional view of the Tories versus the facts when she notes that "both loyalist and rebel included constituents from the privileged circles and also people in the margins of colonial society." It was not a battle between "virtuous rebel farmers who bravely stood for liberty" and "colonial aristocrats who selfishly pursue[d] wealth and position." The leaders on both sides were well educated and wealthy, but "the most disadvantaged in the colonies—the African-American slaves and the Native Americans—mostly sided with the British."[6]

William Nelson suggests that the leaders of both sides were oligarchs, with the difference between them being that the Tories needed British support, not that the Whigs were merely representatives of the common man. William Allen Benton agrees, arguing that the Whig and Tory oligarchies "were essentially identical in their functions, behavior and makeup," with the difference between them being the "bases of their power." As for the common man emphasis, Benton contends that "the Whig oligarchy was safeguarded by property qualifications for the participation in government." Edmund Morgan explains that common people such as some merchants in New York City and some tenant farmers in the Hudson Valley joined with the Tories when they "felt that the local Revolutionary leaders threatened their interests more than the mother country did." In other words, "social groups that felt endangered or oppressed by the Revolutionary party" gravitated to the Tories, irrespective of theory or ideology.[7] Both wealthy and common men became Loyalists for economic reasons.

Religious identification played an important role in choosing sides and "in many cases determined the sympathy of individuals who had no other interest at stake." Interestingly, though the religious lines dividing Whigs and Tories were "quite clearly drawn," they were not drawn with denominational borders. The traditional view is that Congregationalists and Presbyterians were Whigs and Anglicans (members of the Church of England) were Tories. The closest adherence to that notion came from the Anglican missionaries of the Society for the Propagation of the Gospel (SPG), who, like Anglican ministers, had all taken oaths of allegiance to the king. About 90 percent of the SPG missionaries kept that oath and were Tories. Aside from them, the truth is that "every Protestant denominational community, and even Jewish synagogues and Roman Catholic parishes, harbored Patriots, Loyalists, and neutralists," although Catholics and Jews were predominately Patriots.[8]

Largely because they reported to a central government that kept records or to a single, organized mission agency, statistics for the Anglicans are more available and more reliable. According to the most recent and most in-depth study, 101 of the 311 Church of England ministers in the thirteen colonies became active Loyalists and twenty-seven were moderately or passively Loyalist. But seventy-six of them became active Patriots and fifty-four were moderate or passive Patriots despite their oath to support the king. Despite traps and pressure, fifty-nine of them were able to keep their political views and allegiance unknown.[9]

Though religious affiliation clearly played a role, it may not have been the decisive factor for many. Claude Halstead Van Tyne suggests that "few men living south of New York seem to have had their politics influenced by their religion" unless they also had an economic motive. Of the 120 Anglican ministers in Virginia, only 22 percent were loyal; eleven of them "became members of local committees of safety while one became a brigadier general (and not a chaplain, either) in the Continental Army." In Maryland, 40 percent were loyal, but that could be said of only five of twenty-three Anglican clergymen in South Carolina. Chopra notes that in the North, where two thirds of New York and New Jersey ministers remained loyal, there was greater Tory "intensity." As will be seen in later chapters, "some Anglican clerics in the northern colonies associated loyalty to the Church as synonymous with loyalty to the empire." Chopra concludes: "If the

Church of England supplied more loyalist spokesmen than any other single denomination, it must also be observed that the signers of the Declaration of Independence included more men of Anglican faith than any other." In fact, more than half of those signers were Anglican, although none was a clergyman.[10]

Nelson concludes that the key to understanding which side a particular religious group would favor is to look at the "dominant local denomination." Groups that were in "a local minority were everywhere inclined towards Loyalism, while adherents of the dominant local denomination were most often Patriots. In New England not many Congregationalists, in the Middle Colonies not many Presbyterians, in the South not many Episcopalians, were Tories. Conversely, most of the Anglicans in the North were Tories; so were many Presbyterians in the Episcopalian South." In other words, the traditional view concerning these large denominations is not supported by the facts. Nelson's theory also explains why smaller groups aligned mostly with the Tories. Most Quakers, German Pietists, and Dutch Reformed members were "passive Loyalists," and "in New England even the Baptists were accused of 'not being hearty' in the American cause," although Baptists tended to be Patriots in areas where Episcopalians were Loyalists. Perhaps the religious minorities had greater confidence in England's ability and desire to respect their liberty, as opposed to the potential of majority tyranny in the emotionally charged realm of religion. Janice Potter suggests that "some religious minorities, such as the Palatinate Germans and Huguenots in New York, would have reason to equate Britain with religious liberty. Some religious minorities in Massachusetts also could, on the basis of their own experience, link the British connection with liberty." New England in particular was not known for allowing religious liberty for minority groups. The two religious minorities that generally supported the Revolution and thus are the exception to the rule are the Catholics and the Jews. Nelson suggests a possible explanation: "It is possible that the Jews and Catholics were in such suspect and habitual minority that they felt obliged to follow what seemed majority opinion for their own safety." Some wishing to be neutrals chose the Loyalist side as a result of "repressive revolutionary programs" that would not allow neutrality and demanded a choice of sides.[11]

Whether the category is social, economic, or religious, Nelson finds one common factor among Loyalists: "They represented conscious minorities, people who felt weak and threatened," those who felt they "needed protection from an American majority." Holger Hoock makes the same point regarding ethnicity, religion, and occupation. David Fowler affirms that in New Jersey "religious minorities perceived the Crown as a buffer against the tyranny of the majority." Nelson argues that this "assortment of minority groups" might have, in total throughout the colonies, "constituted a majority of Americans," but without necessary unifying factors or leadership. "In this case the Revolution would have been, as it has sometimes been claimed to have been, the achievement of an organized and wilful minority." In an effort to nail down the number of Whigs and Tories with some degree of accuracy, he muses on the long-suggested ratio of one third in favor of the Revolution, one third opposed, and one third neutral, and he suggests that "perhaps half as many Americans were in arms for the King, at one time or another, as fought on the side of the Congress." The presence of the third, "middle group of passive citizens who had no clear point of view, who . . . wanted above all not to be disturbed" complicates this effort. Giving up on the overall problem, Nelson finally limits the discussion to "the politically active population of the colonies." Nelson ultimately applies his own argument about compounding minority groups and settles on a ratio of one third Loyalists and two thirds "revolutionists."[12] Despite the unsatisfactory conclusion, Nelson's theory is intriguing and might be the best explanation of nonideological factors in the choice between being a Whig or a Tory.

It was ideology, however—or at least ideas—that attracted or drove most people into one camp or the other. Griffin notes that Tories "believed the British program of sovereignty spoke to their ideas and their interests, and they remained loyal at great personal cost." Max Savelle provides useful and representative summaries of Whig and Tory ideology. He boils down the Whig ideology to "the steady increase in the power of the representative, or popular, or 'commons' arm of government" with "the concept of individual 'liberty'" at the center. The critical institutions to defend that liberty were representative government and a balance between the legislature and the executive—and of course the Whig ideology included a right of "resistance" or revolution for those who were not satisfied with their level of liberty. In Savelle's characterization of the Tory ideology, "Tories stood against the popularization of government. They stood for a maintenance, even a strengthening, of the political connection with the mother country. Above all, they stood for a maintenance, even a strengthening, of the royal prerogative." "For the Tories, the essential element in the government of the colonies was the prerogative of the Crown. This royal prerogative was a quality that was inherent in the kingship; it was not the gift of the people, and therefore the people could neither diminish it nor take it away."[13] The Tories therefore affirmed the authority of the king, denied a right of revolution, and strongly opposed American independence.

Nelson supplies a somewhat different, more abstract, but equally helpful interpretation of the differences between the Whig and Tory ideologies. He sees the key distinction being the degree of emphasis on society versus the individual. Nelson argues that the Tories stressed the value and supremacy of society, with a man's worth largely determined by his contribution to and accord with his fellow men. He suggests that "their theories about society were usually mere projections of their concern for the individual." Like Savelle, Nelson emphasizes the centrality of liberty: "To the [Whigs], liberty was a concern of utmost importance, and liberty was to be found in the assertion of the rights of the individual against the priests and princes who would oppress him. The Tories were not indifferent to liberty, but they defined it differently. They believed that men were in more danger of being enslaved by their own unreason than by Church or State."[14]

Patriot Benjamin Rush provides insightful contemporary summaries of the motivations of each side. Of the Tories, Rush says:

> There were Tories (1) from an attachment to power and office. (2) From an attachment to the British commerce which the war had interrupted or annihilated. (3) From an attachment to kingly government. (4) From an attachment to the hierarchy of the Church of England, which it was supposed would be abolished in America by her seperation [sic] from Great Britain. This motive acted chiefly upon the Episcopal clergy, more especially in the Eastern states. (5) From a dread of the power of the country being transferred into the hands of the Presbyterians.

Rush leaves out the obvious: love of country and culture by proud Englishmen. Of his own faction, the Whigs, Rush says:

> It cannot be denied, but that private and personal consideration actuated some of those men who took a part in favor of the American Revolution. There were Whigs (1) from a desire of possessing, or at least sharing, in the power of our country. It was said there were Whigs (2) from an expectation that a war with Great Britain would cancel all British debts. There certainly were Whigs (3) from the facility with which the tender laws enabled debtors to pay their creditors in depreciated paper money. (4) A few men were Whigs from

ancient or hereditary hostility to persons, or families who were Tories. But a great majority of the people who took part with their country were Whigs (5) from a sincere and disinterested love of liberty and justice."[15]

Regarding the fourth group, Tory minister Jonathan Boucher claims that "private grudges gave rise to public measures. Such motives . . . lie beyond the reach of ordinary historians." He then goes one step further: "I am not conscious that I should assert more than I can prove were I to declare that the revolt itself originated in private resentment."[16] From Rush's perspective, though political and economic motivations were important on both sides, most Whigs were motivated by principle.

Loyalist Jonathan Sewall's explanation of the reason people became Whigs is less noble and high-minded. He is convinced that there are only two ways that people owning "a sufficient Share of landed property, in one of the finest Climates in the World; living under the mildest Government, enjoying the highest portion of civil and religious Liberty that the Nature of human Society admits, and protected in the Enjoyment of these, and every other desirable Blessing in Life, upon the easiest Terms, by the only Power on Earth capable of affording that protection" could or would give up that happy life and throw off that protection. Many were "hoodwinked, inflamed and goaded on" by "turbulent Spirits" and "desparate [sic] Demagogues" to see an imaginary advance of tyranny and threat to their liberty. In short, they were manipulated by republican propagandists to fear a "mere Delusion" of a threat to their happiness and to support "Chimerical Grievances" against a benign protector who was falsely accused of bad intentions. That was at the beginning, but "now many are intimidated by the Threats of their Countrymen, and a Dispair [sic] of protection" from the committees enforcing the will of those demagogues. They were previously afraid of England taking away their liberty and now are afraid of the Patriots. In either case, Sewall cannot believe that people "so scituated [sic] for Happiness" would voluntarily take up the Whig cause; they must have been fooled or forced. Whether or not Sewall's charge was correct, it is important to note that "content with the old order of things was the normal state, and that men had rather to be converted to the Whig . . . views than to the Tory" position.[17] Sewall's opening description of the life of Americans under British authority and protection along with a statement of respect for law and order constitutes his explanation of the motivation of Loyalists.

Rush also identifies different types of Tories and Whigs in terms of their conduct. He suggests that there were "furious Tories who had recourse to violence"; "writing and talking Tories"; "silent but busy Tories" who disseminated what the writers produced; and "peaceable and conscientious Tories who patiently submitted to the measures of the governing powers, and who shewed nearly equal kindness to the distressed of both parties during the war." Rush similarly divides the Whigs into four groups. Interestingly, his commentary indicates that he did not at all approve of three of the four types. First, there were "furious Whigs, who considered the tarring and feathering of a Tory as a greater duty and exploit than the extermination of a British army." Rush says that these men were "generally cowards, and shrunk from danger when called into the field by pretending sickness or some family disaster." Second, there were economically "speculating Whigs," who "infested our public councils, as well as the army, and did the country great mischief." The third group was the "timid Whigs," whose hopes "rose and fell with every victory and defeat of our armies." The fourth type, of which Rush was presumably a member, was the "staunch Whigs." Rush reports that these "were moderate in their tempers, but firm, inflexible, and persevering in their conduct."[18]

Rush the Whig and Sewall the Tory agree that there were many who were neither Whigs nor Tories. Sewall argues that "a very great Majority of Merchants and Traders throughout the continent . . . could they be protected in a Neutrality . . . would gladly remain quiet." These were some of the people that Sewall said were Whigs out of fear of the Patriot committees. Scholars note that although the committees "possessed no constitutional legitimacy," they "literally enforced the Revolution." Maya Jasanoff refers to the most famous of them—the Sons of Liberty—as a "street gang." Not only merchants and traders but also clergymen and members of certain other occupations were not allowed to remain neutral. Rush suggests that this third class "had no fixed principles and accommodated their conduct to their interest, to events, and to their company." They tried to play each side off against the other and moved "toward the point of least resistance." But, Rush contends, they "were not without their uses. They protected both parties in many instances from the rage of each other, and each party always found hospitable treatment from them." Overall, by Rush's accounting, the Whigs were the largest class, and this third class was "a powerful reinforcement to them" once the war began going the revolutionaries' way. Chopra affirms the existence and primary motivation of this in-between group, contending that "the proximity of the British army and the threat of local coercion" had greater influence on the choice of many than ideological commitments. In particular, those who "refused or hesitated to choose rebellion . . . risked physical harassment, social isolation, and legal ostracizing from local enforcement agencies." Many were coerced into support for the Patriot cause by threats to their families and property.[19]

There were therefore several types of Whigs and Tories and a variety of motives for choosing to be a Whig or a Tory, some of which were material and others a matter of principle. Some people may have been manipulated or intimidated, and consequently had the choice essentially made for them. When they did choose, Whigs favored the popularization of government, emphasis on personal liberty, and the aggrandizement of the individual. But how would that play out in terms of their views of the structure and function of government? Whigs argued for "the substitution of regular units of representation systematically related to the distribution of population; . . . alterations in the definition of seditious libel so as to permit full freedom of the press to criticize the government; and the total withdrawal of government control over the practice of religion." They believed in "civil supremacy" over the military (as opposed to military independence), and they opposed the concept of standing armies. Until the Declaration of Independence, American Whigs supported the king as a constitutional monarch whose "chief business was to protect the Americans from parliamentary or ministerial oppression. His prerogative was a check on power rather than power itself." And they made it clear that they would be ready to overthrow his rule "if ever he should step out of his constitutional role." In fact, the threat of "ministerial aggrandizement seemed particularly pressing" in the American colonies, "for there . . . the executive branches of government . . . held, and used, powers that in England had been stripped from the crown in the settlement that had followed the Glorious Revolution as inappropriate to the government of a free people."[20]

American Whigs looked wistfully at the idea of the Glorious Revolution, with many considering it a sort of starting point rather than a consummation of the quest for liberty. "After extensive controversy there emerged an agreement that the British constitution was fixed and that finite limits were imposed on governmental power, an essential position given the nature of colonial political institutions and their constant efforts to expand the limits of their own authority." In part that led the colonial assemblies to claim to be endowed with all of the rights of the House of Commons. In part it meant that government must be "balanced" between the legislature and the executive. In part it legitimized a right of resistance and justified revolution when government exceeded its proper limits. Whigs were taught the right of resistance by the after-the-fact apologist for the Glorious Revolution: John Locke. A "Lockean notion about the contractual basis of government" was commonplace and appeals to Locke "a completely natural performance" among Whigs. The Tory press recognized his influence and mocked the central Lockean doctrines of a "state of nature" and equality: "Now, if the Whigs establish their republic, they 'will reduce all men into a state of nature,' and perhaps the next step would be to cut off the legs of the tallest, that no man might look over the head of his neighbors."[21]

Whig pastors in particular imbibed Lockean theory with enthusiasm and poured it out to their congregants to justify rebellion.[22] Indeed, Savelle claims that the "classic American statement of the right of revolution was that pronounced by pastor Jonathan Mayhew in his famous sermon of 1750 [*A Discourse Concerning Unlimited Submission and Non-Resistance to the Higher Powers*]." Mayhew acknowledged his intellectual debt to Locke and his premises were Lockean. There were, of course, many other important sources for Whig thought, but it is not within the scope of this overview chapter to discuss them with specificity.[23] The players in this study emphasized and cited Locke, not Trenchard and Gordon or other English or continental libertarians. The Patriot preachers overwhelmingly if not exclusively cited the celebrated and sagacious Locke, and the Loyalist ministers treated Locke as their primary if not exclusive philosophical adversary.

According to the Whigs, government was limited and could be resisted by force if it overstepped its bounds. By the mid-1770s, American Whigs believed that condition had been met. It is also beyond the scope of this introductory chapter to address all of the particular issues and complaints that led the Americans to engage in rebellion against the British government. Virtually all of them will be addressed in succeeding chapters as the Tory clergymen respond to and answer them. For the purposes of this introduction, one multifaceted issue will serve as a core cause of the American Revolution from the Whig perspective: taxation. Increases in and enforcement of taxes levied on the colonies by Parliament resulted in acts of defiance, violence, and destruction of property that ramped up tension and confrontation. That necessitated greater use of policing force by the British government and in turn more confrontation. Familiar historical examples abound, such as the intimidation of stamp agents, the Boston

Massacre, the Boston Tea Party, and the events at Lexington and Concord. More importantly for the study of political thought, however, numerous views concerning various types of parliamentary taxation highlighted the fundamental differences in principle between the Whigs and Tories. As Van Tyne observes, once the British repealed all of the "obnoxious acts ... except the tea duty" and replaced the objectionable Francis Bernard as governor of Massachusetts, there "was nothing now to fight for except a principle. Then it was that the difference between Whig and Tory political philosophy became defined."[24]

When Parliament lowered the tax on tea to such an extent that British tea became cheaper to buy than that of any other country, Benjamin Franklin saw an ulterior motive. Britain's "wise scheme" was to entice Americans to give up their protests, buy the tea, and thereby "keep up the exercise of the right" of Parliament to tax the Americans. Franklin said, however, that the Americans acted from principle, not interest, and that 30 pence a year in tea tax would not be "sufficient to overcome all the patriotism of an American."[25] Whigs did not emphasize the price of goods due to taxation but rather the principle of whether Parliament had a right to tax the colonists at all. Famously, the American Whigs claimed that the British constitution guaranteed "no taxation without representation."[26] John Joachim Zubly declared: "Every impartial man will allow that this is the foundation of the whole dispute." Part of the dispute between Whigs and Tories lay in the meaning of the word "representation." To Tories, representation meant that the classes of the community were represented in Parliament. For them, the appropriate phrase was "no taxation except that voted by the House of Commons." To Whigs, representation meant that there was a seat in Commons occupied by a person elected by the people of a geographical community—that each person taxed had an opportunity to vote for a member of Commons making the tax decision. Because of the difference in meaning, the two sides often talked past each other.[27]

The Whigs also distinguished between types of taxes. Some denied Parliament's right to tax the colonies internally but recognized its right to tax them externally. Some distinguished between taxation for revenue purposes and taxation designed to regulate the trade of the British empire. Others denied Parliament's right to levy any taxes at all on the Americans.[28] "Beyond the question of constitutional law was the question of expediency. The Whig held that the claim of the right to tax was fraught with too much danger to be admitted even if it were constitutional" because of the possibility of abuse. Once the right was granted, miniscule taxes today could become oppressive taxes tomorrow. Tories "pointed to the fallacy of contesting the use of power simply because of the possibility of abuse."[29] By that logic, government—including the colonial assemblies—could never be granted any power because they might abuse it.

It is important to note that many, if not most, Tories shared the Whigs' disdain for some of the acts of Parliament and policies of government ministers. The Tories were Americans too; they had to pay the taxes, and they suffered from ministerial overreach. As Nelson says, "The British government's decision at the end of the Seven Years War to reform colonial administration and to tax the colonies threw the American Tories into confusion. They were as indignant as other Americans at what seemed an unjust and arbitrary exercise of British authority" and "their indignation as Americans ran ahead of their alarm as Tories." In addition, they were on board with what initially appeared to be an *American* cause, but not when it became a *revolutionary* one. He admits that a few Tories "mildly defended the Stamp Act," but most of them "condemned the Stamp Act as wholeheartedly as did the Whigs."[30]

A couple of representative examples will serve to make the point. Just before the repeal of the Stamp Act, the venerable Tory Thomas Bradbury Chandler declared: "Every Friend therefore to the Happiness of the Colonies, or even of Great Britain, who is acquainted with the Case as it really is, must wish that the Parliament would relax of its Severity." Nearly ten years later, on the precipice of conflict, he admits that the "peace and happiness of the American colonies had been, for some time, interrupted and disturbed, by certain acts of the British Parliament." He wants the colonies "released from parliamentary taxation" with an "assurance of our willingness to contribute, in some equitable proportion, towards defraying the public expences" under a new "*American Constitution*" under, in turn, "the superintending authority of Great-Britain." Jonathan Boucher calls the Stamp Act "exceptionable," complains that "this terrible Stamp Act" is "in every Sense, oppressive, impolitic & illegal," and calls the Royal Proclamation of 1763 limiting colonial expansion westward "very impolitic, as well as unjust." He further charges that the "best & dearest Rights" of Americans "have been mercilessly invaded by Parliament" and calls opposition to the Townshend Acts "the most warrantable, generous, & manly, that History can produce."[31]

The Tory clergymen were not blind apologists for the British government. Their willingness to be critical of actual British excesses is one of the factors that makes their sermons and pamphlets compelling and credible. They agreed with the Whigs on many of the problems, but they disagreed strenuously regarding what actions were appropriate in response to British offenses. Fundamentally, Loyalists "wished to resolve any disagreements within the existing constitutional framework."[32]

According to William Allen Benton, a third middle-ground term is necessary in light of the fact that most Tories originally held some Whig views and some went from being enthusiastic Whigs to active Loyalists. He calls the latter "Whig-Loyalists." "The Whig-Loyalists functioned as Patriots before the American Revolution and then became supporters of British rule in America." Ironically, given the traditional view of the Whigs being the faction of the common man, Benton argues that these men moved seamlessly from one camp to the other on the basis of "principles which upheld oligarchy." After discussing six "categories of belief and conduct" between Whiggism and Toryism, he asserts that "the Whig-Loyalists were neither ambivalent nor indecisive. During the course of the revolutionary struggle they made decisive changes of affiliation in keeping with their ideological beliefs."[33] Though they shared or sympathized with Whig complaints, they could not go so far as to support revolution or independence. Arguably, the preeminent Whig-Loyalist was John Joachim Zubly.

According to Randall Miller, editor of a collection of Zubly's writings, Zubly was the only Whig pamphleteer in Georgia. He also "espoused a radical Whig constitutional interpretation" and served in the Continental Congress. Miller conversely claims that "much truth obtains in the charge" that Zubly was "the archetypal Loyalist." He suggests that both can be true because Zubly was a Whig-Loyalist. Indeed, all of Zubly's extant pamphlets support the Whig cause, including *The Law of Liberty*, which was a sermon preached before the Second Provincial Congress of Georgia on July 4, 1775. In that sermon, he calls for "a most conscientious regard to the common laws of the land. Let our conduct shew that we are not lawless." He urges what he later urges as a Loyalist: restraint, negotiation, and peaceful protest. "Let us convince them that we do not complain of law, but of oppression; that we do not abhor these acts because we are impatient to be under government, but being destructive of liberty and property, we think them destructive also of all law."[34]

This preacher with impeccable Whig credentials suddenly became a Tory when talk of independence in the Continental Congress became more serious. As Miller explains, Zubly became a Loyalist because "he loved America and so sought to avoid her destruction in a civil war. Zubly [like other leading Loyalist ministers] believed that reconciliation and reform were possible within the empire." Zubly's primary Loyalist expressions were not published in pamphlets but in newspaper articles. There he excoriates the Patriots for their violence, their violation of civil rights, and ultimately their assault on "law and liberty." He sees what he had warned against in *The Law of Liberty*: "remedies that [are] worse than the disease." Zubly is representative of many Loyalists who "felt equally torn between [their] sympathy for colonial rights and [their] aversion to rebellion and violence." They were "peaceful, sober-minded citizens, who perhaps had more than half sympathized with the Whig movement thus far, but the thought of civil tumult and even war had checked their noble rage" in a way that it had not checked that of the Patriots. "Most significantly," says Griffin, "these men and women also considered themselves American."[35]

An episode from the Revolution illustrates the two sides. When well-known Patriot Joseph Warren died at Bunker Hill, a letter was found in his pocket from his classmate and friend, Congregationalist pastor Lemuel Hedge. In the letter, Hedge, a Loyalist, "professed a sincere interest in the liberty of his country, although he admitted his doubts in regard to the issue of the Revolutionary struggle."[36] In the eighteenth century, having doubts was the polite way of saying that one did not believe in or agree with something. The same concern for liberty impelled one man to the battlefield of a revolution and led his friend to seek a less radical and more peaceful solution.

There is a sense in which most Loyalists could be labeled Whig-Loyalists. They "loved America with a sincerity not surpassed by the most high-minded Whigs,"[37] and they were willing to recognize and criticize errors made by the British government. In the long run, that willingness may be a key factor in identifying them as Loyalists rather than Tories. They were loyal to the Crown, but not blindly. Their recognition and discussion of British errors will be examined in greater depth in Chapter 5. They were willing to see and disapprove of British injustices, but they were not willing to take up arms against their sovereign, preferring to seek a negotiated, conciliatory settlement.

Terminology

During the heat of conflict, both sides tried to define the other in the public mind. In response to the Boston Port Act of 1774, refusal to send provisions to relieve the inhabitants of Boston was "branded as Toryism." In May 1776, the Boston town meeting sent instructions to the Massachusetts delegates to Congress: "'Loyalty to [the King] *is now treason to our country.*' Here was the keynote to the whole future treatment of the Tory by the Whig. The Tory was no longer regarded as a political opponent to be coerced, but as a traitor deserving retributive justice." In their resolutions, the Whigs took the upper hand rhetorically and ironically accused the Tories of rebellion. After the Declaration of Independence, "every Tory was an enemy in camp, a suspected traitor and a wretch to be charged with all the ills of the state." A correspondent of the New Haven *Connecticut Journal* defined a Tory as "'a maintainer of the infernal doctrine of arbitrary power, and indefeasible right on the part of the sovereign, and of passive obedience and non resistance' on the part of the subject." Representing the Tory side, Loyalist minister Richard Mansfield produced a sarcastic and bitter suggested "Catechism" for the Whigs:

QUESTION: What is a Tory?
ANSWER: A Tory is nowadays one that is a friend to government, keeps his oath to be true to the King and his lawful successor.
QUESTION: What rule have you to know what makes a Tory which is sufficient to punish him as such?
ANSWER: The infallible rule is by his frequent citing texts of scripture to prove that kings are God's ministers and the like. . . .
QUESTION: But do you not use arguments . . . to convert them to be Whigs?
ANSWER: None but such as these, viz., . . . if the Tories don't join us and fight with us, they will not be a whit better off than we at the last if the King's forces overcome them. . . .
QUESTION: What are the special benefits that accompany and flow from anarchy, pulpit drummers [i.e., dissenting clergy], and independency?
ANSWER: They are these: the pleasure of punishing Tories; the free enjoyment of all false doctrine, heresy, and schism; hardness of heart; contempt of God's word and commandments; privy conspiracy and rebellion.[38]

One can glean from this that Mansfield thought that disregard for Scripture, inability to make a rational case, reliance on threats, sadism, heresy, and rebellion were characteristic of a Whig.

The Whigs clearly won the rhetorical and propaganda battle. They won in large part because they shut down and literally destroyed Tory avenues of communication. But they also won because they had "talented" propagandists such as Samuel Adams, because they had agents such as the Sons of Liberty keeping the passions of the people inflamed, and because they had a more inspiring and exciting message. The Tory message was the obligation to obey the law and the rather "humiliating idea" of subordination. Their message was "hardly inspiring and made no converts." The Whig message of independence was dynamic and "flattered the people," as prominent Tories admitted. "The trouble with Loyalism in the American Revolution was that it was a *negative* thing; it was not a burning belief, but rather an *absence* of belief; and there will always be trouble getting men to rally round a vacuity." The only thing that really inspired the Loyalists was their sense of being martyrs to a cause due to the harsh treatment they received.[39] But again, that was gained by suffering and by being on the receiving end of coercion, not by positive actions or victories.

"Whig" and "Tory" are the traditional names for the two sides in the argument in America during the Revolutionary period. Having outlined the nature and positions of the American Whigs and Tories, I now abandon these titles for several reasons. First, "Whigs in America preferred to call themselves Patriots, the Tories preferred to call themselves Loyalists." In particular, those who remained "friends of government" or "the loyal party" usually "denied the name [Tory] and called themselves Loyalists."[40] Because there is nothing inherently objectionable in those titles, we might as well accede to their preferences. Second, at the time, the name "Tory" was considered an epithet, a stigmatizing insult, and there is no reason to perpetuate it. Third, distinct titles clearly separate the American political factions from the British political factions. Finally, "Patriots" and "Loyalists" refer more directly to their positions taken regarding the climactic and seminal event of their dispute: the American Revolution. One side saw themselves as patriots of a new country, and the other saw themselves as loyal to the present one.

For the bulk of this study, those supporting rebellion and independence will be called Patriots and those opposing rebellion and independence and arguing for adherence to the legal authority of Great Britain will be called Loyalists. Generally, these two terms will be capitalized because they refer specifically to these American groups and not to patriots or loyalists in general.

Bishop Controversy

Because this is a study of the writings of Loyalist clergymen, it is appropriate to briefly discuss an issue that roiled the ecclesiastical waters some time before the American Revolution. After the French and Indian War, "Anglicans and Presbyterians clashed repeatedly for religious and political advantage." In particular, Anglican and Congregationalist ministers fought over whether the Church of England should assign a bishop or bishops to the America colonies. Donald Chidsey argues that "there can be little doubt that the Lawn Sleeves [Bishop] Controversy, the hottest issue in America at one time, had a great deal to do with bringing about the Revolution."[41] That may be a bit overstated, but the controversy certainly contributed to hard feelings between Patriot Congregationalist pastors and Loyalist Anglican priests, to fears of increased British control over religion in America, and to the Patriot propaganda machine.

Arguably, the real core of the issue in the 1770s was competition between the Congregationalist and Presbyterian dissenting churches in America and the Anglican or Episcopal church. Both dissenters and Church of England adherents could trace their American history to the beginning of its colonization: the Jamestown settlers were Anglican; the Plymouth settlers were dissenters. But the Pilgrims and Puritans came to these shores to escape persecution from the Church of England, so they had more than a passing interest in the expansion of Anglicanism in America. "Most alarming to old-line New Englanders was the American campaign by missionaries of the Church of England from the Society for the Propagation of the Gospel" in New England. In addition, "converts [to Anglicanism] also knew that Anglican expansion represented a diffuse cultural war against the Congregational Way." Thomas Ingersoll notes that "in 1773 the orthodox Church [of England] seemed formidable."[42]

By the time of the Revolution, there were 660 to 800 Congregationalist churches (mostly in New England), more than 500 Presbyterian churches (mostly in the middle colonies), and more than 400 Anglican churches spread throughout the colonies. Importantly, the number of Anglican churches was growing at a rapid pace, especially beyond the church's established base in Virginia and Maryland. By war's end in 1783, a total of 300 Anglican churches had been founded outside of those two colonies by the missionary efforts of 600 clergymen from the SPG. Between 1760 and 1770, the Anglican church "nearly tripled its earlier rate of increase" and trailed only Congregationalists and Baptists in the rate of increase. "Likewise, in the 1760's, there was a dramatic upsurge in the number of colonial candidates for Anglican ordination, even though this process required an expensive trip to London." Nelson suggests that in addition to spawning rationalists, the Enlightenment in America spurred the growth of Episcopalians as congregants grew to prefer the "conviviality of the Anglicans" to the "severe discipline of the Presbyterians and Congregationalists." Indeed, the Church of England grew steadily in Connecticut, a "strongly Congregationalist colony," and established forty-five new churches there. The "number of confirmed Anglicans in the colony rose from 150 to more than 2,000" as early as 1739 even though the law discriminated against the Church of England.[43]

A contemporary of the time reported, for example, that "the Episcopal Church increased mightily in Connecticut . . . to the great annoyance of the old Puritans." By the mid-1700s, membership in the Church of England was becoming "socially desirable in the Middle Colonies and fashionable even in Boston." Loyalist minister Charles Inglis argued that this growth was due to Anglican clergymen's "adherence to the Dictates of Conscience" and "Preaching the Gospel unadulterated with Politics" while "the Pulpits of Dissenters resounded with scarcely any Thing else than the furious Politics of the Times, which occasioned Disgust in the more serious & thinking."[44]

Whatever the reason, once Anglicanism began to make inroads into New England, the dissenters were indeed annoyed and reacted strongly. They entertained visions of tests for office, taxes for the support of bishops, and persecution—in other words, those things that motivated their ancestors to throw "themselves as it were into the arms of Savages and Barbarians" and to land on "the then inhospitable shores and desarts [sic] of America." Jonathan Mayhew reflected the views of many dissenters of the day when he asked:

> Will they never let us rest in peace, except *where all the weary are at rest?* Is it not enough, that they persecuted us out of the old world? Will they pursue us into the new to convert us here? . . . What other new world remains as a sanctuary for us from their oppressions, in case of need? Where is the COLUMBUS to explore one for, and pilot us to it, before we are consumed by the flames, or deluged in a flood of episcopacy?

By the 1760s, the Church of England had achieved "astonishing success" in New England areas such as Connecticut, and the dissenters felt threatened by its expansion, believing that its advance meant the loss of their religious freedom. The "underlying issue" between the Anglican church and dissenter churches was "whether a powerful and influential Anglican church was compatible with religious liberty." The prospect of an American bishop became the symbol for this dispute. As a contemporary observer later reported: "The New Englanders felt that the authority of the government of England and the National church must be crushed or their Puritanism be overthrown. It was this spirit largely which originated the late rebellion in America."[45] This latter statement may also be a bit overstated, but there is no denying that the Bishop Controversy had some effect on the eventual Revolution, whether or not it was a central cause.

In the mid-1760s and again in the early 1770s, Episcopal clergy petitioned Parliament for the creation of an American episcopate and the establishment of American bishops. To the dissenters, the establishment of a Catholic bishop in Quebec "seemed to herald Anglican episcopacy in the colonies, now with an autocratic Roman model in Quebec to imitate." The stated—and insistent—purpose of the Episcopal clergy, however, was almost exclusively spiritual and simply a matter of religious liberty. As Nancy Rhoden has noted, "They appealed to a denominationalist perspective by claiming that they wished to be put on an 'equal footing' with other North American religions." An address from New York and New Jersey Episcopal clergymen to Episcopalians in Virginia explained why American bishops were needed: "Our Clergy were left without a proper Direction and Government: Ordination could not be obtained, by our Candidates, without great Loss of Time, Hazard and Expence: Confirmation, which our Church esteems as an highly beneficial Institution, was not within the Reach of its American Members: And it was evident that nothing but resident Bishops could free us from these Disadvantages." In the address, the authors repeatedly stressed that they did not propose bishops "vested with any Degree of temporal Authority, or that any Taxes should be imposed upon the Colonies." The proposed bishop would only have jurisdiction "of an ecclesiastical or spiritual Nature, and confined to the episcopal Clergy; and . . . their Support was to be provided in England." Recognizing that rumors of a plot were circulating that the real intent was to introduce a politically powerful bishop who would endanger religious liberty for dissenters, they answered that "to imagine that the Society had any secret Plan, materially different from their declared one, is an unjust, injurious and groundless Suspicion; such as has not the least Shadow of Evidence to warrant it."[46]

Turning to the reasons a bishop was needed, the address highlighted direction, ordination, and confirmation. First, they confessed a need for superintendence "to regulate, direct and guide us." Second, they complained that it was too costly and too dangerous for candidates for ordination to have to go to England. In support of that argument, Thomas Bradbury Chandler attached a note saying that fifty-two candidates sailed for England seeking ordination in 1767, and ten of them—"near a fifth Part of them"—died in the attempt. Charles Inglis wrote many letters laying out the need for more clergymen and the expense and danger of traveling to England to become one. One church seeking to fill its pulpit in Connecticut sent one candidate who was ordained in England but "perished on the return passage." A second "died on shipboard," and a third was "taken by the French, and passed the remainder of his life in prison." Seeking merely "Equality of Privileges," they noted that "all other Churches are allowed the Means of providing for themselves, in this Respect [ordination], in the easiest and cheapest Manner." Third, they asked, why should members not have access to "the ancient Rite of Confirmation"? In his own sermon on the issue, Jonathan Boucher contends that it "matters not that many Christians, who are of a different communion, think lightly of confirmation. As long as there are many thousands of good subjects, who believe it to be essential to Christians, no reason can be given why they should not be tolerated as well as other Christians are in the rites and doctrines of their respective religions."[47]

A prominent theme in the address is the matter of fairness. In another note, Chandler claims: "If any Presbyterian or Congregational Society in the Colonies had suffered in this Manner; much more, if all of them were rendered liable to suffer in this Manner, through the Want of such a full Toleration as was allowed to all other religious Denominations, I am much mistaken, if the whole British Dominions would not resound with, at least, Lamentations and Complaints." Given the track record of these denominations, this is undoubtedly true. The authors addressed a second aspect of the fairness issue: "The Honor of our Church also requires, that it should stand on as respectable a Footing, as other religious Societies; and that it should not be destitute of such Privileges, as are enjoyed by the most inconsiderable Sects in his Majesty's Dominions." Several ministers argued that the Church of England was the official established religion of the British empire, so it was completely illogical that it would not be given at least equal treatment with other sects. Finally, drawing a parallel with the dissenting churches on the matter of leadership, the authors argued: "Were for Instance, the Presbyterians not allowed to have Presbyteries, for the Purposes of their Discipline; were they permitted to have no Preachers, without such Expences and Delays as must attend the Introduction of ours; they would consider it as an insupportable Oppression." That is also unquestionably true. For the record, the clergy of Virginia responded to the address by explaining that they would not be opposed to "*an American Episcopate, introduced at a proper Time, by proper Authority, and in a proper Manner.*"[48] But they did not think that the present appeal met those criteria.

As a Virginian, Jonathan Boucher was on the receiving end of the address, but he was a staunch and vocal supporter of the effort to procure a bishop. In his sermon "On the American Episcopate" delivered in 1771 in the midst of the dispute, Boucher hits many of the same themes, but he gets to the heart of the issue in his own inimitable way. He suggests that the rejection of applications for an American episcopate "has been singular and unprecedented. That an established Church, which gives ample and liberal toleration to sectaries of every name, should herself not be tolerated, is a phenomenon in political history peculiar to the American world." Boucher charges that opposition to the American episcopate is "the only real attack upon religious liberty now existing in the British dominions." He explains this highly charged and inflammatory remark: "Religious liberty, as far as it concerns the present question, consists in this, that they who maintain bishops to be of apostolical institution should have their bishops, and that they who maintain the same of presbyters should have their presbyteries."[49]

Rhoden suggests that some in minority religions may have "hoped colonial Anglicans might receive a bishop, so that the Church of England could grow 'as a Balance to Presbyterians' and thereby prevent Presbyterianism from endangering religious liberty in America." Perhaps that is true, but for the dissenters whose ancestors suffered at the hands of the established church, the scars of the past were too fresh and the wounds ran too deep. As Mayhew's comments indicate, some feared an expansion of the Church of England in America that would result in the kinds of persecutions their forefathers fled to America to escape. Some objected to the anticipated cost; some objected to having "a peer, a lord" introduced in America's officially unclassed society. Still others focused on potential political concerns. Assuming that this was a plot by government ministers, opponents reasoned that "if Parliament could create dioceses and appoint bishops, they could collect tithes and crush heresy." John Adams said of the controversy that it "spread an universal alarm against the authority of Parliament." "If Parliament could tax us, they could establish the Church of England," with all that goes with it, and "prohibit all other churches."[50] So for Adams, the authority of Parliament to tax Americans and its authority to establish bishops in America were closely interrelated. Both had to be opposed in order to maintain liberty.

In the end, American Episcopalians did not need the British government in order to establish an American episcopate and select an American bishop; they got one after the Revolution in the new United States. The battle over bishops had several lasting effects. Although it is difficult to assess how significant it was in causing the Revolution, "the bitterness the controversy had aroused was absorbed into the general argument of the Revolution." The bishop question was one issue that united Old Light and New Light Congregationalists and Presbyterians against Anglicans. Because of that bitterness and unity, Anglican clergy in particular became targets for "popular fury" and "scapegoats for popular mobs," especially in New England colonies that had few royal officials to persecute. The entire Anglican church in America "became tainted by association as pamphleteers labeled them 'Tories.'" In addition, Robert Calhoon argues that the "uproar over proposals for bishops in the colonies, the deep-seated suspicion [exacerbated by the bishop issue] that Anglicans wanted to destroy religious liberty in America, and the allegation that Anglicans preached unlimited submission to constituted authority obscured the authentic political implications of Anglican preaching and belief."[51]

For our purposes, the most important effect of the Bishop Controversy was the creation of an organized group of Loyalist ministers (Nelson says "an organized group of propagandists") to resolutely and effectively oppose revolution and independence. This was the political debut of some of the key figures in this study. A convention of New York and New Jersey clergy sent a "memorandum" to the SPG in support of the establishment of American bishops. Leading members of that convention and authors of the message were Thomas Bradbury Chandler, Charles Inglis, and Samuel Seabury. Those three "agreed 'to watch all publications either in newspapers or pamphlets and to obviate the evil influence of such as appeared to have a bad tendency by the speediest answers.'" Myles Cooper was one of the contributors to the memorandum, and he made several trips south from New York to enlist the support of the southern clergy. Jonathan Boucher and James Horrocks, president of the College of William & Mary, rallied support for a bishop among the Virginia and Maryland clergy. Cooper and Boucher also went to Philadelphia to discuss "an Anglican political programme" and a "plan for joint action" in the north, south, and middle colonies.[52] The Bishop

Controversy provided an opportunity for these ministers to dip their toes in political waters and accustomed them to working together for a political cause. This political activism and cooperation reached its apex in the rhetorical fight against the Revolution.

Persecution

The Loyalist clergy made their case in a context of threat and persecution. One recent study calls the Loyalists "the most immediate victims of the war." The Loyalist ministers accused the Patriots of hypocrisy in their demands for liberty and individual rights because they denied liberty, freedom of speech, freedom of religion, and due process of law to anyone suspected of loyalty to England. Prominent scholars have observed that the Loyalist press articulated "a profound sense of moral estrangement from the values that the revolutionaries claimed for themselves and that permeated their republicanism" and that the rebels engaged in practices "that contrasted sharply with the ideals of their cause." For example, the author of a recent study of loyalism asserts that one of those practices—confiscation of Loyalist property—was "contrary to the social ideal that every individual deserved the community's defense, and it violated the right to free speech" because it was the property of those who spoke against the rebel cause that was seized. In addition, "it was contrary to the belief that every individual has the right to hold independent views even at odds with those of everyone else." He concludes that the "act of liquidating property" was "an embarrassment to their [the Patriots'] high ideals."[53]

Persecution of Loyalists by those complaining about tyranny went far beyond confiscation of property. Unlike that of the Patriots, the tyranny faced by the Loyalists was not theoretical or potential but all too real. Theirs was not the "tyranny" of a voluntary tax on tea but the forced loss of all property. Theirs was not an imagined threat of impending Catholicism but the actual closing of their churches and the prohibition of their liturgy. Theirs was not the inconvenience of traveling to a royal court in pursuit of justice but being kidnapped, dragged to another state, denied due process rights, and tried by partisan mock courts with no legal authority—or being subject to confiscation of goods and property or imprisonment without even the pretense of a trial. The tyranny that they experienced saw many of them sent to prison or publicly assaulted merely for expressing an opinion. It was a tyranny that denied them their livelihood and left them and their families destitute.[54] For too many, the tyranny suffered by the Loyalists resulted in death. One-fourth of all Anglican clergy in America were exiled, and one fifth of them died during the Revolution.[55] For the most part, the tyranny that the Patriots bemoaned consisted of attempts to tax them or severe acts taken by the British government in response to Patriot violence and destruction of property.

Not surprisingly, Loyalist ministers made an effort to publicize unjust, unfair, and illegal treatment and to publicly denounce Patriot leadership for actively sanctioning or conveniently overlooking it. The persecution (there is no other word for it) suffered by Loyalists ranged wide in severity and frequency. It might take the form of verbal insults; it might result in death. Some of it was ordered, some was approved and encouraged, some was just allowed, and some was simply ignored by Patriot authorities ranging from local committees to George Washington. Some was the work of soldiers, some of mobs, and some of neighbors. Some was the devilish work of ruthless, self-interested bands of ruffians acting on their own—but they were rarely punished. In his definitive study of violence during the American Revolution, Holger Hoock suggests: "We will never be able to quantify the violence that American Loyalists endured. . . . Violence was as much about states of mind as it was about its physical characteristics." In fact, says Hoock: "The Revolutionaries relied on terror—acts of violence and the threat of violence—to crush dissent."[56] Even Loyalist women had their property plundered and were "verbally abused, imprisoned, and threatened with bodily harm even when they had not taken an active role in opposing the rebel cause."[57]

Perhaps equally disturbing is the fact that many clergymen simply wished to remain neutral, but the Patriots generally would not allow neutrality. The celebrated days of prayer and fasting proclaimed by the Patriots may have had pious intent for some, but they also had the ulterior motive of exposing those ministers who were not enthusiastic supporters of the rebel cause. Loyalism scholar Claude Halstead Van Tyne explains that "the proclamation by the Continental Congress of a day of fasting and humiliation and prayer was the signal for the persecution of those who refused to obey." The Committees of Safety watched for participation by "doubtful persons." In particular, they sent agents to see which ministers observed the day and presided over services. A majority of Loyalist clergymen "dated the commencement of their troubles from the first fast day" (July 20, 1775).[58]

Days of prayer and fasting were designed to expose those ministers who were, to this point, neutral—not Loyalist activists. The original day of fasting and prayer "began the identification of these Loyalist clergymen." At least six clergymen died as a result of the abuse or imprisonment that followed. Six other clergymen sent a letter to the bishop of London explaining that they had been trying to remain publicly neutral in the growing conflict and keeping "our pulpits wholly clear of anything bordering on this contest." They reported, however, that "the time is now come . . . when our silence would be misconstrued and when we are called upon to take a public part." They said that it was due to the July 20 day of prayer and fasting, as "refusal to pray for the colonial cause would be considered a hostile action."[59]

The July 20 proclamation was not the only one that was used to reveal Loyalists. Earlier in 1775, Reverend John Wiswall of Maine tried to remain silent about the conflict until he refused requests for days of fasting and prayer in support of resistance to the Coercive Acts and for a collection for Boston. Shortly after, he was accosted by "a Body of men armed with Muskets and Bayonets," was "greatly insulted and abused, and in great danger of being shot to death." After being held for a time, he escaped to a British ship without money, clothing, or his wife and three children. His wife and daugher subsequently died. His supposed crime was refusing to support the rebel cause with days of prayer and fasting. Events other than days of prayer and fasting were used to unmask closet Loyalists among the clergy, including a false report of a British attack that drew 40,000 minutemen—but no clergy—in response. The absence of clergy "was judged to be sufficient proof of their disaffection to the liberties of America," and brutal attacks on clergymen by "the mobs" ensued.[60]

The most common, open, and widespread of these methods of smoking out anyone harboring Loyalist sentiment or being insufficiently enthusiastic about the Patriot cause were the "test acts" passed in all thirteen states. While the tests varied in substance and severity from state to state, their ultimate purpose was "separation of the political chaff from the political wheat"—that is, uncovering Loyalists.[61] Generally, jurors (those who passed the tests) took an oath to support the American cause and not to support the British, renounced allegiance to King George, and promised allegiance to their state. Much of this effort was aimed at the clergy.

As a matter of practice—not exception—Americans who would later celebrate their Bill of Rights denied to Loyalists virtually every right in the list. Though the Patriots claimed to be building a new society based on rights, Loyalist ministers demonstrated and criticized the hypocrisy of that claim in practice. At the hands of self-appointed groups and mobs, Loyalists suffered ostracism, proscription, loss of property, banishment or exile, personal assualts and threats, prison or other means of confinement, and death. Loyalists were denied freedom of religion, freedom of speech, freedom of the press, due process of law, and other rights. More importantly at the time, those demanding their rights as Englishmen felt free to deny the rights of Englishmen to anyone who disagreed with them. Loyalist ministers used that fact to argue for the moral superiority of the British side in the conflict. To be fair, the British army also violated the rights of Americans and sometimes committed brutal offenses.[62] But unlike the Patriots, such was not the policy of the British government, and their offenses were primarily directed at combatants who actively rebelled against the established government.

Twenty-first-century studies echo the conclusions of long-respected works on loyalism in detailing the persecution suffered by Loyalists at the hands of the Patriots.[63] Jim Piecuch introduces his recent study as "an often unflattering portrayal of the Whigs" and a "more favorable" view of the Loyalists, then explains: "An objective analysis of the sources permits no other interpretation." He concludes that the Patriots justified murder and hangings by accusing the Loyalists of the same, but this was a myth that eventually "became accepted as truth." "Once the myths are pruned away," he argues, "the historical record tells a very different story." For him, the real story is that of people who were "beaten, tarred and feathered, imprisoned, harassed, and sometimes murdered" for remaining loyal to their king. Their property was confiscated, and they were banished from or fled their homes.[64] His summary judgment is that the "Loyalists' story is one of fidelity, courage, and persistence in the face of adversity, and it is every bit as heroic as the story of the Whigs' fight for independence."[65]

Key Players

By my calculation, drawing from the most reliable sources that I can find, there were at least 182 Loyalist clergymen in America at the beginning of or during the epic struggle between the American colonies and Great Britain. Conventional wisdom says that they should nearly all be ministers of the Church of England. From what I can conclude, however, there were about 138 Anglicans or Episcopalians, which is 76 percent of the total. By my count, there were 16 to 21 Congregationalists, 4 Methodists, 3 Presbyterians, 3 Dutch Reformed, 2 Baptists, 2 Sandemanians, a Quaker, and 2 ministers for whom we have no denominational information.[66] The Congregationalist number is indeterminate because five ministers for whom we have no denominational information served churches in the Congregationalist strongholds of Massachusetts, New Hampshire, and Maine and are not listed in Anglican records. It seems logical to assume that they were Congregationalists. It would also seem logical that more Quakers would be Loyalists, but there are two factors to consider. First, Quakers were generally neutral rather than aligning with either side. Second, most Quaker publications were general pronouncements made by groups without identifying specific individuals, so we do not know the stance taken by most individual Quakers.[67]

This study includes significant commentary from about a dozen of these 182 Loyalist ministers. Five of them were arguably the most prolific writers and the most influential voices: Jonathan Boucher, Thomas Bradbury Chandler, Charles Inglis, Samuel Seabury, and John Joachim Zubly. Interestingly, there are four Anglicans and one Presbyterian in the group, roughly reflecting the overall Anglican versus non-Anglican denominational breakdown within Loyalism.

Jonathan Boucher was born in England, but he moved to Virginia at age sixteen. He went to England for ordination and returned to Virginia to take over the Hanover parish. From there, he moved to St. Mary's parish and then eventually to Maryland and St. Anne's rectory in Annapolis. His final parish in America was Queen Anne's (St. Barnabas) in Maryland, from which "he was ejected at the Revolution" in 1775. A mid-eighteenth-century historian says that Boucher "was accounted one of the best preachers of his time." In addition to preaching, Boucher operated a school to augment "his slender income" that included George Washington's stepson, Jackie Custis, among its students. This was the beginning of a friendship with Washington that was abruptly terminated by the Revolution. Robert Calhoon suggests that Boucher's "most significant achievement was his pioneering work in educating Negro slaves." "Boucher taught several of the most promising slaves to read and then, using them as assistants, began large-scale Sunday-afternoon instruction of blacks in the rudiments of Christianity. He baptized several hundred adult slaves, and at one time more than a thousand received instruction. Thirteen slaves were regular communicants in his church at St. Mary's parish."[68]

In the mid-1760s, Boucher went through a period of serious theological doubts, but he emerged stronger and more committed to the faith. He gained some notoriety, though negative, for defending the right of Catholics to freedom of conscience. A fortuitous marriage improved his social status, while his position as an advisor to the governor, along with his efforts in public battles over clergy salaries and the Bishop Controversy, elevated his political reputation. "His wit and intelligence made him a useful political figure" and ultimately an effective advocate of Loyalism.[69] More than twenty years after he left America, Boucher published a collection of his pre-Revolutionary sermons in 1797, dedicating it to his prominent former friend, George Washington. There is evidence to indicate that copies of his original sermons were lost or destroyed, and he "reconstructed" them from memory with the benefit of twenty years of hindsight.[70] This discovery has cast a cloud of controversy and doubt over the use of Boucher's sermons by historians. In my opinion, scholars must be aware and careful when using these sermons, but there is no reason to dismiss or avoid them, particularly in the field of political thought. There is no reason to believe that the viewpoints and arguments expressed by Boucher in the reconstructed texts are materially different from those originally delivered to his congregants. As long as one discounts Boucher's seemingly uncanny prophetic powers and focuses on the core issues and arguments, there is insufficient cause to deprive ourselves of the thoughts of one of the most compelling and important Loyalist voices.

Thomas Bradbury Chandler was born in Connecticut and raised a Congregationalist, but he converted to the Church of England while an undergraduate at Yale. He studied theology "in preparation for ordination under Samuel Johnson" and "became one of Johnson's protégés." He gained notoriety in the Bishop Controversy and was a leading figure in several conventions of Anglican clergy. His pamphlet, *The American Querist*, "enjoyed immediate public interest in the colonies; appearing in 11 editions in New York." It was publicly burned by the New York Sons of Liberty. Another of his pamphlets, *A Friendly Address to All Reasonable Americans*, was also burned on the ironic grounds that it was somehow more of a threat to American liberties than the practice of burning an unpopular pamphlet. After the pivotal armed conflicts at Lexington, Concord, and Bunker Hill, Chandler left for England in 1775. Chandler returned to America and his former parish in Elizabeth Town, New Jersey, after the war in 1785. He was chosen to be the first colonial bishop recognized by the Church of England (in Nova Scotia), but he did not want the post and was able to decline it because of his declining health. "He lived long enough to see Inglis assume the episcopal office but not long enough to see the sweeping changes that were soon to come to the United States after 1790."[71]

Many of the Loyalist pamphlets were written under pseudonyms, largely for the safety of the author. Those written by Chandler were for a time attributed to Myles Cooper, as "Cooper was accused of writing almost every production that appeared on the Loyalists' side of the controversy." In reality, it appears that "only a few" were actually written by Cooper, and most of those attributed to him "were written by his colleagues." Those colleagues submitted claims to the Royal Commission after the Revolution and took "full credit for everything they wrote." Cooper never made such a claim, but Chandler did, and Chandler also admitted in his correspondence to writing the pamphlets now attributed to him, so it is "now certain" that Chandler was the author of several of the better-known Loyalist pamphlets referenced in this study.[72]

Though born to Scottish parents, Charles Inglis was born and educated in Ireland. He came to America at age twenty-two and, after teaching for two years and being ordained in England, was assigned as the SPG missionary to Dover, Delaware. He eventually moved to New York City, where he became assistant rector at the prestigious Trinity Church. This position put him "at the centre of political and church activity" and gave him contact with notable clergymen such as Chandler and Samuel Seabury. Like the others, he participated in the fight for an Episcopal bishop. Unlike Boucher and Chandler, he stayed in New York through the war years as rector of Trinity Church "to visit the sick, baptize the children, and offer support to the poor." Governor William Tryon started a loyalist newspaper and appointed Inglis one of two managers of "the political part" of the paper. He published pamphlets and sermons, first openly and then surreptitiously when able to evade the destructive efforts of the Patriot committees. Particularly enthusiastic efforts were taken to stop circulation of his "True Interest of America Impartially Stated," a response to Thomas Paine's *Common Sense*. Chopra calls Inglis the "most articulate Anglican cleric in New York," and Nelson concludes: "Except for Jonathan Boucher, he was perhaps the most profound of the Tory writers in the period of the Revolution." Inglis left America with the evacuating British troops in 1783, but he returned to Canada in 1787 as the first Anglican colonial bishop appointed by the Church of England.[73]

Samuel Seabury was born in Connecticut, graduated Yale in 1748, and, after being ordained, took a parish in New Brunswick, New Jersey, in 1754. Three years later, he took the parish in Jamaica, New York, where he spent the next ten years before becoming rector of St. Peter's in Westchester County, New York. A nineteenth-century biographer of Alexander

Hamilton, Seabury's pamphlet nemesis, called Seabury a "man of strong will, clear perceptions, untiring diligence, learned and eloquent, . . . chief among those who organized and led an opposition to the Congress and all tendencies to independence in New York, and the adjoining counties. . . . He was a stout churchman, of strong convictions, and, by those convictions, a loyalist." Seabury was such a popular preacher that his church was described as "always crowded & often so that all have not room to Sit." Calhoon claims that "Seabury's *Letters of a Westchester Farmer* was the most comprehensive and sustained polemical effort by any doctrinaire Tory to repudiate the pre-Revolutionary movement, demolish its constitutional arguments, discredit its methods of protest, and expose its coercive tactics and presumptions." Nelson concludes that "Seabury was perhaps the best propagandist, except for Tom Paine, that the Revolution produced on either side."[74] Both comments are intended as compliments, albeit backhanded.

Correctly suspected to be the "Westchester Farmer," Seabury was carried away to Connecticut by a mob and held prisoner for six weeks. He remained in New York through the war years and stayed in America after the war was over. After the war, Seabury moved to Connecticut, where ten Episcopal clergy elected him to be the first bishop of Connecticut and of the American Episcopal Church. Seeking consecration as an Episcopal bishop, Seabury sailed to England. Because he was an American citizen, he was unable in England to take the required oath of allegiance to the king, so Seabury was consecrated as a bishop by the Scottish Episcopal Church in 1784 and returned to establish his see in New London, Connecticut, in 1785.[75]

John Joachim Zubly was the non-Anglican among the key Loyalist clergy. He was born in Switzerland but was ordained at the German Reformed church in London. After emigrating to America, Zubly assisted another German Swiss minister in Georgia and preached in settlements in Georgia and South Carolina. Upon meeting famed evangelist George Whitefield in 1746, the two became "friends for life." A trip north to raise money for Whitefield's orphanage significantly widened his circle of "prominent" political and religious acquaintances, and increased his interest in "religious affairs outside Georgia." After "a brief stint" as a pastor at Purrysburg, Zubly "prospered" for a time at Wando Neck before settling in as the pastor of a Presbyterian church in Savannah "which had many leading Georgians in the congregation." This, along with the "fortune in land and slaves" that he amassed through "shrewd investments," led to the expansion of his "social and political power" and his entry into politics. Zubly became known for his "mastery of homiletics" and his "firm grasp of modern and classical languages," and he "won respect as a scholar widely read in history and political theory as well as in theology."[76]

Although not "a democrat or even a friend of republics," Zubly's political activism led to his being a delegate to Georgia's Second Provincial Congress and "reluctantly" agreeing to serve as a member of the Second Continental Congress. Although he went along with many parts of the Whig program, Zubly firmly opposed rebellion and independence. Eventually forced out of the Congress for openly embracing the Loyalist side, Zubly tried to keep a low profile until he refused to take the oath of allegiance to the Congress. He was arrested and declared "an enemy of the state. The Revolutionary government in Georgia, which was strapped for funds and eager to force obedience from lukewarm 'patriots,' chose to make an example of the harried minister by confiscating his estate and banishing him from Georgia." He fled to the backcountry, to return only when the British retook Savannah. He returned to his "ministerial duties and generally tried to avoid political involvement" until his death two years later.[77] Zubly is unique among the key clergy. Although several of the Loyalist ministers opposed the early controversial British actions, Zubly is the only one who wrote extensively as a Whig and then again as a Loyalist.

A Word about Method and Structure

From the end of this opening, context-setting chapter, primary sources dominate this study. Any emphases (italics or capitalization) in quotations are original unless otherwise stated, and readers need to be aware that spelling and punctuation were not yet standardized in eighteenth-century America, so readers of the quotations should not assume errors on my part or that of the editor. In the next five chapters, the Loyalist ministers make their case against the American Revolution and independence on various grounds of argument. For the most part—almost without exception—they are allowed to speak for themselves free of secondary commentary except for some clarifying and summarizing remarks.[78] My intent is for them to make their own case for the reader to evaluate, as eighteenth-century readers were asked to do.

Chapter 2 covers the biblical arguments made by the Loyalist ministers. It illustrates the value of studying this overall question from the perspective of clergymen. As ministers, they offer a unique and important perspective in light of the biblical literacy of the people and the prominent position of clergy in colonial American society. They argued for an historical, grammatical literal reading of the Old and New Testament scriptures, and they admonished the Patriot preachers for illegitimately finding political liberty in the text and for taking liberties with the text. For years, the Patriot pulpit has been recognized by scholars as a driving force and major recruiting device for the Revolution. But the Loyalist pulpit and printed sermons were similarly effective for the other side until suppressed by Patriot mobs and committees. Janice Potter argues that "there is evidence that the Loyalist message influenced at least some rank-and-file Americans. In the two years before independence literally hundreds of Loyalists signed addresses, declarations, or associations in which they stated, sometimes in simple language, their view of the Revolution. It is interesting that they supported the basic ideas and aims of the more educated and well-known Loyalist spokesmen." She also points to the "fact that Loyalist refugees . . . shared the ideas of these propagandists" as evidence "that Loyalist writers had a significant impact on the views of their readers" and suggests that "there may have been many in their closets secretly praying for the king" in order to avoid persecution.[79] Their effectiveness is also at least partly evidenced by the frantic efforts to shut them down. Ultimately, the Loyalist argument is incomplete without its biblical element. This is at least one reason why scholars generally agree that the key clergymen were the most effective of the Loyalist spokesmen.

Chapter 3 deals with arguments from the nature of government. This is the shortest chapter because the Loyalists did not emphasize theory or appeals to human philosophy. They strongly stressed authority, but the authority of government, not the authority of classical or modern political philosophers. Their own reason, grounded in biblical authority and the record of history, guided their thought—not Plato, Aristotle, Locke, or Sidney. They were not hesitant to argue with Locke, but for the most part they did not summon or rely on a philosophical champion for matching citations. Because they were highly educated and well read, they clearly were influenced by the thoughts of others, but they generally borrowed from them unconsciously and without acknowledgment. Theirs was unapologetically a largely traditional understanding of the nature of government and man's relationship to it, and it was guided by a confident belief that the British system was superior.

Chapter 4 examines the legal arguments of the Loyalist clergymen. As highly educated, well-read leaders in their communities, these ministers had studied and understood the law. Their legal arguments are arguably as sophisticated and nuanced as those of the few lawyers who published Loyalist pamphlets. Because they were generally uninterested in theorizing and philosophy, and because they believed that the British system of law and government was the pinnacle of human legal achievement, they wrote confidently of the status quo and critically of theoretical notions. Particularly effective were their regular reminders that the Americans—who began by claiming their rights *as Englishmen*—were subject to the British legal system and, regardless of desire, were not free to act on the basis of imagined law.

Chapter 5 reflects the Loyalist ministers' analysis and evaluation of the American situation in the mid-1700s. What is the relationship between England and the American colonies? What about errors that have been made by Great Britain? What about King George—his character, his actions, and his relationship to Americans? Who is to blame for the deterioration of relations? What about efforts toward conciliation? Are they sincere or sufficient? What about the Continental Congress—its genesis and its authority? Is the Congress working in the best interest of Americans?

Chapter 6 presents the Loyalist clergymen's criticism of colonial actions against Great Britain and against Americans. The chapter begins with their challenge to the legitimacy and wisdom of the three "nons"—nonimportation, nonexportation, and nonconsumption. Growing out of this discussion is condemnation of the treatment of Loyalists at the hands of the Patriot committees and mobs—in particular, violations of their rights. That is followed by their specific argument against the Revolution itself and their expectations of American victory or defeat. Their analysis of the immediate and ultimate cost of the Revolution in human, moral, and financial terms is presented, along with warnings and chidings concerning America's alliance with France. Finally, their argument against American independence is detailed.

After Chapter 6, a brief epilogue reminds readers of the primary arguments and summarizes the overall position of the Loyalist ministers.

2 Biblical Arguments

> One plain and principle doctrine of Christianity.
> —*George Micklejohn*

The most appropriate place to begin a study of the biblical arguments against the American Revolution is with the hermeneutics and views concerning proper preaching held by the Loyalist ministers. Hermeneutics (one's method of interpreting the Bible) played a critical role in determining which side of the conflict clergymen took. In their sermons, as a general rule, the Loyalist preachers appealed more to the Bible and held to a more literal and contextual interpretation of the relevant texts of Scripture than did the Patriot preachers. In addition, the Loyalists typically took passages at face value without adding to or subtracting from the text, while the Patriot preachers adjusted texts to fit their purpose by adding qualifying language. Patriot preachers of course believed that their interpretations were correct, but they did not claim that their interpretations were based on a literal reading, or that they took the passages at face value.[1]

Three eminent scholars have recently published books about the use of the Bible in early America in which they discuss the various views of critical passages of Scripture such as Romans 13 and I Peter 2 that were put forward by ministers on both sides of the American conflict. They do not suggest that the Patriots took the passages literally or at face value. Daniel Dreisbach says that they had a "nuanced interpretation of Scripture, articulated in the wake of the Protestant Reformation," as opposed to a literal interpretation articulated in the historical context of the writing of those passages. He further notes that those preachers who supported revolution argued that key biblical texts were to be "qualified by the narrative and practices" in the Bible and that those preachers "typically *began* with key biblical texts," but followed them with "examples and arguments" drawn from sixteenth- and seventeenth-century Europe (emphasis added). In fact, Dreisbach notes, "violent clashes between Protestants and Catholics in the mid-sixteenth century" motivated Reformed thinkers to reconsider their view of the key Scriptures teaching nonresistance. Reformers incensed by violence and persecution in England, the Netherlands, Scotland, and France found a literal reading of Romans 13 to be unsatisfactory in light of the suffering around them, and as a result, they departed from a "conventional reading of Romans 13:1." According to Dreisbach, Samuel Rutherford—a source that he contends had significant influence on the Patriot preachers—drew from "political tradition," "the ancient classics, and the works of the church fathers and Reformers" in forming his theology. In Dreisbach's twenty-page section on resistance theology, there is much discussion of political theory and history, but few and brief references to Scripture.[2]

In his discussion of Romans 13 and I Peter 2, James Byrd reports that "Patriots read these passages through the prism of republican ideology" and they tried to "shift attention from [Paul's and Peter's] words to their actions."[3] In other words, they did not take them literally or at face value. In his discussion of the argument of the Patriots, Mark Noll chooses three preachers as representative. He refers to the biblical expositions of one as "creative exposition," "hasty exegesis," and "flights of fancy." Of the second, he questions "the pertinence of [the] text to the American situation" and suggests that it is "not obvious" that the teaching was "responsibly biblical." Noll describes the third as a "calm, deliberate performance" that was "thoughtfully constructed." Nonetheless, Noll notes that this preacher began his look at Romans 13 with a declared intention "to reconcile seeming contradictions; to make self evident truths (flowing from the attributes of God, and loudly proclaimed by nature) agree with some plain declarations of scripture," and with a proposition found "in nature" and "from reflecting on 'the intensions of God.'" First, one should note the emphasis on nature. Second, there is no need to make the self-evident truths agree with the plain declarations of Scripture unless those truths come from outside the plain declarations and appear to be at variance with them. Indeed, Noll's third preacher brought to bear outside evidence, and instead of attempting to reconcile other texts and other information with the literal text, he denied the validity of a literal reading of the text. Noll concludes his discussion with his own commentary that "exegetical precision was not required in order to enlist the Bible for the patriot cause."[4]

Those holding to alternative views of Romans 13 and I Peter 2 did not claim to be simply restating what the biblical text says. Rather, they expended much effort to explicate views that do not leap off the page but rather require lengthy argumentation and some nuance. The Loyalist ministers held to a more direct interpretation. It is perhaps symbolic, but also instructive, to recognize that, as Dreisbach notes, the motto of resistance theology was the nonbiblical phrase "Rebellion to Tyrants is Obedience to God."[5] In contrast, the catchphrase of the Loyalist ministers was "Let every soul be subject unto the higher powers"—the direct text of Romans 13:1.

Regardless of which approach one prefers, it is clear that the clergymen from the two sides of the argument about the propriety of the American Revolution had very different interpretive approaches to instruction and commands contained in the Bible. The views of three of the most prominent Loyalist ministers illustrate and illuminate the prevailing hermeneutic of those clergymen who opposed the Revolution.

Hermeneutics and Preaching

In his final sermon in America, Jonathan Boucher looks back on his method for determining right from wrong in the Anglo-American crisis: "With sincerity in my heart, and my Bible in my hand, I sat down to explore the truth. With these guides, and none but these, the process is not difficult." He then identifies the link between that study and his preaching: "I entered on the study for the express purpose of first instructing myself, that I might with more propriety afterwards instruct you."[6] Boucher elsewhere explains "the process": he reports that he seeks "the true sense and meaning of the text" and holds that to find the "true and precise meaning of any passage of Scripture, it is in general necessary to know the circumstances of the writer, and his end and aim in writing."[7] He reports that he "critically examined the New Testament in the original language; and considered the sublimer doctrines of revealed religion, not as subjects of philosophical disquistion, but as truths or facts, which the Scriptures assert. In this manner did I *search the Scriptures*."[8] Boucher's approach is basically what theologians today would call the "historical/grammatical method": attempting to understand the author's intended meaning in the original language and within historical and literary context. Boucher comes to the Scriptures with a measure of humility, insisting that "a minister of God" should be "taught by him [God] who knoweth what is fit and good for us better than we ourselves" and that "we are not to judge of the Scriptures of God, as we do of some other writings."[9] So for Boucher, one must determine the clear sense of a passage of

Scripture and then take that message as God's instruction and not question it or debate its merits.

In his letters, Charles Inglis gives additional insight into how a conscientious eighteenth-century divine might approach such a task. It requires a lot of study, as Inglis reports: "I go on in my usual Way, devoting all my leisure Time to Study." Then, assuming that a full understanding of a text requires analysis in the original language, Inglis says: "My Mornings, before Breakfast are employed in Reading Hebrew."[10] To further enrich this study, Inglis notes: "I have lately got over Walton's Polyglott Bible & Castell's Lexicon, which are an invaluable Treasure to a Clergyman. This will naturally lead me to pursue my Study of the Hebrew with more Diligence; & learn to read at least the other Oriental Languages. The Samaritan I can read already."[11] A year later, Inglis writes to Samuel Johnson to affirm the usefulness of his book of Hebrew grammar "to the young Hebrecian" and compares it to other such grammar books, including those in Greek and Latin.[12] Inglis explains that his desire to "understand the Sense of the Sacred Writers" results in research "which costs me much Labour; as I consult the best Expositors, ancient & Modern, besides reading the Original, as I go along." He found it worth the effort, though, "as it will give me a critical Knowledge of ... the sacred Writings; & it is certain that a thorough Knowledge of the Scriptures is the most essential Qualification of a good Divine."[13]

Boucher and Inglis are concerned about the politicization of preaching, the increasing propensity of preachers to misinterpret the Bible to suit their own purposes, and the apparent desire of preachers to be popular. Boucher calls the political sermons of his contemporaries "more popular," "more frivolous," "more unsound," and "less learned" than "such compositions used to be."[14] He bemoans the fact that where Loyalist ministers are concerned, "offence is taken, not so much because some of us preach on politics, as because we preach what are called unpopular politics. Preachers who are less anxious to *speak right*, than *smooth things*, are ... numerous among us."[15] He laments that as a faithful minister, he is obligated to preach "necessary, rather than agreeable sermons" and what is "most salutary and useful" rather than what is "most palatable and pleasant."[16] He concludes that "to be very popular, it is, I believe, necessary to be very like the bulk of the people, that is, wrong-headed, ignorant, and prone to resist authority."[17]

Inglis expresses the same concern when he asks, "Shall we listen to the popular Declamations that would excite to the Breach of God's Law?" He explains that he will leave some matters "to Divines—so such I mean, has have not kicked the Gospel out of their pulpits, nor substituted news-papers and politics in its place."[18] He claims that Anglican churches were growing "in some places, particularly in Connecticut" because of the Loyalist clergy's "adherence to the Dictates of Conscience by persevering in Loyalty, & Preaching the Gospel unadulterated with Politics." That was in contrast, according to Inglis, with the Patriot pulpits, which "resounded with scarcely any Thing else than the furious Politics of the Times."[19] Inglis felt so strongly about this that when he was turned out of his church by "the Rebel officers," he put himself at risk by refusing to give them the keys, "for I could not bear the Thought that their Seditious and rebellious Effusions should be poured out in our Churches."[20]

According to Boucher, far too many American preachers were interpreting Scripture conveniently in support of a particular agenda and thereby abusing Scripture to illegitimately serve their interests. He simply calls for "common justice" to be done to texts. Boucher charges: "A worldly temporizing spirit ... is now again unhappily gone forth in great force among the people of the Colonies; not sparing even the Sanctuary.... There are many, whose sole aim is to reconcile their religion with their worldly interest," even "among those who serve at the altar."[21] Adopting the tone of an Old Testament prophet, he warns: "But, wo [sic] unto that people who studiously place temptations in the way of the ministers of God to *handle the word of God deceitfully!* and wo [sic] unto those ministers who are thus tempted to *cause the people to err, by their lies and their lightness!*"[22] In the midst of his criticism of these ministers, Boucher utters a prayer that he would not fall to such temptation: "God forbid that, either *for filthy lucre's sake*, or merely with the view of *pleasing men*, I should ever handle the word of God deceitfully, and teach things which I ought not!"[23] Inglis expresses a similar fear: "We dare not ... prevaricate, or trifle with the living God; or handle his Word deceitfully."[24] For Boucher, the anchor that keeps him from drifting with the winds of "human policy" is "the word of God," which, "like mount Zion, *abideth fast for ever.*"[25]

Boucher is critical of those who, in his view, have cast off the anchor of proper treatment of God's word. He is concerned about "the disservice done to religion, when acknowledged scholars and dignified clergymen so far forget themselves as to become sophists" and "when an *ambassador of Christ*, unmindful of the sacred duties of his *high calling*, basely prostitutes all these distinguished privileges, by *walking craftily*, and becoming a mean time-server."[26] This takes place when preachers elevate something other than the word of God to the highest position and then judge God's clear revelation in the Bible by that external standard. Boucher identifies and denounces two such standards. The first is the vague notion of "feelings." Boucher warns against elevating the "imaginary voice" of one's feelings above the Scriptures and against evaluating the truth or falsehood of the Scriptures according to their agreement or disagreement with this "novel, undefinable, something called men's 'feelings.'"[27] It is too easy to follow illusions or feelings "rather than the sober steady light of the word of God" because it does not flatter our pride.[28] Emotions, says Boucher, are undefinable and unreliable sources of truth. He warns against undue emphasis on what was in his time called enthusiasm.

The second, arguably more dangerous, external standard resulting in abuse of Scripture is an elevated and unfettered emphasis on reason. Boucher does not object to the use of reason; he himself makes extensive use of reason and rational argument. Indeed, one must use reason in order to read and understand Scripture. He objects to elevating reason above revelation by making reason the determinant of legitimate revelation or reasoning in such a way as to obscure the clear meaning of a passage in favor of a preferred meaning. From Augustine through Aquinas through the Reformers, there was a significant place for reason, but always in service of revelation. In Boucher's opinion, the preachers he criticized turned that order on its head and elevated reason above revelation and in judgment of it. He confesses that early in his career he had fallen prey to "those writers who attempted to reduce the doctrines of Revelation to the standard of my own reason" and was "misled" by pride.[29] Boucher eventually saw the fallacy of this approach, but he observes: "All the good old doctrines of our venerable Divines, founded as they are on Scripture and on sound Philosophy, are now made to give way to (what we are pleased to call) the deductions of Reason; as if it were possible that sound Reason should ever be at variance with Revelation."[30] For Boucher, such a notion is absurd.

Samuel Seabury shared Boucher's concern; in fact, he preached an entire message on hermeneutics and the relationship of reason to revelation.[31] In the *Advertisement*—essentially the preface—to his sermon on II Timothy 3:16, Seabury says that his twofold purpose is "to recall people to the study of the scriptures themselves, and to the proper use of their reason and understanding." More specifically, his aim is to connect those two goals, "to point out the proper use of human reason in studying those writings, and to give some hints for the better understanding, and more profitable reading of them."[32]

He begins by identifying the Bible as "the history of God's dealing with mankind; and of those revelations of his will which he hath been pleased to make," then argues that man could not attain this knowledge by the "utmost exertion" of his own reason. This world provides knowledge only "of body or matter" and "there seems to be no step or clue to carry reason up from the consideration of body or matter, to the discovery of a being of a pure, immaterial, unbodied nature, such as God must be." He adds that "whenever reason attempts an investigation of these matters by its own strength, it is lost in clouds and obscurity." Seabury concludes that "the knowledge of God is owing to some original revelation that he was pleased to make of himself and of his nature . . . and confirmed and explained by subsequent revelations, such as he saw useful and necessary for the world."[33] For Seabury, reason depends on observation, experience and instruction and, therefore, cannot tell us anything about a "*purely spiritual . . . self-existent* being"[34] such as God without the aid of revelation from that being.

Seabury, like Boucher, contends that sound reason cannot differ from revelation. As he puts it, "no revelation from God can be contrary to human reason" as long as "reason be free from prejudices, and unclouded by vicious affections." That, of course, is a critical qualification; apparent discrepancies between revelation and reason must be due to flawed or corrupted reason. Seabury also points to another important distinction: "There is a vast difference between a thing's being contrary to our reason, and above its reach. Many things in this material world, that come under our daily observation, are yet above the comprehension of our reason." Man must recognize his inherent limitations; he is a finite being, and his "capacities are limited." He asks: "Shall we refuse to give credit to the revelations of God, merely because we cannot fully comprehend them?" Seabury warns that "education or negligence" can cause our reason to become "clouded with superstition, or enslaved by vicious affections, or warped by prejudice, or fettered with an undue deference to the dictates or opinions of others." Consequently, "it is, therefore, a matter of importance, that we daily cultivate and exercise our reason and understanding in a point of so much consequence: that we preserve the mind free, and open to the convictions of Truth, and ready to follow where that leads."[35]

Boucher considers the two external standards of feelings and reason to be invalid and uncertain standards when compared to the clear and direct teaching of the word of God. They come together to unhinge what Boucher considers to be "direct and clear" teaching in the Bible on the subject of politics: submission to authority. Boucher notes that the apostle Paul sees submission to authority as "so essential" that "he recommends it to Titus [Titus 3:1, 8] as a topic on which he should not fail frequently to insist." Furthermore, it is "as direct and clear a commission for a Christian minister's preaching on politics, in the just sense of the word, on all proper occasions, as can be produced for our preaching at all on any subject."[36] Turning to Romans 13, and from all indications Jonathan Mayhew's deconstruction of it, Boucher complains that "light and liberality"—reason and feelings—have produced "loose and debauched opinions" that have in turn replaced "unerring standards of right and wrong." Specifically, Paul wrote definitively as he was inspired, but this is interpreted by some as if he allowed for whatever exceptions they prefer. Their "casuistry" makes what Paul damned as a *sin* (that is, a rebellion) into a "meritorious duty."[37] Because Mayhew, a Locke imitator, cleverly devised a way to make what men feel appear to be rational, Boucher warns:

> At this rate, we shall rest our faith, not on the inspired and heaven-dictated dogmas of St. Paul, but on the subtle and uncertain deductions of Mr. Locke, and his numerous imitators. If resistance to the supreme power of a nation be indeed a virtue, and the practice of it our duty, I confess I can no more see how the reputation of the Apostle is to be saved than I can see how the peace of the world is to be secured.[38]

Because their teachings are diametrically opposed, Paul cannot be right if Locke and Mayhew are right, and Locke's reason must be determined to be superior to revelation from God if he and Mayhew are right.

Seabury similarly condemns commentators who "have warped and forced particular expressions of the scriptures, to make them comport with their own preconceived opinions." This has produced the "evil,—that particular passages and expressions of scripture being understood according to the forced sense which some commentator has given them, are brought to establish certain tenets to which they have no manner of relation." This is particularly true, he observes, because commentators have followers and "admirers" who treat the commentary as "at least of equal authority with the text itself." Seabury ends his discussion of hermeneutics with a statement that is both critical to and reflective of the general position of the Loyalist ministers: "Above all things, when we apply ourselves to the study of the scriptures, we ought to bring with us a candid, unprejudiced mind, ready to embrace and follow the truth where ever it shall lead; ... ready to submit to the will of God in all circumstances, and to obey it in every particular."[39]

Three final observations concerning the Loyalist's hermeneutics must be briefly addressed. First, the Loyalist ministers believed the writers of the Bible were literally inspired by God in what they wrote—not in the sense that one might say an artist or composer was inspired, but directly, specially, and authoritatively. Consequently, the Bible was literally divine in origin and carried a certainty and authority that was not to be questioned or doubted.[40] As one preacher puts it, "To those who deny what the scriptures positively assert, while they reject the authority of the Bible, it is not worth while to plead with them in support of any authority."[41]

Second, Boucher particularly and specifically rejects the commonly practiced and occasionally expressed hermeneutic of many of the Patriot preachers, that "the Scriptures cannot be rightfully expounded without explaining them in a manner friendly to the cause of freedom."[42] In an extensive argument concerning the meaning of liberty, Boucher notes that "the word *liberty*, as meaning civil liberty, does not ... occur in all the Scriptures." The Scripture text for Boucher's best-known sermon was a passage wrongly interpreted to apply to political liberty, and he apologized to his audience for having to cite it in that false context in order to respond to Patriot claims: "I entreat your indulgence, whilst, without too nicely scrutinizing the propriety of deducing from a text [Galatians 5:1] a doctrine which it clearly does not suggest."[43] Another making this point was John Joachim Zubly, who preached an entire message on "The Law of Liberty" in which he emphasized that the liberty spoken of in the Bible and associated with Christianity was liberty from sin and from ceremonial religious law.[44] Interestingly, at that time, Zubly's purpose was to support Patriot objections to British actions. In a fit of inconsistency, he applied those passages about spiritual liberty to the political situation as would a Patriot.

A final observation regarding the preaching of the Loyalists is that they frequently used Old Testament stories to find applications—not interpretations—to illustrate their arguments. A number of the Scripture texts for their sermons are not overtly or apparently political, but they find principles in these "Scripture parallels" that inform or help to clarify various aspects of the political situation of the day. In one sermon, for example, Boucher writes: "I do not hesitate to confess it was for the sake of digressions of this sort that the subject was chosen; indeed the having an opportunity to introduce such remarks, and to make such applications, is the chief recommendation to me of these Scripture parallels."⁴⁵ It is important to note that he distinguishes between the strict and specific interpretation of a passage—its actual meaning—and a possible wider application of principles regarding human relationships and human nature found in the narrative.

Having established the basic approach to the Bible of the Loyalist clergymen, their argument drawn from the Bible remains to be explored. For the Loyalist ministers, some biblical passages had direct and prescriptive relevance to the political questions of the day, some contained principles that might be applicable or helpful, some illustrated major or minor arguments, and some had to be addressed in response to Patriot usage.

Romans 13

As one familiar with the Bible might expect, Loyalist preachers often turned to the two passages that most directly and succinctly address the matter of government and our relationship to it: Romans 13 and I Peter 2. Partly, I suspect, because these passages were so familiar as to be thought clichéd and self-explanatory, and partly because so many Loyalist sermons were destroyed, there are not many extant Loyalist sermons with Romans 13 or I Peter 2 as the primary guiding text. That being said, sermons of the Loyalists are replete with references to these two texts; these references tend to be stated in matter-of-fact language that takes the commands as "clear and direct."

One sermon based on Romans 13 that survived the Patriot purge is George Micklejohn's "On the Important Duty of Subjection to the Civil Powers." Romans 13 famously begins: "Let every soul be subject unto the higher powers. For there is no power but of God; the powers that be are ordained of God. Whosoever, therefore, resisteth the power, resisteth the ordinance of God; and they that resist shall receive to themselves damnation." Micklejohn begins his sermon by lamenting that many have "lately so unhappily wandered" from "the paths of duty and allegiance" despite the fact that "this important duty of subjection to lawful authority, is one plain and principal doctrine of christianity" and that "it is here delivered to the world by an inspired Apostle of CHRIST." This encapsulates the Loyalist position well: subjection to authority is a plain, principal, and authoritative command. To reinforce the element of authority, Micklejohn observes that because God gave Paul "the distinguishing title of '*a chosen vessel to Himself*,'" this command "comes to us by the *Authority* of the same God and SAVIOUR, who has given us every other precept that we meet with in holy scripture."

Furthermore, "no rank nor station in life, can possibly exempt any one from the strictest obedience to it: For it is directed to all men in general, without any exception."[46]

Micklejohn then turns to "a second very material argument, arising from the words of the text," namely that God is the source of governmental authority: "*for there is no power but of God: the powers that be, are ordained of God.*" God, says Micklejohn, does not need to give reasons for His command, but He "graciously" informs us that "the authority they [higher powers] are invested with is from HEAVEN . . . ! They are God's vicegerents upon earth" and are "the ministers of God to us, for good."[47] As the Loyalists tended to do, Micklejohn takes the passage at face value and says, as Paul does, that those with governing authority *are* ministers of God for good. Patriot preachers who dealt with Romans 13 tried to turn Paul's description in verses 3 and 4 of governing authorities and what they *do* into qualifications or benchmarks that rulers must meet—to the satisfaction of the observer—in order to qualify as legitimate authorities to whom subjection is due. They thus adjusted the text and said that governing authorities "should be" or "must be" ministers of God for good, rather than what the text says: "he [the ruler] is the minister of God to thee for good" (my emphasis). This is a subtle but critically important distinction.

To drive this point home, Micklejohn turns to the ultimate example: Jesus Himself. Referring to John 19:10–11, Micklejohn notes that Jesus, "when *Pilate* was boasting of that power he had over him, . . . puts him in mind from whence he had received his authority; and gives him this mild and instructive answer, *Thou couldst have no power at all against me, except it were given thee from above.*" Keeping in mind that Pilate was a governor representing a militaristic, pagan empire that had conquered Israel, Micklejohn says: "Here we learn from the mouth of our *Redeemer himself,* whence is derived that dignity and sacredness, which belongs to those who are invested with any public power and office." In case anyone might claim greater authority or mistreatment so great that they could claim an exemption to the command, Micklejohn observes: "Here we behold the God of the universe submitting to that supreme authority *he himself* has conferred upon man; and acknowledging the reverence due to that very power, which was shortly to pronounce the sentence of death against him."[48]

Micklejohn appeals to Jesus's example in what he considers "a still more striking and remarkable instance of submission and respect to the Civil Powers, which our blessed Lord, upon another occasion, condescended to shew." He points out, in a reference to the temple tax question in Matthew 17:24–27, that Jesus was rightfully exempt from paying the temple tax, but "notwithstanding our Lord might have justly claimed this privilege and exemption; yet . . . he willingly declines it; and, *Least we should offend them*," Jesus pays the tax with a coin from the mouth of a fish. Jesus thus worked "a miracle, rather than not satisfy the demands of public authority; lest, by refusing compliance himself, he might countenance others in disobedience and rebellion!"[49] For Micklejohn, everyone, without exception, owes subjection to the higher powers because those powers received their authority from God and are His representatives.

Following his discussion of the "heinous crime" of disobedience to God's command to be subject, Micklejohn's third point in his sermon on Romans 13 is to "briefly consider the dreadful conquences [sic] that must attend it. This the Apostle gives us, in these few, but awful words, *They that resist, shall receive to themselves DAMNATION; not only condemnation in this world, but eternal vengeance in the life to come.*" Micklejohn argues that God often gives commands without identifying an accompanying punishment for disobedience, "but this was a matter of so much consequence to the general comfort and happiness of the world, that the *divine wisdom* thought it necessary for us, while we read the sacred injunction, to have before our eyes that future misery which must follow the violation of it: So that, if the love of God, and reverence for his commands, should fail to produce this becoming submission, a regard for our own *Everlasting Interest* might possibly prevail." He then suggests that "there cannot possibly be offered a greater insult to *Almighty* God, than thus contemptuously to disregard his will, and dispise [sic] those sacred powers whom he has ordained and appointed to carry on the best and noblest purposes in the world."[50]

Micklejohn's treatment of verses 3 through 7 of Romans 13 is more general, in the form of a summary concern for a dutiful response to those holding governmental positions. He holds that "every the least Insult offered to magistrates and governors, is an act of the basest ingratitude against those who are, under god, our protectors and guardians." They provide security from danger and "the safe and comfortable enjoyment of all the blessings of private life, and all the advantages we derive from civil society." Consequently, we are obliged to them and "how very enormous and shocking is the offence, when in the discharge of their laborious office, they are treated with insolence instead of honour, and meet with threatnings [sic] instead of thanks!"[51] Having warned of God's command to be subject to authority, of the fact that God ordained governmental authority, and of God's punishment for lack of subjection, Micklejohn urges his listeners and readers to give honor and respect to those in government as a matter of gratitude and appreciation, as well as instruction from God's "chosen vessel," Paul.

As illustrated above by the example of Jonathan Boucher, others made reference to Romans 13, even though it was not the primary text for their message. In one of his references to Romans 13, Thomas Bradbury Chandler puts the burden of proof on those who preach resistance by asking whether God "has given any dispensation to the body of the people, under any government, to refuse *honor*, or *custom*, or *tribute*, to whom they are due; to contract habits of thinking and *speaking evil of dignities*, and to weaken the natural principle of respect for those in authority?" Chandler answers his own question by maintaining that, "on the contrary," God commands submission and, "require(s) us, on pain of *damnation*, to be duly *subject to the higher powers, and not to resist their lawful authority*." Given that severe penalty for disobedience, Chandler asks the following chilling question: "if it should finally appear, that the claim of the *British* parliament is just, and according to law, [would] it be not a necessary consequence, that the colonies have resisted that *power*, which is *ordained of God*, and are in the high road to open rebellion?"[52]

Chandler is also one of several[53] who notes that Nero was the Roman emperor at the time that Paul wrote the command to the Romans that "every soul" be in subjection to the governing authorities. According to Chandler: "No tyrant was ever more despotic and cruel, than Nero, and no Court ever more corrupted than his; and yet to the government of this cruel and despotic tyrant, and his corrupt ministry, peaceable submission was enjoined by an Apostle, who had due regard for the rights and liberties of mankind." Given this context for Paul's instruction, Chandler further argued that "were we the subjects of the Grand Turk," we ought not to "disturb or threaten an established government, by popular insurrections and tumults."[54] In eighteenth-century America, the "Turk" was code for the worst of tyrants.

For almost all Loyalist ministers, the message of Romans 13 was clear, direct, and without exception. Two of them are the exceptions that prove the rule—and prove the importance of one's hermeneutic in approaching a text. Myles Cooper writes that if he had "lived in the Days of Nero," he "would have united with Mr. A———s [Adams], Mr. H———k [Hancock], yea, even with the Generation of Vipers, and . . . have done his utmost to tumble Nero from his Misnud [elevated seat]. Thank God, *Non tali auxilio, nec defensoribus istis Tempus eget* [not such aid nor defenders does the time require]." It is instructive to note that as he begins this statement, he asks for forgiveness or an exemption from "St. Peter and St. Paul." He thus recognizes that the position he takes runs contrary to that of those apostles in I Peter 2 and Romans 13. It is also important that he introduces his position with the confession that it is based on his "present Opinions and Feelings."[55] Cooper, then, knows that participation in overthrowing a ruler—even one as bad as Nero—is not what the apostles teach, and thus can be explained only as an emotional response. His final statement in Latin indicates that he opposed the Revolution because he did not think that Britain's actions were sufficient to warrant it.

John Joachim Zubly was a supporter of the American cause up to the point of rebellion and then became a Loyalist. He believed that the British government had been oppressive and somewhat tyrannical, but although disobedience might be called for, rebellion was not the proper response. Because he essentially bridges the two sides, Zubly's approach to Romans 13 and his use of it illustrates the different hermeneutics used by each. In his earlier, Whiggish sermons, Zubly reflects the Patriot practice of adding to and adjusting the text in order to make their case. He begins his look at Romans 13 with: "The gospel gives no higher authority to magistrates than to be 'the ministers of God, for the good of the subject.'"[56] One should notice immediately that Zubly says magistrates are *to be* ministers of God, not that they *are* ministers of God, as Romans 13:4 says.

This is the common subtle, but strategic, change in the text that the Patriots depended on for much of their argument. This makes being a minister of God a qualification in order to be considered a magistrate rather than the magistrate's identity and function—something to aspire to rather than what one is in essence. It is akin to the difference between saying that someone is a human being and saying that someone must prove to be a human being by meeting certain qualifications. This is critically important for the Patriot position because it allows the observer to decide whether or not someone is a legitimate magistrate based on whether or not the subject approves of the magistrate's actions. It makes the individual subject the ultimate judge of what it means to be a minister of God and of what constitutes his good. But men of goodwill disagree on policy; one man's tyranny is another man's responsible action. Furthermore, man's view of what constitutes his good may differ significantly from God's view. Paul does not say that magistrates govern for the good of the subject as approved of by the subject, just that they govern for the good of the subject from God's perfect perspective. For example, God may determine that an individual may have to fight a battle with cancer for his or her ultimate good, but virtually no one would view it as good in the midst of the fight.

This change in the text also means that some who are called magistrates are not really endowed with authority from God; not all are, as Jonathan Mayhew puts it, magistrates "as such." Once this possibility is recognized, then the door is opened for the desired conclusion of the Patriots as expressed in Zubly's next sentence: "From whence it must surely follow, that their power is to edify, and not to destroy: When they abuse their authority, . . . they deserve not to be thought ministers of God for good; nor is it to be supposed, when they act so contrary to the nature of their office, that they act agreeable to the will of God, or in conformity to the doctrine of the gospel."[57] But this puts into the hands of the subject a power that God never gives him. The critical question is, who gets to judge whether a magistrate is legitimate or not? The subtle textual change allows for the idea that the people are the proper judges. The actual text makes God the judge. If the people are the proper judges, then rebellion may be an option. If God is the proper judge, then only He may remove a magistrate by extralegal or nonlegal means.

This same small change also affects the succeeding verses in Romans 13. Given the notions that magistrates have to qualify by their actions to be legitimate and that individual subjects have the authority to make that judgment, Zubly's other Whiggish application of Romans 13 logically follows:

> The case I would state thus, "Whether any duty or impost supposed to be laid on in an illegal manner, and inconsistent with natural and civil right, from motives of conscience ought nevertheless to be paid?" and to elucidate this, I observe, the general rule is this: "Render therefore to all their dues; tribute to whom tribute is due, custom to whom custom; fear to whom fear, honour to whom honour." Rom. xiii:7. There is something due to government which cannot be refused without injustice, and more than which cannot be demanded without tyranny and oppression.[58]

Zubly's position here depends on the previous assumption that governing authorities can be deemed illegitimate. But this again begs the question: who decides? And on what basis? Does God give men the right to decide whether or not to be subject to authority on the basis of "natural and civil right"? If so, where does God give that right? Who has the right to determine the legality or illegality of taxes—private individuals or magistrates raised to office by the rules of the political system? Who has the right to determine what is "due" to government—individuals or the body endowed with the legislative power?

Zubly later, as a Loyalist, takes a different view of Romans 13. In an essay written for the newspaper in 1780, Zubly argues that "there cannot be worse beings in hell, or out of it," than those who start and fight a rebellion "without cause" in their own country and that they "must appear conspicuous and next in rank . . . to Lucifer and the fallen angels, who without cause introduced rebellion in the creation." After this astonishing remark, and because he is now expressing opposition to rebellion, Zubly simply quotes Romans 13 without changing any of the wording: "Whosoever therefore resisteth the power resisteth the ordinance of God, and they that resist shall receive to themselves damnation, Romans 13:2."[59] In his commentary, he still includes the qualification "without cause" because, like Cooper, Zubly might approve of some rebellions, but he did not think that British actions provided a sufficient cause for this one. The qualification weakens his argument in reference to the literal text, but it nonetheless demonstrates that when taking the Loyalist position, ministers kept the biblical text intact.

I Peter 2

I Peter 2:13–17 rivals Romans 13:1–7 in terms of explaining the purpose and role of government and the relationship between individuals and government. We have sermons based on I Peter 2 by two of the most prominent and influential Loyalist ministers: Samuel Seabury and Charles Inglis. Both men establish, as an historical context, that "the Jewish Nation" had been "seditious," "frequently raising Insurrections," "turbulent, factious and rebellious," and "making Religion the Cloak of Disloyalty"; and that this conduct was "particularly exceptionable."[60] They contrast this behavior with God's command of submission delivered by the apostles Peter and Paul. It should not surprise the biblically literate that both sermons include references to Romans 13, and indeed that both sermons move seamlessly back and forth between the two texts. Seabury specifically says that the two texts are "parallel" commands. Both Inglis and Seabury also emphasize the importance of the providence of God in placing people under particular governments and their subsequent obligation to submit to—and to honor—the authority that God has placed over them.[61]

Given that foundation, Seabury begins his discussion of the relevant verses (13–17) by getting right to the command: "The Apostle first attends to, and inculcates upon Christians, due and peaceable Submission to that Authority under which they live; whether it be exercised by KINGS as Supreme, or by Governors sent by them, and acting by their Authority." He connects Peter's directive with that of Paul in Romans 13 and reminds his audience that "the Injunctions of both these Apostles are drawn from the Fountain of Truth," which is the authority of Jesus.[62] Inglis, on the other hand, begins with the significance of Peter stipulating that one must be submissive to government "for the Lord's sake" and that such submission is "the express 'Will of God.'" Inglis moves quickly to the reason that Peter gives for the command and concludes that the "Honour of Christ, and the Success of his Gospel, depended on its Professors observing this Line of Conduct—I may affirm, that they also greatly depend on it even now."[63] This latter statement clearly was designed to stress the relevance of the instruction to the events of the day.

Both Inglis and Seabury find great significance in the fact that Nero was the Roman emperor when the apostles gave their instruction. It is important enough to their argument and to the general issue for me to include extended quotations from each. Inglis argues:

> NERO was Emperor of Rome when St. Peter wrote this Catholic Epistle; and notwithstanding the vicious Character of that Prince, he delivers the Precept in my Text—"honour the King." This was to be a general Rule for all Christians. The personal Character of the Magistrate was not to interfere with the Civil Duty of the Subject: Even when bad, it did not dissolve the Obligation of the latter. . . . The Christian therefore, is here injoined [sic] to honour the Person who is vested with legal Authority, and whom the Providence of God hath placed over him.[64]

Inglis, then, uses the example of Nero to focus on the irrelevance of the character of the ruler in terms of the subject's obligation to submit and even the honor the ruler. The implication for Inglis's audience would of course be that as bad as George III might be, he is not nearly as bad as Nero—and not even Nero's "vicious Character" excused rebellion. Seabury's use of Nero's example was directed toward his vicious and unjust actions:

> When St. PETER and St. PAUL wrote their Epistles, they were under the Government of Heathen Emperors and Magistrates, who persecuted

them, and the other Christians,—depriving them of their Possessions, beating, banishing, and killing them,—without any Crime proved against them, but merely because they were Christians. And yet it was to these Emperors and Magistrates,—even to *Nero* and *Caligula*—that the Apostles commanded Honor and Respect, at all Times; and whenever it could be done consistently with Obedience to God, Duty and Submission.[65]

The irony—intended or not—in Seabury's statement is that his charges against Nero and Caligula were the same as those that the Loyalists leveled against the Patriots. If one were to replace "Heathen Emperors" with "committees" and "Christians" with "Loyalists," it would be an apt description of Loyalist treatment at the hands of the rebels. But Seabury's fundamental point is that the apostles teach and command submission to all rulers irrespective of the justice or injustice of their actions.

In both of these sermons, the announced text was actually specifically I Peter 2:17: "Honor all men. Love the brotherhood. Fear God. Honor the King." Both preachers spend time addressing the particulars of this verse and then use it as a platform for summarizing the subjection command in both I Peter and in Romans. Inglis notes that Peter "connects the respectful Honour and Obedience we owe to our Sovereign, with that filial, reverential Fear which is due to our Creator; not only because they are characteristic of a real Christian, and should be inseparable; but because our Welfare, Peace and Happiness, temporal and eternal, depend on the Discharge of them." In other words, because God has chosen to dispense benefits through an earthly king and has made subjection to him mandatory, those who fear God will subject themselves to the king's rule. Seabury adds another view of the relationship between the admonition to fear God and to honor the king: "If we fear God we shall obey his Command from a Principle of Duty to him."[66]

But what does it mean to honor the king? Inglis provides a detailed answer: "To honour the King, is to entertain respectful Sentiments of his Authority and Person—to speak always with Deference of both—to promote the Peace and Stability of his Reign, and pay a chearful Obedience to his Laws—to check, as far as we are able, the Calumnies which Sedition or Malice would propagate to his Disadvantage, to oppose the Proceedings which would disturb or endanger his Authority—and to promote these Sentiments and Conduct among others."[67] Inglis maintains that this duty "extends to the Subjects of all regular States," irrespective of forms of government. He admits that some forms are preferable to others, but "neither our Saviour, nor his Apostles have decided where that Preference is due." In other words, Christ and the apostles did not interfere in political affairs or with "the Political Constitution of States," but simply laid down the command to "'be subject to the higher Powers,' and honour those who are vested with supreme Authority; whether that Authority be lodged in One, in a Few, or in Many."[68] The specific regime or type of regime does not matter; the duty of the people is to submit and honor.

What does this specifically mean for an Englishman? Seabury provides a detailed answer: "The last Command in the Text is to *honor the King*.—In the Empire to which we belong, the supreme Authority is vested in the KING, the *Lords* and the *Commons* of the Realm, conjunctly called the PARLIAMENT; and to the Laws of this supreme Authority absolute Submission and Obedience are due . . . upon the Principles of Religion . . . otherwise the Commands of God will be violated."[69] Seabury here makes the king—to whom the Americans regularly and fervently pledged allegiance—a part of the Parliament, whose power over them the Americans disputed and denied. In doing so, he cleverly applies the injunction to honor the king to a duty to honor the Parliament. The king was, in fact, a part of Parliament in the sense that his approval was necessary in order for any bill to become law; in the case of George III, he dominated the Parliament through his ministers who "commanded overwhelming majorities in both houses."[70] Continuing this line of reasoning, Seabury proceeds to emphasize that "no Law can be enacted" without the king's "single Approbation" and none can be executed without his "Commission." His primary point is that it is invalid for the Patriots to claim allegiance to the king while denying the legitimacy of laws passed by Parliament. Seabury ends this discussion by reminding his audience that the king "is *the Viceregent of God*" and therefore worthy of "*the highest Honor and Respect, that are due to any Mortal.*"[71]

Although it is not the text for his best-known sermon, Jonathan Boucher concludes "On Civil Liberty; Passive Obedience, and Non-resistance" by simply quoting I Peter 2:13–17. He does so without elaboration, trusting to the clarity and power of the word of God and to the groundwork that he has laid for the reader. He does make one alteration in the text for purposes of emphasis: he puts the words GOVERNORS and SENT in all capital letters. This is meant to encourage the reader to more closely identify its message of submission with the particular American situation. It is no coincidence that, ending with the quotation of these particular verses, the final statement in Loyalist Jonathan Boucher's signal sermon in answer to the Patriots is: "honour the king."[72]

Liberty

Boucher preached "On Civil Liberty" in answer to a sermon on the same text and subjects by Jacob Duché. The text that Boucher inherited from Duché was Galatians 5:1: "Stand fast, therefore, in the liberty wherewith Christ hath made us free." Whereas Duché used the verse to urge parishioners to stand up to the British in support of political liberty, Boucher expounds the verse in its context to establish that it refers to spiritual freedom from the law and from bondage to sin. Regarding the Jews, liberty here "denoted an exemption from the burthensome services of the ceremonial law"; regarding the Gentiles, "it meant a manumission from bondage under the *weak and beggarly elements of the world*" (Galatians 4:9); and "as it respected both in common, it meant a freedom from the servitude of sin."[73] Boucher declares: "The passage cannot, without infinite perversion and torture, be made to refer to any other kind of liberty; much less to that liberty of which every man now talks, though few understand it." In fact, he continues, as meant by the Patriots, liberty "is never used . . . in any of the laws either of God or men." Rather, "flowery panegyrics on liberty" are "the productions of ancient heathens and modern patriots: nothing of the kind is to be met with in the Bible, nor in the Statute Book. The word *liberty*, as meaning civil liberty, does not, I believe, occur in all the Scriptures." Boucher, then, begins his argument by severely criticizing the Patriots' improper interpretation and application of the central text. He charges that the text has been used "for no other reason that appears but that the word *liberty* happens to stand in the text."[74]

Building on this argument concerning improper use of the concept of liberty, Boucher moves to the practical consequences of the liberty addressed in Galatians 5:1. He reaffirms that "the liberty inculcated in the Scriptures, (and which alone the Apostle had in view in this text,) is wholly of the spiritual or religious kind." He then observes: "This liberty . . . certainly gave them no new civil privileges. They remained subject to the governments under which they lived, just as they had been before they became Christians, and just as others were who never became Christians; with this difference only, that the duty of submission and obedience to Government was enjoined on the converts to Christianity with new and stronger sanctions."[75] Paul reminds his readers that they have gained liberty in Christ, but that liberty leaves them in exactly the same political situation as they inhabited before. In fact, given the unique capacities provided by that spiritual liberty which was gained, Paul elsewhere strengthens rather than weakens the responsibility to submit to and obey the government.

Boucher expands on this theme of submission and obedience: "Obedience to Government . . . is particularly incumbent on Christians, because (in addition to it's [sic] moral fitness) it is enjoined by the positive commands of God: and therefore, when Christians are disobedient to human ordinances, they are also disobedient to God." The ensuing discussion is clearly in the context of Romans 13, including: "If it [the government] be less indulgent and less liberal than in reason it ought to be, still it is our duty not to disturb and destroy the peace of the community, by becoming refractory and rebellious subjects, and *resisting the ordinances of God* [Romans 13:2]."[76] He concludes this part of his argument by noting that throughout, the Scriptures are "summarily recommending and enjoining a conscientious reverence for law whether human or divine."[77]

For the reason explained by Boucher, the Loyalist clergymen rarely talked about political liberty. They did not believe it to be a biblical concept—or, at least, emphasis—and they believed that God was more concerned with submission to authority. As an eventual Loyalist with strong Whig sympathies, John Joachim Zubly is of two minds where the question of liberty and the Bible is concerned. During his Whig period, Zubly, like the Patriot preachers, applies a number of texts speaking of spiritual liberty as if they spoke of political liberty. Because his basic approach to Scripture—his hermeneutic—is that of the Loyalists, however, he often gives the proper interpretation of a verse as he gives an inappropriate application of it. He says, for example, that given the repeal of the Stamp Act, "it may not be improper to subjoin: Fear God, honour the king, stand fast in your liberty, and be not entangled with the yoke of bondage." In the same message, he quotes Romans 6:16 about being a slave of God, warns against being "slaves unto lust," and declares that "to be free indeed is neither more nor less than to be heartily engaged for him whose service is perfect freedom." He concludes his sermon about the Stamp Act by stressing that only through salvation and serving God "shall we be a people really free and truly happy; then will the son make us free, and we shall be free indeed."[78]

That last remark is a paraphrase of John 8:36: "If the Son shall make you free, then are you free indeed," which he also quotes in his sermon on "The Law of Liberty."[79] His primary text for that sermon, which was preached before the Second Provincial Congress of Georgia (a Patriot group) in 1775, is James 2:12: So speak ye, and so do, as they that shall be judged by the law of liberty." In explaining the meaning of the verse, Zubly makes it clear that this is a reference to spiritual liberty. He says: "The law which the apostle speaks of in our text, is not a law of man, but of Him who is the only lawgiver, that can save and condemn." He points out that "the dispensation of the gospel, under which we live, is called the law of LIBERTY" and that "whenever he [a man] feels the happy influence of the grace of the gospel, then this 'law of liberty makes him free from the law of sin and death.'" He further explains: "By the law of liberty he is made free from sin" and "there is another reason why the gospel is called a law of liberty, which is to distinguish it from the ceremonial law under the Mosaic dispensation."[80] Like Boucher, Zubly teaches that the liberty spoken of in these verses is spiritual liberty of two types: freedom from sin and freedom from the Mosaic Law.

In this same message, and in the midst of this argument, Zubly the Whig applies the verses as if they had political meaning. He quotes John 8:36 in the context of "the civil state," man's "social condition," and "national freedom." In the previous sermon, he said that its context is salvation and serving God. He says of his primary text (which he earlier said was about salvation): "It seems [in James 2:12] as though the apostle had an eye to some particular branch of the law of liberty, i.e. the love which we owe unto our neighbour." That leads to discussion of "the rights of mankind" and his criticism of "a divine right to kings to govern wrong." In so doing, Zubly asks: "Does the gospel cease to be a law of liberty, because some of its professors pervert it into an engine of tyranny, oppression and injustice?" He earlier said the gospel was about freedom from sin and death. Zubly also cites the passage that Boucher says is irrelevant (Galatians 5:1) and declares: "The gospel . . . bids us to 'stand fast in that liberty wherewith the Son of God has made us free.' . . . Freedom is the very spirit and temper of the gospel."[81] Yes, but what kind of freedom?

John Joachim Zubly shows the ability to produce a Patriot application even from a Loyalist interpretation of a passage of Scripture. This is perhaps no more evident than Zubly's reference to the book of Philemon. That book would seem to be a problematic portion of the Bible for a Whig—one that he would ignore. In Philemon, the apostle Paul, who introduces himself as a "prisoner of Jesus Christ," sends a runaway slave, Onesimus, back to his owner, Philemon. The apostle, who presumably is familiar with the gospel, does not order or even ask Philemon to free Onesimus. If political freedom is an important biblical principle and a central part of the gospel—the "very spirit and temper" of the gospel—why does Paul not demand Onesimus's freedom? Zubly actually references the book without seeing the need to solve that puzzle. He cites Philemon 14 in order to conclude: "Surely then the spirit of the gospel is very friendly to the rights and property of men."[82] Perhaps that is true, but the "property" referenced here is a man—a slave. Zubly has Whig sensibilities before the Revolution, so the emphasis in his pre-Revolution sermons is on political liberty, even though he knows that he is applying biblical texts about spiritual liberty to support his cause. Once the Revolution begins, Zubly cannot find a way around the many clear and direct passages that prohibit rebellion. He speaks out against rebellion and is targeted by the Patriots for being insufficiently patriotic. As he becomes a Loyalist, Zubly's emphasis turns away from liberty to submission to authority and criticism of rebellion.

Boucher and other Loyalist ministers were also outspoken critics of some of the early acts of Parliament. However, like Zubly, they could not make the jump to justifying rebellion. Referring to his protests against the Stamp Act, Boucher later describes his own dalliance with an overemphasis on liberty in spiritual terms: "I too bowed at the altar of Liberty; and sacrificed to this idol of our groves, *upon the high mountains, and upon the hills, and under every green tree* [Deuteronomy 12:2]."[83] Boucher believes that liberty became a focus of false worship to many in America and distracted them from obedience to the commands of God.

Example of Jesus

Turning focus from God the Father to God the Son, Boucher takes his argument to the example of Jesus. Boucher finds instruction not only in the teachings of Jesus but also in the general example of Jesus, concluding that "every thing our blessed Lord either said or did, pointedly tended to discourage the disturbing a settled government."[84] Circumstances were "meritorious and honourable" and ripe for an overthrow by the standards advanced by the Patriots: "At the time when he was upon earth, his country groaned under an unjust and most oppressive bondage. It had just been subdued by a people, whose chief motive for over-running the world with their conquests was a lust of dominion: and it was as arbitrarily governed, as it had been iniquitously acquired."[85] What more reason or justification could a revolutionary want? In addition, Old Testament prophecy had promised the Jews a Messiah, which they interpreted as a temporal prince who would deliver them. All the signs pointed to revolution and to Jesus as the commander in chief. Matthew, Boucher notes, went out of his way to say that Jesus was "'born king of the Jews' [Matthew 2:2], that is to say, the person who was their king by birth." Furthermore, "it is well known that in no instance whatever did our Saviour give greater offence to his countrymen than he did by not gratifying them in their expectations of a temporal deliverance. . . . It was one of the chief grounds of the enmity of his countrymen towards him, and the only plausible pretence on which he could be arraigned."[86]

In addition, "they would have set him on their throne in that way by which alone we are now told authority over a free people can properly be obtained, viz. by the suffrages of the people. To assert his claim *de jure* against those who held it *de facto*, they would fain have taken him by force . . . to make him a king [John 6:15]."[87] Finally, He "who could have commanded more than twelve legions of angels" did not lack the power to effectively resist Pilate, "who, from the basest of all motives, gave sentence, that a person in whom he declared he found no fault, should be put to death."[88] Jesus had the right to be king; His people were under real tyranny; the people consented; and He had the power to remove injustice. Boucher has led his readers to ask themselves: why did Jesus not lead a rebellion?

Despite the ideal circumstances and justification according to "human reckoning," Jesus did not, of course, lead a rebellion. Boucher notes that though they did not believe "interference" (involvement) in civil affairs was "contrary to Christianity, it no where appears, that either our Saviour, or any of his apostles, ever did interfere with the affairs of any government, or the administration of any government, otherwise than by submitting to them."[89] Furthermore, Boucher suggests that His suffering and humiliation on the cross proves that Jesus was not afraid to do whatever it took for the glory of God and the good of mankind. One final justification for revolution is added: "His constant discouragement, therefore, of a scheme so well calculated . . . to emancipate his country (had he estimated . . . the condition of subjects under government, according to our ideas) would have been inconsistent with that love to mankind which he manifested in every other action of his life." So why did Jesus not do it? For Boucher, the answer is simple:

> The only rational conclusion . . . is, that he thought it would be better, both for Judea in particular, and for the world in general, that . . . the

> people should not be distracted by a revolution, and . . . that there should be no precedent to which revolutionists might appeal: his words were not meant to bear merely a local and circumscribed, but a general and extended application, when he directed his followers to *render unto Caesar the things that are Caesar's*: his practice was conformable to this precept; and so would ours be, were we but practically convinced that *it is enough for the disciple to be as his master, and the servant as his lord.*[90]

On the one hand, Jesus did not want to distract people from His true mission to provide spiritual freedom. On the other hand, He had called His followers to be subject to government, and He simply practiced what He preached. If we claim to be His followers, then we should do the same. Boucher sums up the Christian's responsibility to Jesus in this area: "As Christians, solicitous to tread in the steps in which our Saviour trod, the tribute of civil obedience is as much due to our civil rulers, even though they should happen to be invaders like the Romans, and though, like Herod, the ministers of government should chance to be oppressors, as the duty of religious obedience is a debt which we owe to *the King of kings, and Lord of lords.*"[91]

Finally, Boucher disagrees with those Patriots who argue that submission to authority—particularly in matters of contention—is degrading and humiliating. Citing the example of Jesus, Boucher denies that submission is "a degrading and servile principle." He says, rather, that it is "the very reverse"—that it has "superior dignity" due to its "celestial origin."[92] How could following the practice of God on earth (not to mention His command) be degrading?

Other Loyalist preachers did not develop arguments from the example of Jesus that were as long and detailed as Boucher's, but several of them did appeal to His example. As was mentioned in the discussion of Romans 13, George Micklejohn pointed to the words and actions of Jesus before Pilate and to His explanation of why He would pay the temple tax, even though He was technically exempt. In response to the latter (Matthew 17:24–27), Micklejohn asks: "And who is there that will presume to offer insult to the powers that are in authority, or shew the least resistance, when he considers how remarkably our Lord was pleased to honour them?"[93] Like Boucher, Micklejohn emphasizes that Jesus had sufficient power to successfully oppose "the civil powers." He concludes that if Jesus could feed the five thousand as He did, He could certainly have prevailed in a contest with civil authorities, "but instead of shewing resistance, we behold Him here manifesting the most tender concern and regard for the support of their authority." Micklejohn then asks the obvious question which results from the example of Jesus (God): "Shall man then presume to refuse that submission which God himself has thus condescended to pay?" Micklejohn's answer is that Jesus's example "ought to have an irresistable influence" and that it was "intended for our imitation . . . to leave us an example that we might follow in his steps."[94] Micklejohn does not mention it, but the apostle Peter makes that very point in I Peter 2:21.

Samuel Seabury highlights Jesus's command to "*render unto Caesar the Things that are Caesars, as well unto God the Things that are Gods* [sic]." Charles Inglis also quotes this passage, Mark 12:17, in support of his own observation that "our blessed Saviour" joined together honor and obedience to the king with the fear of God. According to Inglis, Jesus went beyond mere submission to earthly authorities to completely separate His followers from any kind of rebellion:

> To clear himself from all Imputation of Sedition, he told Pilate that his "Kingdom was not of this World" [John 18:36]. His Kingdom did not interfere with earthly Kingdoms—its Spirit and Design were totally different, and it was to be promoted and administered by other Laws and Measures. His Apostles unanimously inculcated Submission and Obedience to the higher Powers.[95]

As Inglis notes, all of the apostles drew the same implication from the example of Jesus as well as from His words. Inglis implies that his audience should follow suit.

Old Testament

In addition to the example of Jesus, the Loyalist preachers found examples and illustrations from a number of Old Testament passages. Like the Gospels recounting the life of Jesus, the Old Testament is largely narrative, and clergymen on both sides in the American crisis utilized the stories to make or to illustrate arguments, with occasional proverbs mixed in. Presumably their congregations found the stories interesting and engaging, and the proverbs easier to digest, than unbroken exhortation and admonition frequently based on difficult passages.

Some of the preachers simply reached into the Old Testament—usually

Psalms or Proverbs—to grab hold of a helpful verse. Thomas Bradbury Chandler, for example, punctuates his discussion of the duty of submission by asking whether it is "not a matter both of worldly wisdom, and of indispensable Christian duty, in every American, to *fear the Lord and the King and to meddle not with them that are* GIVEN TO CHANGE?" This is an uncited quotation of Proverbs 24:21, which is a warning against associating with rebels. The stated text for Samuel Seabury's "Discourse on Brotherly Love" is Psalm 133:1, but he merely uses that verse as a jumping-off point rather than discussing it in depth. In fact, his primary point is not what the verse says but rather what he believes is the historical context for the verse. He argues that the psalmist (David) had seen "party and faction, and . . . civil war"; "Rebellion indeed had once reared its horrid front, and displayed its bloody banners . . .; but public justice had routed, had crushed, had punished the hedious [sic] monster, and peace, order and happiness were restored."[96] This, he says, is the context of the passage, which he takes as an indictment of those who disrupt unity.

Charles Inglis often cites or quotes isolated passages from Job, Proverbs, Ecclesiastes, Isaiah, and Daniel, as well as lesser-known books such as Malachi and Hosea, to make or bolster a particular point. He does explicate two Old Testament passages in depth, however: I Samuel 8 and Deuteronomy 17:14–20. I Samuel 8 is arguably the most important passage on civil government in the Old Testament, and Deuteronomy 17 provides helpful information to a proper understanding of I Samuel 8. Inglis did not really choose to comment on this passage; he did so in answer to claims made by Thomas Paine in his popular pamphlet, *Common Sense*. In his assault on monarchy as a form of government, Paine asserts that "the will of the Almighty, as declared by Gideon and the prophet Samuel, expressly disapproves of government by kings."[97] Inglis astutely shows that Paine's interpretation of Judges 8:23 and of I Samuel 8 cannot be correct: "That simply desiring a King, could not be a crime, is undeniably evident; because the Almighty had long before expressly permitted it, had directed the mode of chusing a King, and prescribed the line of conduct the King should observe, when chosen. This is done in Deuteronomy xvii. 14–20." Inglis then spends two pages laying out the instructions given to future kings of Israel in Deuteronomy 17.[98]

Because Paine's view cannot be correct, Inglis reasons that their crime must be "something else," namely "in the *manner* of their asking a King—in the *principles* on which they acted—in a *disregard* of the venerable old prophet—but chiefly, in a *neglect* of the *directions* above mentioned

[Deuteronomy 17]." Inglis explains that "the people tumultuously assembled to desire a King, who would resemble the despotic Kings which surrounded them" and that the main point was that the people rejected a king "such as the Almighty had directed them to chuse," thus effectively rejecting God as their king. Inglis then argues that the monarchies around the Israelites were despotic and that Samuel tried to warn them against that "manner" of monarchy in verses 10–18. According to Inglis, Paine suggests that this is a general proscription of monarchy, but it is in reality a warning against despotic monarchy. Inglis moves ahead to the kingship of David to demonstrate a proper monarchy. He observes that "Saul's successor was 'a man after his [God's] own heart,' by a zealous attachment to, and punctual execution of, the Mosaic law in his regal character."[99] In other words, David was the kind of king that Deuteronomy 17 described. Inglis takes up the important task of defending monarchy from a biblical perspective, and after blunting Paine's attack via I Samuel, Inglis quotes twelve other passages of Scripture—from both the Old and New Testament—"merely to lay the plain truth, the genuine testimony of Scripture on this point, before such as might not be at the pains of examining it themselves; and might therefore be misled by our author [Paine]."[100]

Jonathan Boucher makes even more extensive use of the Old Testament, including six sermons based—and centered—on Old Testament passages. His best-known sermon is not based on the Old Testament, but in it he begins his discussion of authority and subjection in the Garden of Eden. He points out that "the first instance of power exercised by one human being over another is in the subjection of Eve to her husband," and he argues that "Adam could not have assumed, nor could Eve have submitted to it, had it not been so ordained of God. It is, therefore, equally an argument against the domineering claims of despotism, and the fantastic notion of a compact."[101] Authority and submission were established by God for His purposes. They are not rooted in inherent superiority or superior might; nor are they rooted in consent. Boucher further says that this also proves "that it [government] may and must be submitted to by a fallen creature, even when exercised by a fallen creature, lost both to wisdom and goodness." The fact that rulers are fallible, unwise, and bad does not remove the responsibility to be subject. As for a Lockean notion of consent by equals, Boucher asserts: "The equality of nature . . . was superseded by the actual interference of the Almighty, to whom alone the original underived power can be said to belong."[102] The original power belongs to God, not to "the people." Boucher seems to recognize that his primary adversary is not Jacob Duché, whose sermon he is answering, but the source of Duché's and the revolutionaries' theories: John Locke. Locke's name is sprinkled throughout the sermon (at least nine times), and five single-spaced pages of arguments against Locke were added to the 1797 published version of the sermon.

One of Boucher's sermons with an Old Testament text is also in answer to a Patriot sermon, this one by William Smith and based on Joshua 22:22. Both sermons were preached and published in 1775. In Joshua 22, the Israelite tribes that settled beyond the Jordan River built an altar as a witness or reminder of their connection with the rest of Israel, but it was initially thought to be a sacrificial altar for false worship and independence from Israel. Consequently, the other tribes organized an army to attack them and restore them to the nation. Before there was fighting, the supposedly rebellious tribes explained the purpose of the altar and said, "If it be in rebellion, or if in transgression against the Lord (save us not this day)." Smith's application of the passage to the American situation was that the American colonies were like those tribes beyond the Jordan and that they had erected only altars of affiliation with the British and an altar of liberty, so the British need not respond with force or suspect a desire for independence on the part of the colonies.[103]

Boucher argues that it was reasonable for the remaining tribes to treat the altar with suspicion and to send a force to enforce the law. That is particularly true because "it was their duty to vindicate the laws of God, lest, by forbearing to punish the disobedient few, they should bring down his wrath upon the whole congregation." Boucher explains the significance of that fact and its application to the Americans. The Israelites objected to the Gileadites' altar because it "exposed the whole congregation" to danger. Likewise, the consequences of the conduct of the some of the colonists would fall on all. If their actions are, as the British believe them to be, "unprecedented, unconstitutional, and rebellious," then they "may be fatal not only to ourselves, but endanger the whole empire."[104]

Boucher also points out some important distinctions between the tribes beyond the Jordan and the American colonies. The tribes appeal to God "only as they are clear of any designs of a revolt." Their altar was indeed an innocent one affirming their unity with Israel, but "we have set up our altar on principles totally dissimilar to those of the two tribes and an half; for, our principle in setting it up at all, is to declare ourselves, in some sense, and to some degree, a separate and independent people; whereas, to have done so would, in their estimation, have been *rebellion*, against which they most earnestly protested." The object of the American altar of "Liberty," he argues, "too clearly is to counteract and resist, if not directly to deny, the supremacy of the Mother Country." It may well be innocent, like the two and a half tribes, but "if we intend peace only, for what purpose are we now everywhere, in the words of the prophet Joel, trained and directed to *prepare for war? why are our mighty men to be waked up? our men of war to draw near?* [Joel 3:9–10]." Boucher concludes with a final challenge to the Americans: "If America can . . . make the same solemn appeal to Heaven that the Gileadites did, viz. that it is not *in rebellion* that our country is now set forth in hostile array, America is without excuse if it be not made." For Boucher, Smith misses the whole point of the story; the Gileadites were innocent and were not in fact pursuing a rebellious course. The same cannot be said for the Americans, but if it could, Boucher reassures his audience, "the Parent Tribes of Israel received the once-suspected Settlers of Gilead with open arms; and doubt not but that your Parent State will imitate this conduct."[105]

Boucher also found applications to the American situation in the story of the dispute between Abram and Lot and their parting of ways, but Boucher was particularly interested in various aspects of the rebellion of Absalom against David. He clearly saw that history as an important source of instruction concerning the practice and elements of rebellion. He preached two sermons on the subject, focusing on particular characters, their actions, and motives. He affirms the Loyalist position by affirming Ittai the Gittite, who, although a "*stranger and an exile*, and of course under peculiar temptations to join in the revolt: yet so far was he from forgetting his duty" that he pledged his loyalty to David (II Samuel 15:19–21). Boucher refers to Ittai as "this firm loyalist." Through the example of Hushai, he takes a shot at republicanism. When Absalom asks Hushai where his loyalty lies, Hushai answers: "*Whom the Lord and this people shall choose, his will I be* [II Samuel 16:18]." Boucher reports: "*The Lord and the people* had chosen, and could choose, David only. Nevertheless, framed and applied as the answer was, it might and it did convey to Absalom the idea that *Hushai* had also adopted the new-fangled notions concerning the power of the people."[106] Boucher clearly was not a supporter of the newfangled notion of republicanism.

The richest Old Testament source for Boucher is the story of another character in the story of Absalom's rebellion: Ahitophel.[107] We know from the beginning that Ahitophel is going to be a negative example, as Boucher chooses II Samuel 17:23 as his sermon text. In that verse, Ahitophel commits suicide. Boucher begins by saying that he holds up Absalom "as a mirror to those of us, who (like him) may be in danger of being led into rebellion, while we suppose we are engaged only in a virtuous opposition." He holds up the story of Ahitophel so "that our Leaders also may see what they have to expect if they, like him, proceed to drive matters to extremities." Because the end of both men was a tragic and violent death, Boucher's not-so-subtle hint warns of the same for those in America who lead or participate in a rebellion. Addressing some of the rhetoric of the Whigs, Boucher notes that "it is in times of popular commotions, when revolutions are meditated, that the doctrines of natural rights and the natural *equality* of mankind are most countenanced." But Boucher connects with another Old Testament story in response to demands for equality and consent when he says "according to the revived doctrine of Korah, Dathan, and Abiram, the governed have the same right to direct and command as those who govern."[108] Given that these three men also suffered extraordinary violent deaths (Numbers 16:27–33), Boucher's disapproval of the newfangled notion of republicanism and political equality is again made evident.

Boucher then turns the argument to focus on God and His providential supervision of events and results. Unlike Ittai and Hushai, Ahitophel joined Absalom in his rebellion, and that was the cause of his downfall. Boucher warns that "*Ahitophel either knew not, or did not consider, how much the Almighty is concerned to defeat unjust and rebellious enterprises.*" God is not an impartial, passive observer. "War is an appeal to God: those, therefore, who engage in an unjust war, appeal to God in an unjust cause: and hence it is natural and rational to expect that God should take part against them, and award the victory to that party which has the most justice on it's [sic] side." God has determined that rebellion is inherently unjust. "To resist and to rebel against a lawful government, is to oppose *the ordinance of God*. . . . He, therefore, who can hope that God, *who is a God of order and not of confusion*, will give his blessing to such attempts, does neither more nor less than expect that he will act in contradiction to his most glorious attributes, and cease to be the friend and father of mankind."[109] God cannot bless a rebellion without supporting opposition to His own ordinance and without violating His own nature. "Sometimes (assuredly for wise and gracious purposes) he may permit iniquitous arms to prosper and triumph over a virtuous cause: but, in general, in wars, as well as in every other public interest, *righteousness exalteth a nation, while sin is the reproach of any people.*"[110]

As he brings his message on Ahitophel to a close, Boucher homes in on his desired response from his audience. Addressing first those with militant tendencies, he notes that, at Ahitophel's advice, Absalom made the breach with David "irreparable" through "such a notorious violation of duty [publicly sleeping with David's concubines], as shewed to all Israel, that he now no longer either wished or hoped for a reconciliation." Boucher mentions this to call to mind lawless American actions, such as the Boston Tea Party, thus suggesting that the Americans are burning their bridges with the British and making anything but a forceful response impossible. Turning to those whose support for the Patriot cause was more tacit or passive, Boucher offers the following admonition: "Let no man therefore flatter himself, that *thus far he may go* wrong, and *no farther*. Unless you can resolve not to WALK *in the counsel of the ungodly*, let what befel [sic] Absalom and his followers be a warning to you how natural the progress is from WALKING TO STANDING *in the way* of sinners, and in due time to SITTING DOWN *in the seat of the scornful*." Once one goes along with violators of God's commands, it becomes easier to be drawn in and more difficult to stand firm at any point. He urges them to have nothing to do with the Patriot cause or with those who promote it. "In such circumstances your safety lies in your retreat, and in having *no fellowship with those who take counsel against the Lord and against his anointed*." In his "Farewell Sermon," Boucher leaves his flock with this same warning, but this time in connection with the opponents of God's work through Nehemiah: "If you listened to my doctrines, you could no longer be the disciples of the Sanballats and Tobiahs, who have at length, step by step, led you to the very brink of rebellion."[111]

Rebellion

It is appropriate that Boucher's last American sermon closes with a warning against rebellion. Loyalist sermons featured negative attacks on rebellion in conjunction with positive exhortations to submit and obey. George Micklejohn emphasizes the effects or results of rebellion. He refers to rebels as "many wretched and unthinking men . . . inconsiderately involving friends, relations and neighbours, in the most direful calamity, and foolishly bringing upon themselves destruction here, and damnation hereafter." He wants "every such rash and misguided person" to be "made duly sensible of the dreadful impiety of so daring and wicked an action, as well as of the certain misery that must invevitably be the consequence." Micklejohn's language is only too clear and requires no clarification. He further declares that "resistance to that lawful power and authority which

God hath set over us" produces only "the wildest uproar," "the most shocking and dismal effects," and "the most wretched scenes of misery and distress." He denies that any good can come from "such wicked means." Micklejohn also laments the fact that though some "only meet the ruin their rashness has sought, yet many others must unavoidably become partakers in the calamity, who were never partners in the crime." He is sensitive to the effects of revolution on innocent persons who do not choose to rebel or participate in rebellion but who suffer many of the same dire consequences as the guilty. At the end of his warnings to those who contemplate rebellion, Micklejohn offers the following injunction: "But particularly let them remember, that the blood which may be shed by their means, will hereafter be required at their hands."[112] God will ultimately hold them accountable not only for disobedience to His command and resistance to His ordinance but also for the blood of those who die and suffer as a result of that resistance.

Samuel Seabury joins Micklejohn in concern for the effects of rebellion, arguing that "the Destruction of every Thing that is good must be the Consequence of Disobedience and Rebellion." He also emphasizes the earthly and heavenly punishment which inevitably falls on rebels. Citing Romans 13, Seabury reminds his audience that the magistrate is "the Minister of God, to execute Vengeance" and that "God himself" punishes those who, "in Contempt of his Authority and Command," resist governing authorities.[113] Charles Inglis aims at a different target in his criticism of rebellion: republicans. He charges that republicans "belie Heaven . . . by claiming its Sanction" for their schemes of "Rebellion and Usurpation." In fact, he considers it "astonishing" that professing Christians "who really believe in a divine Revelation, and acknowledge its Authority . . . should be the Dupes of such Men," become "Trumpeters of Sedition and Rebellion," and "could pursue a Conduct so diametrically opposite to the Spirit of their Religion!" Inglis sees the biblical prohibition of rebellion so obvious and compelling that he says he would think it impossible that any who profess Christianity could participate in it if "melancholy Experience" did not show it to be true. On the other hand, he assures the king's troops in the midst of the Revolution that fighting for the king against a revolution started by republicans is "so good and righteous a Cause."[114]

Inglis emphasizes, however, that he is not diametrically opposed to all forms of revolution. He declares: "I am none of your *passive obedience and non-resistance men*. The principles on which the glorious Revolution in 1688 was brought about, constitute the articles of my political creed; and were it necessary, I could clearly evince, that these are perfectly conformable to the doctrines of scripture."[115] Apparently Inglis does not think that the American cause meets whatever standard he has for a good or righteous revolution. Because he does not produce any of the doctrines of scripture to which he refers, he apparently also thinks that it is not necessary to do so.

Jonathan Boucher echoes some of Inglis's particular criticism of republican rebellion. He charges that the "Northern Colonies [New England] . . . were, with very few exceptions, peopled by avowed Independents; whose principles, whether in themselves well or ill-founded, even those who maintain them will hardly pretend are propitious to those of the British Constitution." Those principles were those of republicanism, specifically those of John Locke. In another sermon, Boucher says of them: "Mr. Locke, however, and his followers, in presenting these principles to the public in their most popular form, have the demerit only of having new-dressed principles which are at least as old as the rebellion of Korah, Dathan, and Abiram." Boucher again connects the republican notions of equality and consent with Korah's rebellion against Moses. Korah led a group of 250 leaders of the congregation and assembly in challenging Moses for exalting himself above the assembly—making it at least a plausible correlation with republicanism. He also expresses a wish that there had been "but one general Interpretation with Regard to the reciprocal Duties of the Sovereign and the People" in "the revealed Will of God," as he sees it "abused . . . to throw a Veil over the Horrors of Anarchy, and Rebellion."[116] The word "anarchy" was generally used by Loyalists as a code word for republicanism. As he sees it, republicans, particularly in the dissenting churches, are justifying their rebellion by an improper and "abusive" interpretation of passages such as Romans 13. Even if their interpretation is adopted that allows for rebellion, Boucher firmly asserts that "it is certain that mankind are no where in the Scriptures commanded to resist authority; and no less certain that . . . they are commanded to be *subject to the higher powers.*"[117]

In a sense, Boucher also shares Inglis's disdain for nonresistance and passive obedience, but Boucher's view is nuanced and he offers his own definition of terms. On the one hand, Boucher refers to "the ridiculous and damnable Doctrines of Non-resistance, and Passive-Obedience" as they were generally viewed; on the other hand, Boucher supports passive obedience as he defines it. In his view, "active obedience" is doing whatever the government commands. "Passive obedience" is essentially accepting penalties incurred as a result of disobedience to government when one must disobey in order to be obedient to God. He argues:

> No government upon earth can rightfully compel any one of it's [sic] subjects to an active compliance with any thing that is, or that appears to his conscience to be, inconsistent with, or contradictory to, the known laws of God: because every man is under a prior and superior obligation to *obey God in all things*. When such cases of incompatible demands of duty occur . . . every well-principled person . . . will submit to the ordinances of God, rather than comply with the commandments of men. In thus acting he cannot err and this alone is "passive obedience"; which I entreat you to observe is so far from being "unlimited obedience," (as it's [sic] enemies wilfully [sic] persist to miscall it,) that it is the direct contrary.[118]

What Boucher calls "passive obedience" is simply subjection that places obedience to God over obedience to government when the two conflict. The believer disobeys the government when he must in order to remain obedient to God, but he remains in subjection to the government (usually meaning taking punishment) rather than rebelling against it. This is the message of Acts 5:29 in conjunction with Romans 13. Boucher puts it this way: "Resolute not to disobey God, a man of good principles determines, in case of competition, as the lesser evil, to disobey man: but he knows that he should also disobey God, were he not, at the same time, patiently to submit to any penalties incurred by his disobedience to man." This approach also leaves open the option to protest. As Boucher explains, both the British constitution and the ordinance of God warn against resistance, but "you are not forbidden either to remonstrate or to petition."[119]

Boucher is adamant that this clearly is not unlimited obedience, as the revolutionary advocates claim. What is missing from the Patriot sermons and literature is the notion of suffering. They assume that any suggestion of obedience without the option of rebellion must be a call for unlimited obedience. They have no concept of suffering unjustly for God's sake as a result of disobedience. Boucher, on the other hand, says that Christianity "is a suffering religion; a religion enjoining suffering, teaching suffering, and rewarding suffering," and that "to suffer nobly indicates more greatness of mind than can be shewn even by acting valiantly." He stresses the obligation and the privilege of following Jesus and His disciples in this regard:

It might be hoped that Christians would not think it grievous to be doomed to submit to disappointments and calamities, as their Master submitted, even if they were as innocent. His disciples and first followers shrunk from no trials nor dangers. Treading in the steps of him who, *when he was reviled, blessed, and when he was persecuted, suffered it*, they willingly laid down their lives, rather than resist some of the worst tyrants that ever disgraced the annals of history. Those persons are as little acquainted with general history, as they are with the particular doctrines of Christianity, who represent such submission as abject and servile.[120]

Boucher thus appeals to Christians to follow the example of Jesus—calling to mind Peter's instruction in I Peter 2:21–23—and scolds those who portray subjection as degrading or dishonorable. On the contrary, Boucher declares: "I affirm, with great authority, that 'there can be no better way of asserting the people's lawful rights, than the disowning unlawful commands, by thus patiently suffering.' When this doctrine was more generally embraced, our holy religion gained as much by submission, as it is now in a fair way of losing for want of it."[121] Thus Boucher addresses both the political and the religious issue, drawing concern for the faith to a level of importance at least equal with political concerns. In so doing, he maintains that the people's rights can still be effectively asserted through submission without compromising the teachings of Christianity.

Perhaps ironically, many of the Loyalist ministers followed Boucher's formula in their dealings with the Patriot committees and provincial congresses. They believed that they could not obey some of the orders handed down and still be obedient to God. Consequently, they disobeyed the revolutionary "authorities" and either fled or took the punishments meted out to them. But they did not fight back. They did not rebel, even though they questioned the legitimacy of the often self-appointed "authorities."

This section on rebellion ends with a Whig who became both a victim of those committees and a Loyalist. Though John Joachim Zubly was an erstwhile Whig and preached a number of sermons sympathetic to or supportive of the Patriot cause, he could not take the monumental step of supporting rebellion. In his best-known sermon, preached after the fateful events at Lexington and Concord, at the cusp of the Revolution, Zubly still claims that the Americans want to retain their ties with England, and he urges them to do so. He views the prospect of rebellion as so extraordinary and so catastrophic that he appropriates Judges 19:30 as a parallel. In so doing, he compares the beginning of rebellion in America with cutting a woman into pieces and sending the pieces throughout Israel. For Zubly, rebellion is a ghastly business.

In the midst of the Revolution, Zubly addresses rebellion itself and the disastrous effects it has had—and presumably will continue to have—on Americans. Zubly affirms that the Americans have real grievances, but he uses a parable in Judges 9:8–15 to illustrate his argument that rebellion against the British is an unwarranted response. His point is that the Americans are cavalierly rejecting very good government for very bad government. Zubly also argues that the Scriptures are clear in their condemnation of rebellion, so the punishment for those who rebel must be severe. To illustrate the point, Zubly alludes to Paul's condemnation of those who violate their conscience "in so small a matter as eating or not eating flesh" (perhaps Romans 14), then suggests that he "who ventures upon resistance to lawful authority, joins to promote all the evils of domestick discord, sheds the blood perhaps of his dearest friend because he remains faithful to his king and country," and brings great evil in the present and for the future.[122] Zubly's point here is clear: matters such as whether or not to eat meat sacrificed to nonexistent idols are debatable, yet Paul castigates those who know what is right and do not do it. Scripture clearly prohibits rebellion and its results are much more catastrophic, so how will one be judged who violates that clear command? Zubly asserts that he has "produced a case from holy writ [Romans 13:2], by which what is deemed rebellion in scripture is most clearly determined, and from which all those that profess regard and obedience to the scriptures may learn under what specious pretence and appearances men may nevertheless incur the greatest guilt, and involve themselves, their country and posterity, into ruin, when they think every thing pleads in favour of their proceedings." Zubly believes that many of those who support the Revolution and the misery it has caused simply refuse to heed biblical instruction: "How dreadful is the case of any person or people of whom it may be said: 'They have eyes to see and see not, they have ears to hear and hear not, for they are a rebellious house [Ezekiel 12:2].'" But Zubly hopes that they will repent, and "it may be they will consider though they be a rebellious house. Ezekiel 12:3."[123]

Sin

As Zubly's example illustrates, another common subject in Loyalist sermons is sin, with particular emphasis on the sin of nations, as opposed to individuals. There was a virtual consensus among Loyalist ministers that the Revolution and America's troubles in general were largely a result of God's judgment on the sins of the American people and those of the British people at large. John Sayre says: "I look on the present unnatural war, as being a judgment of God on the people of Old England, as well as on us Americans, for our many crying offences against his most holy laws, and a loud call to a sincere and immediate return to him and to our duty." According to Jonathan Boucher: "War is the just judgement which God inflicts on a sinful people." Charles Inglis declares to his audience in 1777: "The Judgments of God are now abroad, and his Hand lies heavy on our Land. Our Transgressions have provoked him to visit us with severe Chastisements." As late as 1780, he repeats the warning: "WHENEVER therefore we see those Judgments abroad, and a People visited with them, which is our Case at present; we may be assured that the Hand of God is there, and that he is calling those People to an Account for their Transgressions." Even John Joachim Zubly during his Whig period acknowledges: "If ever ... we should be cursed with a tyrannical oppressive government, our sins must be the cause of it."[124]

Perhaps no minister put greater stress on sin in relation to the American situation than did Samuel Andrews. In a 1770 sermon, Andrews warns that Christianity "is giving Way to human Policy, and is likely to be banished from America." He bemoans the fact, as he sees it, that America is "now half-ready to act a Part which will disgrace the dead, intail [sic] War on ourselves, and Misery on our Children."[125] The reference is to American disobedience to and denial of authority that is likely to lead to outright rebellion. Five years later, after the outbreak of hostilities, Andrews delivered a fast day sermon on the need for repentance that was focused on the national predicament.

In tune with the fast day, Andrews begins by reminding his audience that Americans had "fasted and cryed [sic] repeatedly unto God ... since the commencement of our troubles," but that "God does not appear to regard our cries." A cloud "seems to be just ready to burst with irresistible fury," and neither the Americans nor the British seems willing to find an accommodation. He suggests that if the Americans "attend this fast ... with real repentance for all former sins" and with a true resolution to reform, then God "will, probably, save our land from ruin." But "if we remain obstinately in our sins," then God will not respond favorably.[126] Andrews then leads his audience to reevaluate what might be the cause of their troubles: "Since then, our former expressions of humility, have not been attended with the desired effect;—but our land is *bleeding*, and our dangers, *increasing*; it behoves us now to examine, wherein our former fasts were defective, and to mend those defects in *this*, that the Lord may now be entreated for our land, and save our nation and us from ruin." Andrews recognizes that his audience might argue that they had been appropriately repentant, but that "may delay the salvation of a people for a time, even tho' they should repent of their sins." The problem with that suggestion, Andrews says, is that "our miseries are accumulating, our distresses, increasing, and our punishments, growing upon us." Because it was their sins that brought the calamities on them, it is logical to conclude that they continue and increase because of impenitence. As Andrews concludes, "No reason can be assigned, why he should increase his judgments upon a penitent people, and no example can be produced, where he has done it."[127] In other words, this is not the way God works; He does not increase calamities on those who are innocent. One might quibble with Andrews's argument by pointing to the book of Job, but his conclusion is consistent with the prevailing view of the day and is therefore effective.

After claiming that such action by God would contradict Jeremiah 18:7–8, Andrews begins to ask his audience what their unrepented sins might be. He does not immediately jump to the rebellion; he starts with suggestions more favorable to his people. He suggests that one important sin is slavery. Because he is addressing New Englanders, this is not particularly controversial or likely to cause offense, even though some New England merchants were involved in the slave trade. He cleverly links it with the Patriot cause and sentiments, however, when he asks: "Is it not worth our serious consideration, whether our detaining in captivity, a part of our fellow creatures, can be reconciled with our own principles of liberty, and if not, to examine whether it is not necessary, either to change our principles, or let the *oppressed go free*; for how can we expect, God will work that deliverance for us, which we refuse to give to others?"[128] This introduces an issue addressed elsewhere in this study: the inconsistency and hypocrisy of slaveholders who are arguably the freest people in the world demanding greater liberty while holding others in real slavery.

At this point, Andrews has gained the attention and approval of his audience by calling attention to a recognized national sin, but one that is not particularly threatening to his congregation and one about which they can feel moral superiority. In suggesting other areas of possibly unrepentant sin, he again leads with offenses that his audience would agree with, but he follows with a sin that some might find uncomfortably close to home. He decries "profaneness, . . . needless breaches of the Lord's day, and a neglect of divine worship"—all behavior of which his congregation would disapprove. Andrews then adds to the list of sins requiring confession and repentance (a change in behavior) "a bitter ungodly spirit towards those who happen to differ from us, in opinion, whether the difference, respect things civil or religious."[129] Note the mention of differences of opinions in things civil. Andrews is chastising his people for their treatment of Loyalists and suggesting that uncharitable treatment of Loyalists is at least part of the cause of continued and increasing punishment from God. Andrews asks a damning question: "Is there not reason to fear, that we as a people, are this day determined not to abate in this temper: but to prosecute with relentless anger those who differ in sentiment from us?" To accentuate their shame, he calls on all who "pretend to be christians" to follow Ephesians 4:31, which says: "Let all bitterness, and wrath, and anger, and clamor, and evil speaking, be put away from you, with all malice."[130]

Having stung them with an uncomfortable admonition, Andrews returns to listing sins that allow them to resettle and to feel morally pleased with themselves: "injustice, falshood [sic], oppression, whoredom, and drunkenness." His congregation is unlikely to feel guilty of or vulnerable to these sins, and this restores their comfort level. This effective rhetorical device allows Andrews to drive to his ultimate point—to take his unsuspecting and supportive audience where he wants them to go in their thinking. He reminds them that these days of fasting and prayer ought to be days of "inquiry and examination," especially because God's punishment of them continued unabated. He asks, "Should we not then inquire, whether our cause is really the cause of God?" And "if we have already inquired into this matter—would it be amiss, in an affair of this importance, to re-consider it?" Here is the crux of the matter: are we sure that the American cause is approved by God? He admits that the "general voice is, that we are greatly oppressed," but warns that a kind of madness can develop with thoughts of oppression and calls them to "examine, whether our resentments may not have carried us, even too far" and "whether the laws of God will fully justify, the whole mode of our proceedings."[131]

Perhaps they are justified by men, but will the laws of God justify their extreme actions? How can they answer that question? Andrews now leads them to the Bible and to the fundamental Loyalist biblical argument:

"Let us seriously and impartially try our cause by the word of God—let us carefully, (as they who expect a judgment to come) read over, what is there recorded concerning the higher powers: and the duty of subjects to them—and then, let us resolve, to make these sacred directions, the standard of our conduct: and to do nothing but what we can answer, before the dread tribunal of the final Judge."[132] Andrews's solution to their predicament is to see what the word of God says about their relationship with governing authorities—including Parliament—and to commit themselves to follow whatever it says. For the Loyalist, the sinful cause of America's troubles was clear and unequivocal: Americans were rebelling against God by rebelling against Britain. If they want to end God's punishment and restore God's blessing, then they need to cease the rebellion and return to obedience and submission to the governing authorities.

Andrews then reassures them that he is a "hearty friend to my country" and only admonishing them in this regard so that "we must be safe, and shall soon experience the salvation of God." But what if they do not follow his instruction—or, more importantly, God's command? Andrews asks: "If we do not intend to be governed by this rule, why are we met here before the Lord to day? Or can we expect, but that God will despise this our offering?" Why have you come to church if you are going to reject God's demands? What is the point of a day of prayer and fasting if it is all for show by a disobedient people? Andrews has one more important exhortation for his congregation: "I hope then, that none will be so unwise, as to suspect them to be enemies to their country, who point it to this sacred rule, as the standard of its proceedings."[133] He returns to the matter of the treatment of Loyalists in general, and in particular clergymen who are obligated to preach what the word of God says whether or not it is popular. He apparently sees himself in the place of the Old Testament prophets who spoke the word of God to warn the Israelites of their disobedience and were persecuted and killed (Luke 6:22–23; 13:34) for their unpopular message. Andrews closes his sermon with a summary of his main point concerning sin: "I am not so much afraid of the power of England, as I am of the sins of America. . . . It is our sins which have provoked the Lord . . . therefore it must be repentance alone, which must save us." He exhorts them to "do nothing . . . but what the laws of God approve"[134]—a concise summary of the position of the Loyalist ministers.

Summary

In his seminal sermon "On Civil Liberty," Jonathan Boucher reminds his audience, "It is certain that mankind are no where in the Scriptures commanded to resist authority; and no less certain that... they are commanded to be *subject to the higher powers*: and this subjection is said to be enjoined, not for our sakes only, but also *for the Lord's sake*."[135] This of course is a reference to Romans 13. It focuses attention on God and the fact that subjection is not only for our good but also that God has a stake in the matter of subjection. Man affirms God's ultimate power and authority by adhering to the authority structures that God has established. Boucher builds on this theme with a reference to the Old Testament: "The glory of God is much concerned, that there should be good government in the world: it is, therefore, the uniform doctrine of the Scriptures, that it is under the deputation and authority of God alone that *kings reign and princes decree justice* [Proverbs 8:15]." Boucher wraps up this focus on authority and subjection pointing to God by attacking the central core of the Lockean system: "So far from deriving their authority from any supposed consent or suffrage of men, they receive their commission from Heaven; they receive it from God, the source and original of all power." Consequently, "it is with the most perfect propriety that the supreme magistrate, whether consisting of one or of many, and whether denominated an emperor, a king, an archon, a dictator, a consul, or a senate, is to be regarded and venerated as the vicegerent of God."[136] For the Loyalist ministers, that reality precludes rebellion and puts God against the American Revolution.

3 Theoretical Arguments from the Nature of Government

> I wish and advise you to act the part of reasonable men, and of Christians.
>
> —Jonathan Boucher

The Loyalist ministers were, of course, preachers of Christianity. As one would expect, they often and regularly appealed to the Bible in their sermons opposing the Revolutionary cause. However, the Loyalist clergymen were also observant political subjects and well-educated men who saw an important role for reason in argumentation. When it came to the question of rebellion versus loyalty, they thought that theirs was the reasonable position, and they consequently were not hesitant to make a rational case in their sermons and in political pamphlets. Loyalist ministers also preached sermons in response to published sermons by Patriot preachers. In order to fully answer those sermons, they were required to traffic in reason, nature, theory, and appeal to nonbiblical authority because those were the primary literary weapons of the promoters of the American Revolution. The focus of this chapter is the arguments of the Loyalist ministers that are based on the nature of man, the origin and nature of government, and the nature of revolution.

As a rule, the Loyalist ministers held a less optimistic view of human nature than did the Patriot preachers, who generally taught that man is essentially good. Jonathan Boucher held that men are more likely to be guided or governed by their passions or their temper than by their judgment: "They find the Movement of the Passions a more easy and agreeable Exercise than the Drudgery of sober and dispassionate Enquiry." This is a critically important facet of man's character from a political standpoint because it makes him more susceptible to manipulation. Most men "think only as they are bid to think, and act as they are acted upon." But there are other, even more dangerous, aspects of man's character. In particular, Boucher warns that "AMBITION and Lust of Power above the Laws, are such predominant Passions in the Breasts of most Men, even of Men who escape the Infection of other Vices, that Liberty, legal Liberty, would be in continual Danger of Encroachments, if it were not guarded by perpetual Jealousy."[1] Boucher's observation resembles that of James Madison in *Federalist #51*: "ambition must be made to counteract ambition."

Charles Inglis generally agrees with Boucher's assessment of man, warning that "ambition and a thirst of power are naturally inherent in man." For him, this "condition of human nature" and experience prove the impossibility of a republic working over a large country such as America. Inglis is a little more charitable, however, arguing that human weakness accounts for some of man's evil. Specifically, the weakness of the human intellect is such that men often intend some "real or imagined" benefit but instead do "the reverse." He explains that "men's passions and prejudices mingle with their reasonings, pervert their judgement and hurry them into many things which unbiassed [sic] reason utterly disapproves." Unfortunately, making errors is "the lot of humanity" and unavoidable.[2] Samuel Seabury sees "tender feelings, . . . gentleness and kindness, and meekness and benevolence" in the nature of man, but he warns that passions such as revenge, malice, and anger can sour or taint the better elements of his nature and turn him into "the most mischievous of all animals." The result is "strife, . . . injustice, and oppression, and cruelty, and rapine, and murder, and war, and rebellion, and tyranny." This wicked side of man is so powerful that "the laws of civil society, the laws of God, the tender, sociable and humane feelings of the heart, all concur to restrain the inordinacy of passion, to bridle the lust of revenge; and all these united, and assisted by education, are scarcely sufficient to answer the purpose."[3] The evil side of man is barely restrained.

This statement by Seabury connects the nature of man to the need for civil society. For most political theorists, there is an intimate connection between their view of the nature of man and their concept of the origin of government. The Loyalist ministers were no exception. Along with the need to restrain man's wicked tendencies, Seabury links the origin of government with another aspect of man's nature: man's natural sociability. Citing the biblical teaching that it is not good for man to be alone (Genesis 2:18), he concludes that man is made for society and that this is "the dictate of nature" and "established by the very nature of man." Inglis agrees. He also cites the way that God made man as evidence:

> Are we not, by an act of Providence, in our birth made members of society? A state of society is the natural state of man; and by the constitution of his mind and frame he is fitted for it. Not only his wants and weakness require it, but his inclinations, his noblest faculties impel him to it; and the more perfect those faculties are, the better is he fitted for society. As nature has thus made us members of society, without any choice or will of ours; so, whatever happiness or perfection we are capable of, can only be attained in society.[4]

Having shown that man is naturally a member of society and that man needs society, Inglis correlates man's nature and society with a need for government. He expresses disagreement with Thomas Hobbes on the mechanistic origin of government and agreement with Richard Hooker that government and society are inseparable. With the assumption that man's happiness can only be attained in society, Inglis says "we cannot doubt" that God wills the happiness of men and that He also wills "the means which lead to that end—those means are order and government." Man is born in society, and its ends cannot be obtained but by "subordination, order and the regulation of laws; and where these are, there is government." Condensing what he means by man's inclinations and noblest faculties, Inglis posits that "man is a moral agent, and thereby fitted to be governed by laws." From this, he concludes that government is the will of God and that "it has its origin in the nature and state of man."[5]

God created man to be a social being, so living in society comes naturally to man. God created man with certain characteristics that make government naturally necessary. But what kind of government is best, and what theories best comport with the demands of God via nature? Boucher claims that of all the theories advanced concerning the origin of civil government, only that of the Bible has "no insuperable difficulties." Specifically rejecting the social contract theory, Boucher contends that no man has power over his own life, and therefore he cannot transfer power over his life to another or to others. Man cannot give a right that he does not possess. Boucher argues that only He who gave life—God—can give authority to take it away, and because that authority is essential to government, it stands to reason that government is originally from God. To investigate the idea of a social contract from an historical and biblical perspective, Boucher looks at the establishment of the nation of Israel in the Promised Land in the book of Joshua. He asks where there is any indication or suggestion that it was done by a social contract.

On the contrary, he suggests that the terms of settlement were delivered "not in the cautious style of a contractor, but with all the authority of one who has a right to dictate and to command."[6]

According to Boucher, an "all-wise and all-merciful Creator" established patriarchal rule over man in light of man's "unruly will." God clearly made man to be social, but He knew that men could not live together without the restraint of law and government. Not only does patriarchal government have the "most and best authority of history . . . to support it" but it also is "by far the most natural, most consistent, and most rational idea." This system is the most natural because the "first father was the first king" and "kingdoms and empires are but so many larger families." Boucher suggests that "the first man, by virtue of that paternal claim, on which all subsequent governments have been founded, was first invested with the power of government." Inferring the law from the practice, he concludes that "it was thus that all government originated; and monarchy is it's [sic] most ancient form." He also points out that patriarchy "always has prevailed, and still does prevail" among both the most enlightened and least enlightened peoples. Patriarchy is the most consistent and most rational system because in every country, "the ignorant are more numerous than the wise." Because this is the case, it is never wise for the safety of the country to depend on the determinations of the ignorant majority. God, then, established a system of "natural subordination" in which the more enlightened give instruction and the uninformed receive it.[7]

Charles Inglis narrows the focus from patriarchy in general to constitutional monarchy. Responding to Thomas Paine's attack (in *Common Sense*) on the form of the British constitution, Inglis lays out the basic Aristotelian scheme of three forms (substituting "democracy" for polity) and argues that "the word Tyranny may be applied to the abuse of any of them." Paine, he says, simply calls all monarchy tyranny because "he happens to dislike it," and he "makes no distinction between the right use and abuse of a thing." Inglis then points out that monarchies are "best adapted to extensive dominions; popular governments to a small territory." The implication, of course, is that popular government would not work in a country the size of America. At the end of this discussion, Inglis concludes that "it has been the opinion of the wisest men in every age, that a proper combination of the three, constitutes the best government. It is the peculiar, distinguishing glory of the English constitution, that it is a happy mixture of these; so tempered and balanced, that each is kept within its proper bounds, and the good of the whole thereby promoted." Inglis makes this point a number of times.⁸

Inglis responds to a number of Paine's criticisms of monarchy. Because the celebrated *Common Sense* played a significant role in persuading Americans to oppose the British and to support an independent democracy, it is appropriate to mention a few of those criticisms and rejoinders. Paine insinuated that states without kings are less likely to go to war. Inglis answers with numerous examples of the wars of Greek and Roman republics. Paine cynically charged that monarchy "was first introduced by Heathens." Inglis reminds readers: "So, say I, was Greek and Latin—so was smoking [sic] tobacco; and yet I can dip into Homer and Virgil, or enjoy my pipe, with great composure of conscience." He also notes that democracy, "our author's favourite scheme of government," was also introduced by heathens. Paine added one more religious claim: that monarchy was created to promote idolatry. Inglis responds that the ancient republics, especially Rome and Athens, were "as infamous for every species of the grossest and most abominable idolatry" as any monarchy. Inglis caps off the discussion by asserting: "If a thing is good in itself, I conceive it to be a matter of very little moment, who it was that first introduced it."⁹ Inglis and the Loyalist clergy considered monarchy of the right kind to be a good in itself.

The Loyalist ministers both preferred monarchy and disdained republicanism or any kind of popular rule. Boucher is critical of the "loose notion" that government is "the mere creature of the people" to "erect and pull down" at their whim. He calls this "an unhallowed principle" and links it to the damning desire of the Israelites to do what was right in their own eyes when they had no king (Judges 17:6; 21:25). He directly challenges the presupposition behind the social contract theory: "The supposition that a large concourse of people, in a rude and imperfect state of society, or even a majority of them, should thus rationally and unanimously concur to subject themselves to various restrictions, many of them irksome and unpleasant, and all of them contrary to all their former habits, is to suppose them possessed of more wisdom and virtue than multitudes in any instance in real life have ever shewn." In other words, reason, human nature, and history all testify against the social contract theory. He also rejects the fundamental elements of the theory: man's natural equality and government based on consent in pursuit of the common good. He calls the notion of government based on consent by compact of the people and the notion that all are born equal and not naturally subject to another "equally ill-founded and false" in both "premises and conclusions."[10]

Boucher has both theoretical and practical problems with the notion of a natural equality of man. Practically speaking, "every human being is born the political subject of some other human being" because "infants, the moment they are born, are the natural subjects of their parents" and are also natural subjects of the state in which they are born. The state "is the parent, or in the place of the parent, to all who are born within it's [sic] jurisdiction." In addition, empirical observation tells us that "man differs from man in every thing that can be supposed to lead to supremacy and subjection, *as one star differs from another star in glory.*" This is true even in the state of nature imagined by social contract theorists. "By asking another to exercise jurisdiction over me, I clearly confess that I do not think myself his equal; and by his consenting to exercise such authority, he also virtually declares that he thinks himself superior." Reversing the normal order of social contract thought, Boucher declares that "without government, there can be no society; nor, without some relative inferiority and superiority, can there be any government." Boucher also argues that the "natural equality of mankind" gains its greatest approval "in times of popular commotions, when revolutions are meditated." Linking it with notorious rebels in the Bible, he says that "according to the revived doctrine of Korah, Dathan, and Abiram, the governed have the same right to direct and command as those who govern." The association of the idea of equality with these wicked men is meant as a rebuke of government based on equality.[11]

Boucher finds the idea of government based on consent of the governed in pursuit of the common good to be equally invalid. He argues that mankind has never agreed "as to what is, or is not, the 'common good.'" Every form or mode of government that has been set up and established by common consent in service of a supposed common good has "again been pulled down and reprobated." That has happened because "what one people in one age" have determined to be the common good has by others been determined to be "mischievous and big with ruin." For Boucher, governments do not aim at any particular good; rather, order and stability are characteristic of all good governments. The purpose of government is thus not some positive notion of a common good but rather a negative role of restraining evil so that man can live in an orderly fashion.[12] As long as the "natural subordination" of the "uninformed" to the "more enlightened" exists, "a community possesses all the strength and security of which the regular course of things admits." The job of the subject is to obey and submit, not to evaluate how well a government approaches an objective. Boucher identifies the "principle of obedience for conscience sake"—not the government's proximity to a commonly held goal—as "the firm basis or corner-stone of all good government."[13]

Boucher finds the notion of government by consent of the governed through a compact particularly nonsensical and dangerous. He mocks the "strange consequences" that must follow from the principle of founding government on a compact—namely that the government is "superior and inferior, above and below the people, supreme and dependent." This is not the only aspect of consent and contract theory that he finds illogical and fraught with danger. Boucher reasons:

> If . . . no man could rightfully *be compelled to come in* and be a member even of a government to be formed by a regular compact, but by his own individual consent; it clearly follows, from the same principles, that neither could he rightfully be made or compelled to submit to the ordinances of any government already formed, to which he has not individually or actually consented. On the principle of equality, neither his parents, nor even the vote of a majority of the society . . . can have any such authority over any man.[14]

If a man is born free from any subjection and remains such until he expressly gives consent, then he, and he alone, must give his consent to any law passed by the government, or he has no obligation to obey it. He is not subject to any authority and is essentially a law unto himself.

"Neither can it be maintained that acquiescence implies consent; because acquiescence may have been extorted from impotence or incapacity." If he goes along with a law because of inability to get away with disobedience, then that does not constitute consent and does not excuse attempts to hold him accountable by the government to whom he has not given his consent. The unrecognized government would be violating his fundamental rights. Even if he gives his consent, says Boucher, "explicit consent can bind a man no longer than he chooses to be bound. The same principle of equality that exempts him from being governed without his own consent, clearly entitles him to recall and resume that consent whenever he sees fit; and he alone has a right to judge when and for what reasons it may be resumed." The consequence of this, according to Boucher, is that governments, "though always forming, would never be completely formed" and "that which is now fixed might and would be soon unfixed."[15] Stability is one of the fundamental principles of good government, but government by social contract would be inherently unstable.

Boucher provides a counterargument from John Locke, the social contract theorist who was most influential in America. He quotes Locke as saying, "By consenting with others to make one body-politic under government, a man puts himself under an obligation to every one of that society to submit to the determination of the majority, and to be concluded by it." Rather than consenting to each act, a man consents to be governed by the authority created by the will of the majority and to be subject to whatever determinations it makes. Boucher responds by saying that, by the principles espoused, Locke must prove "that every individual man, on entering into the social compact, did first consent, and declare his consent, to be concluded and bound in all cases by the vote of the majority." Furthermore, any man who made such a declaration "would also completely relinquish the principle of equality, and eventually subject himself to the possibility of being governed by ignorant and corrupt tyrants."[16] In other words, the logical effect would be that the man's right to object to or resist the authority would be removed; he has consented to be ruled by whatever individual or body the majority makes sovereign.

Boucher crowns the argument by maintaining that "Mr. Locke himself afterwards disproves his own position respecting this supposed obligation to submit to the 'determination of the majority,' when he argues that a right of resistance still exists in the governed: for, what is resistance but a recalling and resuming the consent heretofore supposed to have been given, and in fact refusing to submit to the 'determination of the majority?'" Locke is inconsistent in arguing for a right of resistance while at the same time arguing for a duty to submit to the determination of the majority. One or the other must not be correct. "Such a system," says Boucher, "can produce only perpetual dissensions and contests" because the people would have the power to make and "unmake" governments; and once they are taught that unmaking a government is within their rightful power, they would be at least as disposed to do that as to uphold it. Consequently, it would be impossible to run a government by a compact in which a right of resistance is reserved. Furthermore, Boucher says, "there is no record that any such government ever was so formed."[17]

Boucher recognizes, however, that "owing to the weakness and wickedness of mankind, the flattering idea that all power flowed from the people would everywhere find advocates, and everywhere be popular." But though it would inevitably be popular, it is "ill adapted to support a government" and "well calculated to overturn one." Boucher sees the same potential danger in government by the people that Locke's critics have always highlighted: instability. If "the general suffrages of the people could absolve an individual conscientious subject from his allegiance . . . what was to hinder a giddy populace, when the tide should turn, from again acting the same part and deposing" the replacement government?[18] Some might answer that this is the nature of majority rule and that the majority should have whatever government they wish. But, as Boucher warns, it does not require a majority to bring about such change in the name of popular rule, as the history of revolutions demonstrates. Most revolutions are conducted by a relatively small cadre of true believers and not by a majority of the people.

Clearly referring to the American circumstance, he cautions that in practice, the principle of popular rule means that government may be "tampered with, altered, new-modelled, set up or pulled down, just as tumultuous crowds of the most disorderly persons in the community (who on such occasions are always so forward to call themselves the people) may happen in some giddy moments of overheated ardour to determine." Militant and loud minorities can "by certain words and sounds of almost magical potency" make "unthinking multitudes" desire to throw off supposed oppression and "imaginary abuses" that they have not even felt. In so doing, the people remove their government without real consideration of what will take its place. This happens, says Boucher, because "it is very rare to find any people, collectively, considerate and rational; and still more rare to find them moderate."[19] The people are susceptible to manipulation by a vocal minority. This is an inherent potential danger of acting on the belief that the desires or whims of the people are and should be the origin of government. How are those desires to be accurately determined? What if they are counterfeited?

Boucher and the other Loyalist ministers spend a considerable amount of time on the militant radicals who determined to manipulate and control the people. From the Loyalists' perspective, these troublemakers were stirring up the people and convincing them of oppression that they did not feel, all for their own gain. According to Charles Inglis, "The Feelings of the People, of a great many at least, . . . will be exactly such as are excited by Ambition, Discontent, false Principles, or the artful Management of designing Men." In 1774, Boucher admits that he does not know "with any precision" how many people support the Revolutionary cause, "but certainly they fall far short of the numbers which are so ostentatiously boasted of." He maintains "on as good evidence as the case admits" that the American people as a whole do not want separation from Great Britain.[20] These troublemakers or rabble-rousers are discussed at length in Chapter 5.

The radicals were effective at influencing—or manipulating—the people into active resistance. The Loyalist clergymen repeatedly addressed resistance or rebellion or revolution in an attempt to innoculate their congregations and readers against the arguments of the rebels or would-be rebels. Their arguments against the American Revolution in particular are addressed in Chapter 6. At this point, their theoretical reasoning concerning a "right of resistance" and their consideration of the nature of revolution must be examined.

At the base or core of the ministers' argument against resistance and rebellion is a profound sense of duty and honor. Samuel Seabury explains that every person "owes obedience to the laws of the government under which he lives, and is obliged in honour and duty to support them. Because, if *one* has a right to disregard the laws of the society to which he belongs, *all* have the *same* right; and *then* government is at an end." Charles Inglis stresses that "from the very Nature and Design of Government, it is the Duty of [those governed] to honour and obey [those who govern]"; fortunately, God "hath not only made our Duty compatible with our Interest and Happiness; but he hath inseparably connected them together." Similarly, Inglis says that "Government implies Subordination. Where Government is, there must be some who preside or govern—and others, over whom that presidency is exercised." Jonathan Boucher concurs, declaring that "as long as Government subsists, Subjects owe an implicit Obedience to the Laws of the supreme Power, from which there can be no Appeal but to Heaven." He identifies the conscience as the foundation for man's understanding of this reality and of his own duty: "The doctrine of *obedience for conscience sake* is . . . the great corner-stone of all good government; which, whenever any *builder* of constitutions shall be so unwise as to *refuse*, or, not refusing, shall afterwards suffer to be *destroyed*, what can he expect but that the whole fabric should be overturned?"[21]

Boucher saw it as his duty and responsibility to instill and protect that doctrine in difficult times. According to Boucher, "It is the fashion with the unhallowed politicians of these unprincipled times to malign and scoff at this venerable doctrine." In his view, "the low estimation in which this fundamental principle is held is the great evil of our age." Inglis agrees, but he characterizes it as a spiritual failing: "CONTENTMENT with that Station, in which the Will of Providence, and their own Choice hath placed them, is the Duty of all Men. A Disregard of this Duty, so clearly inculcated by the united Voice of Revelation and Reason, is the Source of numberless Evils." Speaking of the "primitive [early] Christians," he by comparison indicts those of his day: "They were Strangers to that Sort of Casuistry which dispenses with the Word of God requiring Honour and Subjection to the higher Powers; dissolves the Tie of Civil Obedience, though confirmed by a solemn Oath; releases Conscience from the Obligation of all these, and then absolves from the Guilt of such Crimes, when Subjects, either through Ambition, Prejudice, or other sinister Motives, happen to dislike the Government, or want to overturn it."[22]

Inglis contends that in pursuit of their own desires, men had convinced themselves that in spite of the Bible, oaths, and conscience, rebellion is acceptable. He attributes it to "a Degeneracy of Manners and Decay of Piety in many," and to a large extent, he blames the Patriot clergy, charging that they "have laid the gospel under a temporary interdict, and adopted principles directly opposite to it; they have thrown aside the spirit and manners of ministers of the Prince of Peace, and acted like votaries of Mars, or disciples of Mahomet." What have they put in place of the gospel? "The pulpits of *Dissenters universally* throughout the continent, and those of a *few renegado Churchmen* [Anglicans] to the southward, have resounded—not with the gospel, but with politics—not with meek lessons of peace, but with zealous exhortations to war."[23] It is well established that the Patriot pulpits were a tremendous recruiting and support mechanism for the revolutionary cause,[24] a fact that was not lost on Inglis in the late 1770s: "That a very large majority of the American Presbyterians have zealously concurred in promoting this rebellion, is a fact so notorious, that it cannot be denied."[25]

Thomas Bradbury Chandler agrees that the views of Americans regarding rebellion had been changed by design. He says that "popular insurrections and tumults" had always been "an unpardonable crime" in "every age and nation," so "most men would be startled and shocked at the proposal of entering into an open *rebellion*." In the colonies, however, "seditious principles, that directly lead to, and must finally bring on, a rebellion, have been gradually instilled" into the people and observes that such is "the common progress, and the effect, of rebellions in general." John Joachim Zubly agrees that this is the normal process of rebellion: "Rebellion may be hatched in a single breast, but becomes formidable by numbers; a few designing men lay the plan, commence violent patriots, and set up a popular pretence the most distant from their real designs, but the most likely to deceive honest men; the unwary are taken in, the unthinking follow, knaves trouble the water in which they intend to fish, the giddy multitude is led on from step to step." Inglis uses similar "step" imagery: "IF Men once deviate from the obvious Path of their Duty, there is no telling where they will stop. . . . Having subdued the first Struggles of Conscience, it afterwards becomes more pliant; and they are gradually carried on from one Step to another." It is their gradual nature that makes such efforts toward revolution so insidious and so effective. He cautions that great evils often come from "seemingly small Beginnings" and that "this is often the Case of Rebellion." Zubly notes that it is "easy to extinguish a spark, it is folly to blow up discontent into a blaze; the beginning of strife is like the letting out of waters, and no man may know where it will end." Boucher complains that "to encourage undistinguishing multitudes, by the vague term of resistance, to oppose all such laws as happen not to be agreeable to certain individuals, is neither more nor less than, by a regular plan, to attempt the subversion of the government."[26]

The Loyalists find the idea that individuals may resist laws that are disagreeable both unwise and repugnant. Seabury raises some of the resultant problems once one has decided that magistrates who do not please us are evil and our obligations to them are void. First, "are we always competent Judges of the good or evil Conduct of those whom God's Providence hath placed over us?" Seabury implies that "evil Magistrates" are not necessarily evil but may simply be those of whom we disapprove. He then asks whether we are infallible judges of what is right and what is wrong. Second, "do not our Passions and Prejudices often mislead us in the Judgment we form of Men in public Stations?"[27] He reminds his audience that the authority of the magistrates comes from God and that subjects are fallible and prone to error in making judgments concerning those magistrates and their policies. Seabury proceeds to suggest that even if magistrates actually fail in their duty, that does not excuse subjects from performing their own duty to submit. "To act thus would be to endeavour to remedy an Evil by doing a greater. It would be to dissolve all the Ties of Government, and introduce Anarchy, and Oppression, and Confusion, because some of the Officers of Government had behaved amiss."[28] One might think of this as an eighteenth-century version of "two wrongs do not make a right."

Boucher also cautions against allowing subjects to make these kinds of judgments and warns of the same dangerous result. He quotes William Falkner's *Christian Loyalty* to that end:

> If it be allowed lawful for subjects, in any case, to take arms against their Sovereign, this must include in them a right of judging whether their present case be such in which they may lawfully resist or no, otherwise they must either have a general power of resistance, and taking arms without any distinction of any cases; to assert which would be all one as to declare them *no subjects*, or *under no government*. . . . But, to assert that the people, or inferiors, are, of right, judges of the cases in which they may resist their superiors, is as much to say, they are bound to subjection only as far as themselves shall think fit. . . . But this cannot be otherwise than a general confusion in the world.[29]

Falkner's point—and by extension Boucher's—is that anarchy must be the result of subjects having or assuming a power of resistance to authority. It essentially means either that they are under no governmental authority or that they are a law unto themselves, which amounts to the same thing. Boucher holds that where "subjects . . . claim it as a matter of right to resist at pleasure, government is in fact already overturned, and all the great bonds of human society are dissolved."[30]

The Loyalists appeal to human nature and to logic in arguing against resistance and rebellion in principle. Seabury asks what government "would endure a Set of Men who held themselves exempt from all the Laws of civil Society?" Boucher reasons that government is, "in it's [sic] nature, absolute and irresistible." A government that can be rightfully resisted has no real authority or power. A government must cease to be absolute and therefore "cease to be supreme" if it makes itself resistible. If it gives up its supremacy, he argues, then "it must dissolve itself, or be destroyed." If it did not immediately discontinue of its own accord, then it would eventually be removed in favor of an effective force that could maintain stability. According to Boucher, the seeds of resistance and rebellion are sown in the nature of man. Mankind, he says, is "far too *prone to be presumptuous and self-willed; always disposed and ready to despise dominion, and to speak evil of dignities.*" Mankind is also "prone to be refractory, and to oppose power" and "to set themselves against those who govern." Sometimes this results from "vain attempts to render that perfect, which the laws of our nature have ordained to be imperfect"—in other words, from unreasonable expectations concerning what government can do. More often, bad and lawless men, "unwilling to regulate their misdirected passions by the restraints of reason, are equally unwilling to let the laws regulate them." These bad men see laws as fetters and "are always eager to *cast their cords* from them, and to *tear their bonds asunder.*"[31] Their lawless cause can only prosper by destroying laws and as a result government itself. Boucher's argument begs the question of whether the leaders of the American Revolutionary cause are bad and lawless men or merely those who have an unrealistic expectation concerning government.

The Loyalists also appeal to well-respected authorities in making their case against resistance and rebellion. In his attack on rebellion, Inglis cleverly quotes a prominent Whig, Joseph Addison, "on the nature and guilt of rebellion." Addison was a Whig member of the House of Commons whose work inspired Whig radicals John Trenchard and Thomas Gordon, Patrick Henry's famous "Give me liberty or give me death" line, and Nathan Hale's iconic regret that he had only one life to give for his country. Addison's Whiggish credentials were solid, so one "cannot suspect him of partiality to *Tories.*" Inglis quotes Addison as saying that "rebellion is one of the most heinous crimes which it is in the power of man to commit." This is true because "it destroys the end of all government, and the benefits of civil society." After listing a number of those benefits, Addison declares that "rebellion disappoints all these benefits of government, by raising a power in opposition to that authority which has been established among a people for their mutual welfare. So that rebellion is as great an evil to society, as government itself is a blessing." Not content with that denunciation, Addison adds that "rebellion is a violation of all those engagements [oaths, obligations] which every government exacts from such persons as live under it." Inglis's excerpts from Addison conclude with: "We may likewise consider rebellion as a greater complication of wickedness than any other crime we can commit" and "a robber or a murderer looks like an innocent man, when we compare him with a rebel." The gist of Inglis's point is, of course, that even the best of Whigs recognize the dangers and impropriety of rebellion.[32]

As he does regarding contract and consent, Boucher takes on the ultimate Patriot source in the dispute over resistance: John Locke. After referring to him as an "inferior" writer, Boucher claims that Locke "when defending resistance, falls into inconsistencies, and is at variance with himself." Referring to paragraph 226 in Locke's *Second Treatise of Government*, Boucher reports Locke's contention that rebellion is not an opposition to persons but to authority. But, Boucher answers, "in political consideration, it is hardly possible to dissociate the ideas of authority in the abstract from persons vested with authority. To resist a person legally vested with authority, is, I conceive, to all intents and purposes, the same thing as to resist authority." Boucher's point is that authority is always represented by a person or persons, so one cannot rebel against one independent of the other. He applies the principle to the American situation by responding to the opening line of "The Declaration of the Causes and Necessity of Taking Up Arms" issued by the Continental Congress in 1775. Boucher says: "The resistance which your political counsellors urge you to practice . . . is not a resistance exerted only against the persons invested with the supreme power either legislative or executive, but clearly and literally against *authority*. . . . You are encouraged to resist not only all authority over us as it now exists, but any and all that it is possible to constitute." He bases his remark on the fact that "Causes and Necessity" denied "that just supremacy which the 'Divine Author of our existence' has beyond all question given to 'one part of the human race' to hold over another" and thus has called all authority into question by denying its source of legitimacy.[33]

In their discussion of rebellion, the Loyalist clergymen expressed great concern about its effects. Anxious about the possibility of conflict between the colonies and Great Britain, Zubly warns that wars "among brethren" are the "worst species" of the "worst evil." It is largely the effects that make rebellion so odious. Zubly declares: "Whoever considers the natural attendants of Rebellion, and the dreadful effects which must unavoidably follow, will readily admit that a greater crime cannot easily be committed against the Supreme Ruler and Judge of all, nor any that spreads greater misery, and therefore deserves severer punishment among men." Note that the real offense is against God, Who ordained the government being resisted, but that the misery it causes to man is another reason for God to punish rebels. Boucher similarly focuses on rebellion's offense to God and its terrible consequences for man. In discussing the prospects for the success of a rebellion, he argues that a war of rebellion is "so palpably unjust, so destructive to human society, and so derogatory to God's authority, that I can hardly think I go too far when I say it is impossible that it should finally prosper." Because God sometimes unexpectedly allows the unrighteous to prosper, he changes to a rate of perhaps one success for every twenty failures.[34]

Zubly builds on the theme of offense to God by emphasizing oaths of allegiance made explicitly or implicitly: "Subjects are under the most solemn oath to their sovereign, and the strictest ties to each other, they have pawned their souls for their fidelity, and called upon the Supreme Ruler of all to punish them with everlasting destruction should they disregard the oath of their God." A rebellion against one's sovereign "must stand condemned by all equitable and decent persons." Inglis focuses on the human toll: "MORE human Blood hath been shed—greater Miseries and Calamities have been entailed on Mankind—and more audacious Impieties and Enormities of every Kind have been committed by Means of Sedition and Rebellion, than perhaps through any other Cause whatever." He calls on his audience to "reflect for a Moment on the horrid Train of Evils which follow Rebellion," including deceit, violence, perjury, blood, distress, misery, ruin, personal revenge, animosity, and rage, as well as the rousing of "dark, malevolent Passions of the Soul" by which "virtuous Principles are laid prostrate." To add to the list of rebellion's evils, he again quotes Addison: "It is big with rapine, sacrilege and murder. It is dreadful in its mildest effects, as it impoverishes the public; ruins particular families; begets and perpetuates hatreds among fellow subjects, friends and relations; makes a country the seat of war and desolation, and exposes it to the attempts of its foreign enemies."[35]

Government is the institution established by God to ameliorate and control many of these evils, and Inglis encourages his audience to consider the benefits of government. Having put the benefits of government in the forefront of their minds, he urges them to recognize the fact that "the Evil which is contrary to each of these Benefits, is brought on Mankind by Rebellion," and he seals his condemnation of rebellion with an ultimate concern: "Add to all this, that when successful, it generally ends in Tyranny, and the most grievous Oppression." Chandler, like Inglis, pays close attention to the plight of the people. He sums up the dire consequences of rebellion in a concise comparison: "When one people is conquered by another in war, private property is restored to its former possessors; but when rebellions are crushed, the most to be expected is, that the lives of those that belong to the lower classes will be spared."[36]

Because of his personal experience, Zubly focuses on the opportunities that rebellion gives to unscrupulous men to prey on others. He observes that "rebellion frequently begins in triumph, but seldom fails to end in infamy. It furnishes a colour for every vice," which evil men exploit for their own gain at the expense of the good. Zubly is alone in detailing the prospects for the virtuous and the wicked at the end of a failed rebellion. As the unhappy conclusion becomes evident, "the cunning endeavour to be secure in every event, those at the helm begin secretly to dread the general ruin and downfall; despair and violence is the natural consequence; the authors of the mischief 'dash,' and provide for safety by flight; those that remain pay the cost; and nothing is left of the baseless fabrick but a curse as extensive as the guilt imprecated by the dupes and lighting on the authors of anarchy and rebellion." According to Zubly, rebellion should be avoided at all cost, even if there are "just causes of complaint" against the government. Zubly produced numerous sermons and public pamphlets in support of the pre-Revolutionary American cause and was even a member of the Continental Congress, but he stopped short of supporting rebellion. What should the people do? Quoting Emmerich de Vattel, Zubly argued: "Every citizen should even patiently suffer supportable evils rather than disturb the publick peace" and all violences are "crimes of state."[37] Zubly's recommendation to the people in a public essay echoes Boucher's biblically based admonition: suffer rather than commit the evil of rebellion against lawful authority.

Boucher's discussion of the effects of rebellion is a succinct summary of the emphases of the other ministers. In line with Inglis's and Chandler's concern for the people, Boucher warns that "to resist and to rebel against a lawful government, is to . . . injure or destroy institutions most essential to human happiness." In conjunction with Zubly's distress over advantage taken by bad men over good men during rebellions, Boucher observes: "A time of general disorder is to bad men what a shipwreck is to barbarians. Like the willow, men of loose principles bend and yield to the stream; whilst the *righteous*, in a deluge of iniquity, imitating the oak, are usually torn up by the roots and swept away by the torrent." Boucher adds one additional concern about the effects of rebellion: that "when it is successful, it becomes not only a precedent, but an encouragement to it's [sic] being repeated."[38] Here Boucher demonstrates an understanding of the cycle of revolution and, again, of the often repeated criticism of Locke's notion of a right of resistance.

There is some disagreement among the Loyalist clergymen regarding the lawfulness of resistance under any circumstances, however. Whether from conviction or sentiment, some of the ministers are hesitant to condemn, and are willing to justify, the Glorious Revolution of 1688 and consequently allow for resistance when it is "justifiable." Charles Inglis wants to "assure the reader further, that I am none of your *passive obedience and non-resistance men*. The principles on which the glorious Revolution in 1688 was brought about, continue the articles of my political creed; and were it necessary, I could clearly evince, that these are perfectly conformable to the doctrines of scripture." Apparently he does not think it necessary, because he does not offer such evidence; nor does he elucidate the particular principles involved in that revolution that exempts it from the biblical commands that he elsewhere trumpeted. Thomas Bradbury Chandler asserts that the grievances of the colonists are "not a sufficient reason for forcible resistance," which might be read as an indication that there could be grievances that indeed are such a sufficient reason. Samuel Seabury calls the Glorious Revolution "necessary" to "secure the rights and liberties of the English nation," but he expresses horror at the thought of another such conflict. Seabury and Chandler both nonetheless condemn rebellion in no uncertain terms in their sermons and pamphlets.

Clearly uncomfortable in excusing any rebellion, John Joachim Zubly lurches back and forth between the two poles. In one paragraph, he says that those who engage in rebellion "without cause" earn seats next to Lucifer in hell. In the next paragraph, he claims that the doctrine of nonresistance and passive obedience "has long and deservedly been exploded, but its opposite, like some powerful and violent medicines, ought to be handled with the utmost caution." To provide examples of the two, Zubly says: "The violation of every law, privilege, and promises, by a poor bigotted, priest-ridden prince, in 1688, brought on a most happy and glorious revolution; the insurrections in 1715 and 1745 were odious rebellions." Like Inglis, he does not explain the difference or why his rational denunciations of rebellion do not apply to the 1688 revolution. This shows the inherent problem in "exploding" the doctrine of nonresistance: how to judge when it is appropriate or allowable. His view here is consistent with his convenient interpretation of Romans 13, however.[39]

Shortly after these statements, Zubly reaffirms that "when subjects take up or continue in arms against their lawful sovereign, without a just and sufficient cause, it is Rebellion," but again, he gives no guidance as to what constitutes a just or sufficient cause. In another essay, Zubly finally gives some instruction. He suggests that "individuals in no case whatever have a right to resist, or endeavour to subvert lawful government. The cases where resistance may be lawful to the body of a nation are few, and it is the interest of all government they should not be multiplied." Only "the body of the nation" may resist, and only in a "few" cases—but what is the definition of "the body of the nation," and what are the parameters for these few cases? Zubly does not say. Why should any have a right to resist "lawful government," and under what circumstances? He clearly is not comfortable with the implications: a few sentences later, he says that though there may be "real grievances . . . yet, they may not warrant the taking up of arms to obtain redress." Not long after that, he adds more qualification: "Government is so sacred, and so absolutely necessary and useful to mankind, that, without the most irresistible evidence to the contrary, the presumption lies always in its favour."[40] What constitutes "irresistible evidence" to outweigh what is "sacred"? Zubly does not say, but whatever his standard, the American situation apparently does not meet it.

Jonathan Boucher, on the other hand, is less approving of the Glorious Revolution and defends the doctrine of nonresistance. He laments the fact that "popular writers" have taken "unwearied pains" since the Glorious Revolution "to bring the doctrine of 'non-resistance' into disrepute." In his view, the notion that the doctrine has been "exploded is indisputably false." It is in the interest of mankind, he reasons, that it not be "generally believed" that resistance is lawful. He concludes: "Were it otherwise, along with the doctrine of 'non-resistance,' government itself must also be 'exploded'; because it is essential to all government to be irresistible." Addressing the Glorious Revolution itself, Boucher suggests that too many supporters of monarchy thought it in their best interest to vindicate the Revolution as "justifiable resistance; hoping thereby (in the words of Mr. Locke) 'to make good their title to the crown in the consent of the people.'" Boucher roundly condemns their actions: "To the shortsightedness, the iniquity, and the danger of such policy, the perpetual unsettled state of the kingdom, shaken by two rebellions since it has been so generally adopted, and our present distractions, bear ample testimony."[41] According to Boucher, justification of resistance in England had produced instability and more rebellions, just as critics of Locke had predicted. Their actions were shortsighted and dangerous, and had borne unwanted fruit.

Boucher rounds out his argument by reminding his audience that whatever men do, or whatever policies they pursue, "the word of God . . . *abideth fast for ever*; and the doctrine of 'non-resistance' is unquestionably 'a tenet of our Church.'" To emphasize that point, he quotes from the 1687 *Book of Homilies*:

> Lucifer was the first author and founder of rebellion; which is the first, the greatest, and the root of all other sins. Kings and princes, as well the evil as the good, do reign by God's ordinance; and subjects are bound to obey them, and for no cause to resist, or withstand, or rebel,

or make any sedition against them, although they be wicked men. It were a perilous thing to commit unto subjects the judgment, which prince is wise, which government good; and which otherwise. A rebel is worse than the worst prince, and a rebellion worse than the worst government of the worst prince that hath hitherto been.[42]

This language that Boucher endorses is definitive and universal; it leaves no room for exceptions. Rebellion is the greatest sin; evil kings rule by God's ordinance; there is no cause that justifies resistance; and rebellion is worse than the worst government of the worst prince. He sums it up by quoting Archbishop John Tillotson: "The Christian religion doth plainly forbid the resistance of authority." As clear and adamant as Boucher is here and in his other sermons, on one occasion—in a public pamphlet—Boucher allows for exceptions to the rule. Even he vascillates: "There are Causes, where . . . the very Principles, the original Principles on which civil Society depends, require, where God and Nature call aloud for Resistance. . . . On such melancholy Occasions, Men of Sentiment, Spirit and Virtue, the only genuine Sons of Liberty, engage in the honourable Cause of Freedom, with God on their Side." Unlike the others, Boucher gives examples beyond the Glorious Revolution, citing "the horrid Catalogue of Oppressions and Crimes, under a Philip the Second, a Katharine of Medicis, and in the List of Grievances . . . of the Reign of the ill-educated, the ill-advised, the unhappy Charles."[43] It is still not clear how or why these situations could override such absolute prohibitions, but perhaps the heart trumps reason in the end.

For the Loyalist ministers, there was no contradiction between what the Bible taught concerning the nature of man, government, and rebellion and what one could learn through reason and nature. In fact, Seabury explicitly links the laws of reason with the laws of man's nature and the laws of God; and says specifically of government: "Here then, at least, the Commands of God, and the Reason and Nature of Things coincide." God, reason, and nature reveal that man is most influenced by the negative aspects of his nature, but that he is naturally a social being. Consequently, God established rulers to allow man to live in civil society, and man has a duty to obey them. Equality and consent are not biblical or rational bases for government, so popular rule is not a proper option. Popular rule invites instability and manipulation by unsavory characters. Popular rule and belief in a right of resistance result in instability and ulimately anarchy. Rebellion is an evil in and of itself, in addition to being undesirable because of its effects. The

Loyalist clergy drew these conclusions by using their own reason and by tapping into the wisdom of the ages. Ultimately, as Christian ministers, their reason acted in service of their commitment to serving God. Zubly summed up their approach to political matters in general and to the American situation in particular: "Act conscientiously, and with a view to God, then commit your ways to him, leave the event with God."⁴⁴

4 Legal Arguments

> All Liberty is at an End. . . . All Law is at an End. . . .
> All Appearance of Justice is at an End.
> —John Joachim Zubly

Whether in sermons or in political pamphlets, Loyalist ministers made legal arguments against the American Revolution and its accompanying features. Although clergymen by profession, they were well-educated Englishmen and had a fairly solid understanding of the basics of the British constitution, British law, the relationship between the colonies and the mother country, and the colonial charters. As educated men, they knew how to do research, and much of their legal argument reflects study on their part. Sometimes their arguments based on the law were advanced in sermons, but they are more commonly found in the public pamphlets that they published after being shut out of their churches. As respected authorities—at least by neutrals and fellow Loyalists—and as those who spoke and wrote for a living, the Loyalist clergymen could develop an effective argument and produce persuasive phrases. Their pamphlets were a powerful tool for Loyalism, and they prompted responses from some of the most prominent names in the revolutionary movement.

Colonial Charters and the Colonial Relationship

Due in part to claims made by Patriot pamphleteers, the Loyalists frequently addressed the colonial charters and their statements concerning the making of laws, and in particular taxes. Early in the growing crisis (1770), Connecticut clergyman Samuel Andrews appeals to the Connecticut Charter of 1622 to oppose the idea that one could "hold the King's Protection, without yielding Obedience to his Authority and the British Parliament." He reminds his congregation that by that charter, they hold their land "and the Rights of English Subjects . . . on Condition 'of Obedience to the Laws of

England, which now are or hereafter shall be made.'" He also points out that this last phrase contains "Words tantamount to the late obnoxious Clause, which asserts the Supremacy of the British Parliament over the Colonies, in all Cases whatever." That "late obnoxious Clause" was the hotly contested Declaratory Act of 1766, which accompanied the repeal of the Stamp Act and asserted Parliament's right and authority to make laws binding on the American colonies "in all cases whatsoever." Andrews maintains that it is "a Doctrine owned by our Fathers, and by all even in the present Day, except in the instance of Taxation; which Exception seems trifling, after granting that our Lives . . . may be taken away by a British Act of Parliament."[1] Andrews here introduces a common theme among Loyalist apologists: Parliament's authority had been accepted in the colonies for more than a hundred years—and in most matters still was.

In "The American Querist," Thomas Bradbury Chandler's queries are essentially statements of his arguments couched in the form of mostly rhetorical questions. Quite a few of his queries concern specific charters or the charters in general. Echoing the claim by Andrews, Chandler asks whether there has "ever been a time, in which the colonies appear to have thought, that the nation had not a full and compleat right of jurisdiction over them, till about the year 1764?" The implication, of course, is that there had not ever been such a time. Getting to the heart of the issue, Chandler asks whether there is "any proof or probability, that, when the first grants of land in America were made by the British crown to British subjects, it was intended by the former, or understood by the latter, that they were to be no longer subject to the supreme legislative authority of the British nation?" Again, he is suggesting that there is no such proof because everyone assumed and believed that, as British subjects, the colonists were still subject to Parliament's authority. Chandler spends ten of his hundred queries on matters related to the charters of six of the individual colonies.[2] Not surprisingly, his examples all support colonial subjection to Parliament or remove suggested exceptions to that rule.

Samuel Seabury, a resident of New York writing primarily to New Yorkers, begins his discussion of the charters with the observation that "the province of New-York has no charter. . . . The claim, then, of the Parliament, 'of ruling and taxing us without our assent,' is not precluded by charter" for New Yorkers. Like Chandler, he also examines the charters of several other colonies to "abundantly prove that the colony charters by no means imply an independence on the supreme legislative authority of Great-Britain" and that they do not preclude Britain's claim of taxing them without consent.[3] Seabury also joins Chandler in making an interesting but unconventional argument regarding charters. Both men note that the first two charters granted for colonization of America in 1606 and 1609 subjected two Virginia companies to "laws made by a council of the proprietors residing in England" and that, under the same charters, "the King might tax all the inhabitants within the grant, by his sole prerogative, without consulting his parliament, and appropriate the monies, thus raised by taxes, for the use and benefit of the crown only." The great significance of this is that the territory covered by these charters extended from latitude 34 to latitude 45, which includes all of the land between Carolina and Nova Scotia, including "the present *New-England* colonies; the inhabitants of which originally settled under the very charters above-mentioned, after having purchased from one of those companies."[4] They mentioned New England in particular because it was the hotbed of the revolt, but they might have mentioned that this territory includes almost all of British North America. In answer to the Patriots, who were fond of appealing to the charters, Chandler and Seabury provide evidence to indicate that the first charters gave complete taxation authority to the Crown.

Seabury also argues that the power to legislate is "not an inherent right in the colonies."[5] After suggesting that many colonies have long been established and subsisted without that power, he cites a number of historical examples to illustrate the point. Jonathan Boucher expands on both of these avenues of argument. He challenges the Patriots' knowledge of the times, the kings, the people, and the purposes related to the charters and in particular "how they were understood, and construed by our Ancestors." He argues that "the inestimable Privileges of a modern Englishman . . . had never been enjoyed, were generally very imperfectly understood, and rarely claimed by our Ancestors," and that "even these legal constitutional Privileges were encumbered with a Thousand legal Customs, which they patiently submitted to." He suggests, furthermore, that the early colonists were much more concerned about religious liberty than civil liberty and that they "would have been contented with half the Privileges their Posterity enjoy, for an Act of Toleration." They also understood that they were "Subjects of an English Parliamentary King" and therefore were under the authority of Parliament as well as the king.[6]

Boucher emphasizes the fact that although the early colonists were given power to make bylaws in local mattrers, "they were nevertheless expressly and formally restrain'd from making Laws repugnant to the Laws of England" and were "universally understood" to owe obedience to all English laws, "from which no King could release them, because no King could dispense with the Laws." Even if the kings had desired to free the colonists from parliamentary authority via the charters, the kings did not have the authority to do so under the British constitution. Boucher further echoes Chandler's contention that "from this parliamentary Authority, they [the colonists] never wish'd until of late, to be emancipated." Boucher concludes his discussion of the charters with a telling point: "Such were the Practices of the Times, when our early Charters bear their Dates, that if they were not granted by parliamentary Kings, they were granted by Tyrants, and we shall gain nothing by recurring to first Principles."[7]

Charles Inglis does not discuss the charters in detail, but he offers this overall assessment: "The British Colonies were settled under charters, those charters were granted by the King, and specified the civil constitutions of the Colonies respectively—the emigrants were as much subjects of the British Crown, as dependent on the supreme legislature of the empire, 'after,' as 'before,' their emigration; and some of those charters explicitly recognize the right of the British Parliament to tax the Colonies."[8] This is a cogent summary of the position of the Loyalist ministers. Under the charters, the colonists are still subjects of Great Britain and therefore subject to its king, its legislature, and its laws—including taxes. Nothing in the charters changed their civic status or made them independent of the mother country.

Even during his Whig period, John Joachim Zubly affirms that "the colonies in *America*, being settled upon lands discovered by the *English*, under charters from the crown of *England*, were always considered as a part of the *English* nation, and of the *British* empire, and looked upon as dependent upon *England*." The affirmation by Zubly and Inglis that the colonists were "dependent" on England leads to another part of the legal argument of the Loyalists: the legal relationship between the colonies and their parent country. Boucher asks the key questions regarding taxation in particular: "Are we Confederates, or Allies, or Subjects of Great-Britain?" The obvious answer, admitted by both sides, was that the colonists were subjects. "In what Code of Laws, are we to search for Taxation, under the Title, and Condition, of Requisition, as we understand the Word? In what Theory of Government, ancient or modern? Is it to be found any where on Earth, but in modern Harangues, modern Pamphlets?"[9] The Patriots argued that Parliament's power over the colonies with regard to taxation was simply a matter of requisition, not command. In other words, the colonies had authority to decide whether or not to voluntarily pay taxes levied by Parliament. Boucher and the Loyalist ministers argue that the legal nature of colonies, in addition to the nature of subjects, proves the Patriot position to be without merit.

Chandler maintains that the Patriot position is "inconsistent with the nature of dependent colonies, and compatible only with the idea of independent states." Even the Whigs disavowed notions of independence at the time and claimed to be subjects of good King George. Chandler challenges the right of colonies to decide which laws of the parent country they will obey and which they will disobey. He asks whether that would "leave any obligation to obedience at all" on the part of self-avowed subjects and whether "in such a case, the *Americans*, being not *English* subjects, can claim the protection of the English laws, or talk of their rights *as Englishmen*, with any propriety." The Patriots countered that Parliament had no authority to make laws for the Americans because the Americans had not empowered them to do so. Seabury calls this "a position subversive of that dependence which all colonies must, from their very nature, have on the mother country." He further argues that colonists have no "natural right" to exercise a legislative power, and that what they have is the result of an "indulgence or grant of the parent state," whose subjects they were and are. As long as the relationship is a colonial one, Britain "retains the power of binding the colonies by such laws as she shall think necessary to secure and preserve the dependence of the colonies on the mother country;—to promote their particular welfare, or the welfare of the whole empire collectively."[10] That, of course, comports with the historical understanding of a colonial relationship: the colony exists for the benefit of the mother country unless and until the colony gains independence.

Boucher adds an interesting contribution to the discussion of the colonial relationship. He denies that the British constitution allows England to "voluntarily withdraw or forbear it's [sic] government over America." Boucher explains: "Allegiance and protection are not merely reciprocal duties, entirely dependent the one on the other. Each duty continues to be equally obligatory, and in force, whether the other be performed or not. There is no authority to prove, that a failure of duty on one side will justify a like failure on the other." What does he mean? Because the normal terms for the colonial relationship is that of parent and child, Boucher illustrates his point by noting that parents do not withdraw their authority over a child because the child disobeys, but rather the child's disobedience causes the parents to expend greater effort to exert their authority over the child. The same is true for the people under the authority of a government. If not, as he observes, "there could be no such crime as rebellion; nor any right in the magistrate to punish it."[11] Rebellious actions by the Americans and their denials of parliamentary authority do not remove the British government's authority over—or responsibility for—the Americans. On the contrary, they only spur greater efforts to maintain control.

The British Constitution and Parliamentary Authority

Boucher's intriguing argument introduces the matter of the constitutional rights and authority of the British Parliament vis-à-vis the British empire in general and the American colonies in particular. The Loyalist preachers believed and taught that the king and Parliament had the British constitution on their side in the struggle with the Americans. Speaking to a corps of soldiers, Charles Inglis enthusiastically declares that there has never been a "more just, more honourable or necessary" cause than the British side of the Revolution and that it is the cause of "legal Government against Usurpation." Speaking of the king, Inglis says that "he hath taken no Step in which he had not the Concurrence of his Parliament, and numerous Precedents to guide him. He exerted no unconstitutional Authority."[12] As this statement shows, the Loyalists see and emphasize a close constitutional connection between the king and the Parliament, and they rebut attempts by the Patriots to separate them. Samuel Seabury says that by the phrase "British parliament," he means "the supreme legislative authority, the King, Lords and Commons, because no other authority in England has a right to make laws to bind the colonies." He observes that in every government, supreme authority must be "lodged somewhere," and in the mixed British system, "that supreme authority is vested in . . . the King, House of Lords, and House of Commons elected by the people." How does that relate to the American colonies? "This supreme authority extends as far as the British dominions extend." Based, then, on the nature of a colonial relationship and on the fact that the Patriots themselves affirmed their loyalty to the king (though not to Parliament), Parliament's authority extends to America. America, "at one and the same time," would have "to be, and not to be a part of the British dominions" in order to be British, but beyond the authority of Parliament.[13]

For Seabury, talk of being loyal subjects to the king while disavowing the authority of Parliament is "whiggish nonsense." "If we obey the laws of the King, we obey the laws of the parliament. If we disown the authority of the parliament, we disown the authority of the King." The reason this is true is that there is an intimate, indivisible connection between the king and Parliament where law is concerned and it is a necessary and superior element of the British constitution. "There is no medium without ascribing powers to the King which the constitution knows nothing of:—without making him superior to the laws, and setting him above all restraint." English subjects do not have the option to obey the king but not the laws passed by the supreme authority, the king with Parliament. "The difference between a loyal subject and a rebel, is, that the one yields obedience to, and faithfully supports the supreme authority of the state, and the other endeavours to overthrow it." The supreme authority of the state is indivisible. Chandler agrees. He says that "subjection to the *Crown* of *England*" has never meant subjection only to the person wearing the crown "in his *private* or *personal* capacity"; rather, the laws as "public instruments" always mean "by the authority of the crown, the supreme authority of the nation, represented by the crown." The Parliament is part of that supreme authority—the Crown—and, where lawmaking is concerned, is the primary part. Even John Joachim Zubly in his Whiggish period affirms: "All the inhabitants of the *British* empire together form the BRITISH NATION, and that the British Parliament is the supreme power and legislature in the *British* nation I never heard doubted."[14]

However, Zubly reminds his audience that the British nation is also under a constitution and that "the now Parliament derives its authority and power from the constitution, and not the constitution from the Parliament." So there are limits to what any particular Parliament can do with the authority given it by the British constitution. Much of the conflict between the colonies and Great Britain centered on and revolved around the legitimate powers of the Parliament over the colonies, and in particular its authority to tax the colonies. As Zubly puts it: "The question between Great-Britain and America, which has already been productive of such alarming effects, is, 'Whether the parliament of Great-Britain have any power or authority to tax the Americans without their consent?' Every impartial man will allow that this is the foundation of the whole dispute."[15] This was indeed at least the face of the dispute.

The ministers who remained loyal to England did not shy away from this question. Samuel Seabury tackles the issue head on: "The position that we are bound by no laws to which we have not consented, either by ourselves, or our representatives, is a novel position, unsupported by any authoratative [sic] record of the British constitution, ancient or modern." He explains that this notion depends on "an artful change of terms" cleverly promulgated by the Whigs. Although it is true that Englishmen are not bound by any laws unless "the representatives of the nation" have consented to them, "to say that an Englishman is bound by no laws but those to which he hath consented in person, or by his representative, is saying what never was true, and never can be true." Seabury notes that a large portion of the English population have no right to vote for representatives and "therefore are governed by laws to which they never consented either by themselves or by their representatives." This is perhaps the most common Loyalist response to this issue. The situation of the American colonists is no different than that of many of the people in England, but the people of England are subject to the laws made by Parliament. Not only is this normal in practice, but it is also constitutional. As Chandler explains, "The English constitution [makes] the king and parliament the representatives of all the people within the kingdom, whether they be actual electors or non-electors," and the people who do vote are often bound by laws that are opposed by the members they elected.[16] If this were not the case, only laws that are unanimously adopted in Parliament would apply to everyone who voted, and no laws would apply to the millions who do not have the right to vote. There are people in every society who, for one reason or another, do not have the right to vote; but free and stable society is based on the idea that the laws apply to all. If a given representative does not give consent by voting for the proposed law, then that does not excuse him or his constituents from being subject to it.

In further response to the notion that representation and taxation go together, Seabury argues that "the first principles of government" show that "Legislation and Taxation go together; and that no government ever yet had a being where they were divided." It is not representation and taxation that go together but simply legislation and taxation. In any government, the power to legislate necessarily includes the power to tax. In England, a tax bill begins in the House of Commons (the seat of electoral representation), but it does not become law until passed by the House of Lords and approved by the king—that is, "till it has received the sanction of the whole legislature," including those elements of the government not subject to election.[17] Implicit in Seabury's commentary is the comparative generosity of the British constitution in giving elected representatives any voice in taxation in the eighteenth-century world.

Chandler approaches the issue from a different angle. He demonstrates that Parliament's power to tax the colonies had been officially confirmed both by legal authority in England and by the American colonies themselves. He appeals to the decision by two eminent British legal scholars, Clement Wearge (solicitor general) and Sir Philip Yorke (attorney general), in 1722 that colonies could only be taxed by their own assemblies "or by *act of parliament.*" He then points to "the congress at Albany in [1754], consisting of gentlemen of the first character from most of the colonies," which decided that "application should be made *to parliament, to empower the committees of the several colonies to tax* them." Chandler asks whether the Congress or the assembly of New York (which approved the plan) could have thought "that the parliament could delegate a power to others, with which they were not vested themselves." The implied answer is that they could not; therefore, the Albany congress officially recognized the power of Parliament to tax the colonies "so very lately as in 1755."[18]

Boucher changes the focus. He is willing to acknowledge that "many wrong things are thus done among us," but he immediately adds that all should also acknowledge and even "boast of, the excellency of our Constitution." Government is not infallible, but the superb nature of the British constitution is a protection against egregious injustice. He says: "That the Parent State has been unwise, I readily grant; contending only, that she has never been unjust." Like other Loyalist ministers, Boucher disagrees with some of the actions of Parliament and shares some of the Patriot concerns. Steps taken and policies implemented have been "wrong" and "unwise," but they have not been unconstitutional or even unjust. Boucher disagrees more strongly with the militant methods used by the Patriots. He admonishes the Patriots that both the British constitution and the ordinance of God warn against resistance, but "you are not forbidden either to remonstrate or to petition." Furthermore, "if you think the duty of threepence a pound upon tea, laid on by the British Parliament, a grievance, it is your duty to instruct your members to take all the constitutional means in their power to obtain redress: if those means fail of success, you cannot but be sorry and grieved; but you will better bear your disappointment, by being able to reflect that it was not owing to any misconduct of your own."[19] Boucher clearly does not see the colonial grievances as very serious, but he calls for legal response one way or the other. The British constitution provides avenues of redress; he advises taking full advantage of them. Even if those avenues do not bring the desired results, failure to receive satisfaction is no excuse for illegal, unconstitutional action on the part of the aggrieved party. Alongside his legal and constitutional argument, Boucher hints at the biblical notions of remaining in subjection to the governing authorities and of suffering under oppression rather than disobeying God's command to be subject.

Continental Congress

No legal subjects drew more attention—or more ire—from the pens of the Loyalist clergymen than the continental congresses (particularly the first) and the various committees in the colonies. Because churches of the Loyalist preachers and the presses willing to print Loyalist material were mostly shut down by mid-1775, it became increasingly difficult for them to disseminate their ideas after 1775. That, combined with the program of active destruction of Loyalist writings conducted by the Patriots, largely explains the relative dearth of criticism of the Second Continental Congress by those ministers. There are nonetheless enough criticisms of the First Continental Congress to suffice for both. Their experience with the congresses themselves was largely theoretical, analytical, and based on principle. However, the policies enacted by the congresses had a significant economic effect on everyday life in the colonies and therefore on the clergymen and their congregants.

The Loyalist ministers opposed nearly every aspect of the First Continental Congress, starting with the supposed need for such a congress. Jonathan Boucher suggests that if a complaint is "well founded, and a real and great grievance," then all of the colonial assemblies will "concur and be unanimous" in making the case to England. If they do so unanimously, "all due attention" will be paid to "their united remonstrances." Boucher is essentially arguing that complaints from thirteen legislative bodies will draw more attention than from one, especially because the legitimacy of those thirteen, unlike the one, is recognized by law. He adds that the chance of a favorable response is encouraged by the fact that so "many and large concessions have often been made" in response to petitions from individual assemblies. The key, as he sees it, is to make sure that requests be "reasonable and proper," that they be "asked for with decency," and that the colonists do not forfeit their right to be heard "by becoming refractory and rebellious."[20]

Having denied the need for a congress, Loyalist ministers criticized the process by which the delegates to the First Continental Congress were selected. Samuel Seabury calls the claim of the Congress to be a full representation of the colonies "insolence." He emphasizes that "not *one person in an hundred* . . . throughout *this* province [New York] at least, gave his vote for their *election*" and that "their appointment was in a way unsupported by any *law, usage, or custom* of the province." Seabury's explanation as to why so few people in New York participated in the election of delegates to the Congress is simple: many "expected no good from this proposed Congress." New York was the seat of loyalism, and many thought that only "the wrong-headed, blustering people among the sons of liberty" and "the vain and pragmatical, [lacking] political principles, who hoped to rise into some degree of consequence" would seek election. Consequently, many did not want to send any delegates to a congress of which they disapproved. Therefore, they did not participate in the election process. Seabury criticizes the process as it went forward designed to produce a Patriot-friendly result. Writing to Patriot sympathizers, Seabury complains:

> You had no right to dictate to the counties in what manner they should proceed. You had no right to suppose that those districts, or those people who did not assemble, were in your favour. The contrary ought to have been supposed; and you ought to have considered those people and districts who did not assemble, as not choosing to have any Delegates in Congress at all.[21]

Seabury is confident in his speculation that less than 1 percent of the people participated because, as he reports, "it is notorious that in some districts only three or four met and *chose themselves* to be a committee [to choose a delegate] on this most important occasion."[22]

Anticipating the argument that it was their own fault for not participating, Seabury moves to another criticism of the Congress: its lack of legal authority. He precludes the nonparticipation argument with two questions: "That they might have assembled, I know; but had *your* committee, or *their* own superiors, any right to *call* them together? Were they under any obligations to obey such notifications?" He answers the questions in the negative himself, then asks another: "You know they were not, and because they did not choose to obey it, must their rights and privileges be given up, to be torn, and mangled, and trampled on by an enthusiastic congress?" Should people suffer because they chose not to sanction an illegitimate authority? Seabury sums it up this way:

> A COMMITTEE, chosen in a *tumultuous, illegal* manner, usurped the most *despotic* [sic] *authority* over the *province*. They entered into contracts, compacts, combinations, treaties of alliance, with the other colonies, without *any* power from the *legislature of the province*. They agreed with the other Colonies to send Delegates to meet in convention at

Philadelphia, to determine upon the *rights and liberties of the good people of this province*, unsupported by any Law.[23]

Jonathan Boucher likewise challenges the authority of the Congress. Addressing the members of Congress directly, Boucher tells them bluntly: "You, it is true, have not been summoned, or convened, by any formal constitutional Authority, or invested with any legislative Powers." He bristles under directives ordered, not recommended, "by persons of whose authority over us it has been our happiness till now to be ignorant," and he explains that "it is not so much the propriety of the thing enjoined to which we object, as the incompetency and want of authority of the persons enjoining it." It does not matter whether the policies imposed are good or bad, wise or unwise; the issue is that those imposing them have no authority to do so. "If, in defiance of the laws, a mere plurality of votes were sufficient to compel a compliance with the determinations of any bodies of men not constitutionally empowered to determine for others, endless confusions and inconveniences would ensue." This, says Boucher, can be dangerous in addition to annoying. Discussing historical examples from seventeenth-century England, he observes that the first error of the people involved was allowing themselves "to be authoritatively dictated to by persons unknown to the laws." Though dangers may not immediately appear, he warns that usurpers know "that when once we have been brought to do a little wrong, by submitting to an usurped and unlawful authority, we shall then feel less reluctance to commit a greater."[24] Before long, he warns, they will expect us to follow them in rebelling against the legitimate powers. He was, of course, correct.

There were other problems concerning the legal authority of the Congress. Seabury broaches the subject in a question: "What right or power has any assembly on the continent to appoint delegates, to represent their province in such a congress as that which lately met at Philadelphia?" He thinks that the electoral procedure used to select delegates is invalid and that the role of the assembly in appointing delegates is invalid as well. According to Seabury, the assemblies themselves have only delegated authority. As merely representatives of the people, they do not have "even the shadow of right" to delegate authority to others. "Delegates, so appointed, are, at best, but delegates of delegates, [or] representatives of representatives" and not representatives of the people. Any assembly that "acted in this manner" has betrayed the people they represent and "has exercised a power which it never received from the people, but which it has usurped over them." Representative bodies are only valid if chosen by the people, not by intermediaries. Seabury here sounds like a Whig. In addition, Seabury argues that even if the assemblies should have a role in choosing delegates, it must be a "joint act of the whole legislature of the province." The people are not bound by any act of their representatives until it has been approved by all of the branches, not just the assemblies.[25]

Seabury follows this line of thought with yet another legal problem related to the First Continental Congress. He says that while it may be debatable whether the legislature of any province has the power to appoint delegates to that congress, he is "certain no provincial legislature can give them such powers as were lately exercised at Philadelphia." Loyalist clergymen took issue with the powers exercised by the First Continental Congress and with the actions taken by that congress. In particular, they argued that provincial legislatures cannot grant the power to make laws for the whole continent or laws that supersede the authority of the provincial legislatures within each colony. Seabury contends that "the legislative authority of any province cannot extend farther than the province extends." So, he asks: "How then can it give authority to a few persons to meet other persons, from other provinces, to make rules and laws for the whole continent?" This is a return to the argument that a body cannot grant authority that it does not have or control. Seabury also points out that the (British) constitution does not establish any continentwide legislative authority other than Parliament. If a body assumes such an authority, it must subvert the character and design of the colonies, and it essentially "annihilates" "their present independency on each other."[26]

Seabury feels so strongly that the Congress is illegitimate and not representative of the people that he regularly refers to it as a "foreign power."[27] He argues that "the people of this province had already delegated their power to the members of their Assembly, and therefore had no right to choose Delegates, to contravene the authority of the Assembly, by introducing a foreign power of legislation." Because the people had delegated their power to one body—a provincial body specific to the colony—they had no additional authority to give to another body as long as the original body existed. They certainly could not empower a body that could overrule the original to whom they had delegated their power. So part of his argument points back to the matter of representation and the method of selecting the Congress. But why is the Congress a foreign power? Is it not American? Does it not act on behalf of Americans? The point is that the Congress and its members are foreign to *New York* or to any other individual colony. Seabury's view here is similar to that of the Southerners in the antebellum period who saw their state as their "country." He emphasizes the fact that the Congress's laws "and decrees" are made "at Philadelphia" by "factious men" or "enthusiastic republicans" from New England, Virginia, Pennsylvania, and other colonies.[28]

As he sees it, New Yorkers and other colonists had lost the ability to govern themselves and were being dictated to by men who did not share the interests and desires of the colony. This argument should sound familiar; it was the very issue that the Patriots were complaining about in conjunction with the Parliament's exertion of authority over the colonies. Seabury admonishes the merchants of New York:

> By enforcing an observance of the determinations of the congress, in this province, you abrogate, or suspend, several of its laws . . .: You contravene its authority: You take the government of the province out of the hands of the governor, council and assembly, and the government of the city, out of the hands of the legal magistrates, and place them in a CONGRESS, a body utterly unknown in any legal sense! You introduce a *foreign* power, and make *it* an instrument of *injustice* and *oppression*.[29]

The Congress is not legal, its "determinations" are not legal, and they overrule what *is* legal: the laws made by the provincial authorities. Writing to the New York provincial legislature, Seabury asks: "If laws made, and decrees passed, at *Philadelphia*, by the *enthusiastic republicans of New-England and Virginia*, are to bind *the people of this province*, and *extort money from them*, why, Gentlemen, *do you meet?*" He wants to know the need for a government of the colony if they are going to bow to whatever comes from the Congress. "There is no such thing as carrying the regulations of the congress into execution, without transgressing the known laws, and contravening the legal authority of the government." Seabury exhorts the New York legislature to do its "duty," to exert its authority, "and to break up this *horrid combination of seditious men*, which has already enslaved this province."[30] Both the Congress and Parliament passed legislation that bound the colonies, but Seabury rails against the Congress while supporting Parliament. The huge difference between the Congress and Parliament, of course, is that Parliament had authority under the constitution, and the Congress did not.

Seabury argues that this fact also hurts the colonies in their dealings and negotiations with Great Britain. He says that the assembly is "known and acknowledged by the laws of the empire," so their "representations would be considered, their petitions or remonstrances attended to." The Congress, on the other hand, is "a body unknown to the government. In a legal sense, they are no body at all."[31] There is no reason to expect the British government to pay attention to the petitions or remonstrances of an extra-legal, unrecognized body. They are certainly under no legal obligation to do so. Seabury further asserts that the colonial assemblies "are also the true, proper, legal guardians of our rights, privileges and liberties," so if Americans wish to protest parliamentary actions, "they are the proper persons to seek for redress." Not only are the assemblies the proper guardians but also, as Seabury maintains, they are the most likely to succeed. They have "the legal and constitutional means," they are "the real not the pretended representatives of the people," and "they are bodies known, and acknowledged by the public laws of the empire." Unfortunately, their authority is compromised and overruled by "a power from without the province": the Congress.[32] If the Americans really want the British to listen to their pleas and complaints, then they should abandon the idea of continental congresses and act through their colonial assemblies.

In addition to the general lack of legal authority on the part of the Congress, Loyalist ministers denied the specific power or authority of the Congress to take the particular actions that it took. Before the meeting of the First Continental Congress, Thomas Bradbury Chandler suggested limits on their potential actions: "Should it appear, that they mean to encourage acts of hostility against Great Britain, or to support the madmen of New-England in their scheme of an Independent Republic: in that case, I affirm, that the Original Contract between them and the most respectable part of their constituents will be dissolved."[33] After the edicts from that congress were issued, Chandler examined the credentials that were laid before them from the various colonies in order to demonstrate that they exceeded their commission. Those credentials include instructions to and for the delegates, limiting the scope of their action.

Chandler's investigation of the instructions given to the delegates from all twelve attending colonies yields some consistent themes in the instructions that are inconsistent with the actions taken by that congress. Working from north to south, he summarizes the instructions and highlights key phrases to prove his point. In New Hampshire, delegates were to "consult and adopt (such) measures, as may have the most likely tendency to extricate the colonies from their present difficulties, to secure and perpetuate the rights, liberties and privileges, and to restore that peace, harmony and mutual confidence, which once happily subsisted between the parent country and her colonies." Rhode Island and Connecticut delegates were given much the same instruction. Even in the hotbed colony of Massachusetts Bay, Chandler reports that delegates were "*publicly* authorized to proceed *no farther* than 'to deliberate and determine upon wise and proper measures . . . for the recovery and establishment of their just rights and liberties, civil and religious, and the restoration of union and harmony between Great Britain and the Colonies.'" He notes that New York and New Jersey gave no particular instructions, but Pennsylvania and "the Three Lower Counties" (Delaware) delegates were given similar instructions to those given to the New England colonies. At this point, Chandler summarizes:

> Thus far all seems to be fair and pacific. The Delegates from these eight colonies are sent to the Congress, for the most laudable purposes, of obtaining the repeal of certain obnoxious acts, and of promoting the restoration of peace and harmony between Great Britain and her Colonies. And in the prosecution of this great and good work, they are generally confined by their instructions, to the use of such means as are *prudent* and *lawful*.[34]

Three themes emerge from a look at the instructions given to delegates from the northern and middle colonies: (1) seek means of repealing certain acts of Parliament, (2) seek means of restoring peace and harmony with England, and (3) do these in a prudent and lawful way.

Chandler then turns to the instructions given to the delegates from the southern colonies. He finds the directives given to the Maryland and Virginia delegates somewhat "ambiguous" because they hinge on the imprecise phrase "*commercial connexion of the Colonies with the Mother Country*." He takes it as a positive injunction to make an effort to facilitate and improve commerce between them, which seems to be the context. In the case of Virginia, however, there is an added purpose: "to procure redress for the much injured province of the Massachusetts-Bay," along with the thematic exhortation "to secure *British America from* (not *against*) the *ravage* and *ruin* of arbitrary taxes, and speedily to procure the return of that harmony and union so beneficial to the whole nation, and so ardently desired by all British Americans." This is the only mention of the Boston situation in the directions given to the delegates of the twelve colonies. After commenting sarcastically on the "ravage and ruin" that the "poor" Virginians had supposedly suffered, Chandler reasons that suspending all commerce with Great Britain can hardly be considered productive of the harmony and union proposed. "The breaking of a connexion between two distant bodies can have no tendency to produce an union between them; and the setting up a fixed opposition on either side, is not the most likely way to obtain harmony." Finishing with North and South Carolina's instructions, Chandler emphasizes their use of the words "legal" and "prudent" in calling for measures to repeal certain acts and restoring rights.[35]

In Chandler's general summary at the end of his analysis, three themes again emerge. First, he notes that "the general and grand design was, as was asserted before, to obtain for the colonies an exemption from taxation by the British Parliament." Second, "in the pursuit of this great object, many of the Delegates are expressly directed by their respective constituents, to confine themselves to the use of such means and measures as are proper and lawful." Third, "some of them are very seasonably reminded, that they were to negotiate, not for an *independent* community, but for British America; that is . . . for North America, considered as a part of the British dominions."[36] From the perspective of the Loyalists, none of the directives given to the delegates was faithfully followed, and none of the colonies' expressed goals for the First Continental Congress was achieved.

According to the Loyalists, the Congress itself was illegal, and the means of selecting delegates for it was illegal and unfair. In addition, it not only had no constitutional authority but also exceeded the authority given it by the colonies who created it. So what did the First Continental Congress do that engendered rousing condemnation from the Loyalist clergy? A lot. The general problem has been discussed at length, namely that they "usurped the authority of legislation over all the colonies." It remains to consider the particulars, most of which are listed here by Seabury: "They dispose of the militia, direct our commerce, levy taxes for the support of the poor saints of Boston, regulate our diversions, direct what we shall eat, drink, wear, speak and think, and in May next, are to take the management of the courts of justice."[37] Most of these problems spring directly or indirectly from the well-known nonimportation, nonexportation, and nonconsumption resolutions adopted by the First Continental Congress.

Once again, it is Seabury who succinctly sums up the actions of the First Continental Congress from the Loyalist perspective:

> When the Delegates met at Philadelphia, instead of settling a reasonable plan of accommodation with the parent country, they employed themselves in censuring acts of the British parliament, which were principally intended to prevent *smuggling, and all illicit trade;*—in writing addresses to the people of *Great-Britain,* to the inhabitants of the *colonies in general,* and to those of the *province of Quebec, in particular;* with the *evident design* of making them *dissatisfied with their present government;* and of *exciting clamours,* and raising *seditions* and *rebellions* against the *state;*—and in exercising a *legislative authority over all the colonies.*[38]

The delegates were instructed to seek reconciliation with Great Britain, but instead they appeared to take actions designed to exasperate, alienate, and threaten them. They censured the Coercive Acts (which the Patriots called the "Intolerable Acts") as illegal violations of their rights, sent an arguably impudent declaration of rights to England, and drafted letters to the North American colonies not attending the Congress in an attempt to persuade them to join the Patriot cause. The Congress also endorsed the Suffolk Resolves, which was a series of resolutions adopted by Boston and the other towns of the county of Suffolk. In doing so, the Congress encouraged the creation of militias and the arming of the populace in a fashion deemed belligerent by the British. Seabury complains that those resolves "fomented *a spirit of dissatisfaction to Great-Britain, and of rebellion against the state.*" In explaining these actions to the merchants of New York, Seabury says that the Congress approved the "mad proceedings of the people of Boston" and wrote "inflammatory addresses" and exercised "*an assumed power of legislation.*"[39]

In addition to the principles involved, Seabury also bemoans the effects of the measures of the Congress. Rhode Islanders dismantled a fort and took the cannon to use "*against his Majesty's forces*"; people in New Hampshire, led by a delegate to the Congress, took a fort "belonging to his Majesty" and carried off its powder and arms; a "*provincial Congress*" in Maryland assessed the people 10,000 pounds for the arming and training of troops "*to fight against the King*"; and the people of New England were in the process of raising an armed force for the same purpose. Furthermore, Seabury claims that "money is levied upon us without the *consent of our representatives:* which very money, under colour of relieving *the poor people of Boston,* it is too *probable* will be employed to *raise an army against the King.*" He urges the New York legislature to act and to take back control of the province, and he reminds them that the people had chosen them to legislate and to guard their rights and liberties. He also warns them of the dangers of extralegal military forces: "I cannot conceive a worse state of thraldom, than a military power in any government, unchecked, and uncontrollable by the civil power. And this must be the case, with respect to a militia upon such an establishment as that of Maryland and New England. The laws of the congress, not the laws of the province, will be the rule of its conduct."[40]

The most consequential—and from the Loyalist perspective, obnoxious and offensive—effects of the First Continental Congress came from the committees and associations originally established to enforce its nonimportation, nonexportation, and nonconsumption resolutions. Though they were originally created for this specific purpose, committees began to spring up like extralegal mushrooms to join with the radical committees of correspondence and to exert general and penal authority in pursuit of the Patriot cause. Unfortunately for the Loyalists, these self-proclaimed defenders of the American cause eventually became vigilantes and unchecked tribunals that did not allow individual rights to get in the way of their purpose and objectives.

Committees and Associations

The committees were the primary reason that the Loyalist ministers eventually lost access to their churches, the presses, and nearly all of their rights, property, and livelihood. Because of this, their experience with them was intensely personal and visceral—a fact profoundly evident in their writings. From the beginning, they could see the dangers inherent in placing power in the hands of extralegal, unaccountable groups. As the First Continental Congress was meeting, the first two of a hundred questions in Thomas Bradbury Chandler's pamphlet *The American Querist* were whether "*Americans* have . . . a right to speak their sentiments on subjects of government" and whether "*Americans* have . . . an equal right to express their sentiments, when they happen to differ from . . . the *popular* opinion." He also holds that "attempts to check and discourage freedom of speech . . . are . . . unwarrantable usurpations, tending to introduce and establish bondage of the worst kind." This concern is foremost on his mind because of the experience of Loyalists with the committees of correspondence that preceded the Congress. In later questions, he asks whether "the *sons of liberty* have ever *willingly* allowed to others the liberty of thinking and acting for themselves; and whether any other liberty than that of doing as *they* shall direct, is to be expected during their administration." He then suggests that it would be "safer, both to our liberty and property" to be under British rule and taxes than to be "under the government of the *American sons of Liberty*, without paying any duties or taxes at all."[41] The Sons of Liberty, of course, were an association that was the action arm of the Boston committee of correspondence. The various committees, both before and after the First Continental Congress, squelched freedom of speech and of the press where Loyalists and Loyalist views were concerned.

Jonathan Boucher expresses similar concerns about the committees before the Congress: "To public speakers alone is the government of our country now completely committed: it is cantoned out into new districts, and subjected to the jurisdiction of these committees; who, not only without any known law, but directly in the teeth of all law whatever, issue citations, sit in judgment, and inflict pains and penalties on all whom they are pleased to consider as delinquents." Despite what the law says, it is the "public speakers"—the loudest voices, the demagogues—who are running things, and doing so arbitrarily without checks and at their own pleasure. In another sermon before the Congress, Boucher maintains that "majorities can rightfully determine for minorities, only when the persons composing such majorities are known to and recognized by the laws, and act agreeably to the forms of the [British] Constitution." On the other hand, if they are not recognized by the laws, then any attempt to enforce submission to their decisions is "unlawful and oppressive." Such is the case with the committees. Boucher has the same concerns after the First Continental Congress. He says that "times of heat and violence" combined with "momentary passions" have caused Americans to take unwise and "fatal" actions. "Of this kind," he says, "are the present *resolves of our committees, conventions, and congresses*; passed not only without the authority of any law, but in direct opposition to the known and established laws of the land."[42]

Boucher has some strong language for a situation that he considers extremely dangerous. He warns that Americans are "giving up all the comfort and security of fixed law to the caprice and humour of multitudes and mobs." The multitudes and mobs are the committees and those who back them. Boucher is not comforted by the assurances of the Patriots that their methods are necessary and exercised only against "the enemies of our country." Boucher follows that argument to its logical conclusion and determines that it "would be utterly subversive of all government, and make every man his own judge and lawgiver." Without settled law and authority, every individual would enter a Hobbesian state of nature and be a vigilante exercising judgment on personal enemies. How, he asks, do we determine who these enemies of the country are? If we accept the determination of a committee, what is to keep today's enemies from being voted—or voting themselves—a committee tomorrow and denouncing the original committee members as enemies? Boucher explains: "If, instead of submitting public questions to the public decisions of a Constitutional Legislature, we suffer them to be determined by the private prejudices of unauthorized individuals combined in cabals, we must necessarily unhinge the present regular state of things, and substitute a dominion of parties."[43] It is to prevent and avoid these problems that governments based on majority rule with minority rights are established.

Boucher is essentially anticipating James Madison's concerns about majority tyranny. Boucher puts it this way: "The most sacred rights, no longer fenced by the laws, become the sport of every vicissitude or change in a party: there is no more any established rule of conduct; every thing is thrown into uncertainty, and fluctuates with the alternate prevalency of contending factions." In such a circumstance, which Boucher believes is the condition of America, it is only a matter of time before "those who now endeavour to check the progress of political opinion by pains and penalties, by fines and by imprisonment, may, if this state of anarchy . . . continues, themselves be fined, proscribed, or even put to death." Such is the nature of tyranny, and Boucher believes that the committees are tyrannical. It is the nature of tyranny to attempt to silence opposition, and Boucher, along with other Loyalist ministers, has experienced such attempts at the hands of the committees. He warns against "self-delegated persons" who take it upon themselves to be leaders of the people—an apt description of many of the committees. He also points out the irony of the situation: "We are, for fear of surrendering our liberties to (what we call) the arbitrary pretensions of a British Parliament, now to entrust them to men, or bodies of men, invested with no legal authority: men like ourselves, who have no more right to make laws for us, than we have to make laws for them." For the sake of civil society, order, and rule of law, Boucher argues that "it is better even to be oppressed and injured by a lawful power, than to receive benefit and protection from usurpers."[44] Once again, favors from today's tyrant may lead to death from tomorrow's tyrant.

Boucher ends his denunciation of the committees with the following summary statement: "'The free-born soul revolts' at the idea of submitting to such unauthoritative, lawless behests; and must have been 'long debased, and have drank in the last dregs of corruption, before it can brook' the *damnable doctrine and position, that any government lawfully established may be denounced, or resisted, by any self-commissioned persons invested with no authority by law, on any pretence whatsoever.*"[45]

Samuel Seabury focuses his criticism of extralegal groups on the Continental Association (generally simply called the Association) created by the First Continental Congress and the so-called committees of safety established to enforce its extensive trade boycott. He explains that they used "the *soft, mild, insinuating* term of *recommending* their laws," but "they have *solemnly bound . . . every inhabitant of the colonies . . . to adhere firmly to their Association.*" He adds that they set up enforcement officers and penalties for those who violate their "recommendations." Seabury again emphasizes the illegitimacy of the committees themselves and their selection. As he explains: "to give the weight to those committees, and to make them appear as much as possible like LEGAL OFFICERS *duly elected*, they are ordered to be chosen only '*by those who are qualified to vote for Representatives in the legislature.*'" This is solely for the sake of appearance, however; one ought not to be fooled into thinking that they are legitimate officers with real legal authority. He further asks: "And should half a dozen foolish people meet together again, in consequence of their advertisements, and choose themselves to be a Committee, . . . are we obliged to submit to such a Committee?"[46]

In order to demonstrate the dangers inherent in the Association and the powers it bestowed on the committees, Seabury quotes from the text of the Association agreement:

> When it shall be made appear to the satisfaction of a majority of any such committee, that any person within the limits of their appointment has violated this Association, that such majority do forthwith cause the truth of the case to be published in the Gazette, to the end, that all such foes to the rights of British America may be publicly known, and universally contemned [sic] as the enemies of American liberty, and henceforth we respectively will break off all dealings with him or her.[47]

One should notice that this power is given solely to the committee, and that their decision is to be printed in the newspaper to hold the violator up for public ridicule and ostracism. More to the point, the business boycott would then extend to that American. Seabury is outraged:

> Here, gentlemen, is a court established upon the same principles with the *popish Inquisition*. No proofs, no evidences are called for. The committee may judge from *appearances* if they please—... they may proceed to punishment, and *appearances*, you know, are easily *made*; nor is the offender's *presence* necessary. He may be condemned unseen, unheard—without even a possibility of making a defence. No jury is to be impannelled [sic]—No check is appointed upon this court... nor is it left accountable to any power on earth; so that if a majority of the committee should chance not to have the fear of God before their eyes—the Lord have mercy upon us all![48]

There is no provision for—or allowance of—procedures of due process, and no checks or opportunity for appeal. One should also note the assumption of the importance of belief in God in jurisprudence and trials. There is certainly no guarantee that these committees will be populated by God-fearing men; in fact, such "unbounded power" is likely to attract men of the worst character who see opportunity to take advantage. Seabury warns that they are likely to "sometimes wantonly abuse" this unbounded power, especially because "they are accountable to no superior tribunal;—without any other check on their conduct, than their own honour."[49]

For John Joachim Zubly, all of this was something more than theoretical or potential danger. He experienced it firsthand, and his credentials as a Georgia delegate to the Second Continental Congress did not immunize him from the "justice" of the committee. For the supposed crime of not signing the Association agreement, Zubly was banished from his state, and half of his property was taken from him by the committee. In a letter of appeal and warning to the county grand jury, Zubly outlines many violations of due process, the rights of Englishmen, and the rights of Georgians that he suffered. A few of his remarks will suffice to highlight the illegal activities of the committees:

> A Power to tender an Oath, to deprive a Man of Half his Estate, and banish him from every endearing Connection, is lodged in seven Men, without Appeal, without Check, without Challenge.... A Power which annihilates Grand Juries altogether, and effectually renders Petty Juries useless.... As the Matter is now mended, every Man's Person and Half his Property lies at the Mercy of seven Men, who need not have any Qualification, need not receive or produce any Accusation, or hear any Evidence, nor judge of the Breach of any Law.[50]

Zubly further complains: "I have been ordered to appear before Judges who have no Existance [sic] in our Constitution, under the moderate Penalty, not of being proceeded against and outlawed, but of an IMMEDIATE Forfeiture of my Effects, and of being sent to any Goal [sic] without Bail." His use of the word "moderate" is clearly sarcastic and "goal" is a misspelling of *gaol* (jail). In light of his experiences, Zubly concludes that in America constitutional government is at an end, all liberty is at an end, all law is at an end, and all appearance of justice is at an end.[51] One must remember that Zubly did not suffer banishment and loss of property for violating the particulars of the trade boycott but for simply not signing the Association agreement.

The treatment of Zubly is particularly revealing when one recognizes that he was a member of the Continental Congress. No one was safe, as Boucher warned. Speaking of the New York committee's encroachment on the New York legislature's powers, Seabury asks: "If they treat the *Representatives* of the province in this disrespectful manner, what are the *people* to expect?" He then answers his own question: "We shall not dare to eat, or drink, or sleep, or act, or speak, or think, but in the precise mode which they shall direct." If that sounds tyrannical, Seabury's point is made. He continues: "They have already regulated our trade and commerce, our manner of living, and our diversions; and, if their VINDICATOR is to be credited, the *next* Congress is to regulate our *courts of justice*.—Then will their tyranny be established; a tyranny of the most dreadful kind;—which *makes* laws and *executes* them without *check or controul*."[52]

Is Seabury's language hyperbolic? Zubly and countless others might not think so. Loyalist ministers certainly experienced limits on speaking and thinking as they watched their churches closed, their sermons and pamphlets destroyed, and the presses closed to them or ransacked. Some dared not sleep, as vigilante committees dragged them from their homes and carried them off to banishment, prison, or corporal punishment. Limits on food, drink, clothing, and other daily concerns were connected with the regulation of trade and commerce intended by the trade boycott. In his criticism of the Association, Seabury warns that an otherwise innocent person might be declared an enemy of America and be ostracized and boycotted because he or she "hast drank a dish of *tea* . . . or hast used an English *pin*, or eaten an Irish *potatoe* [sic]." To demonstrate that their "liberty and property are made subject to the laws of the Congress, and the will of the committee," he notes that any merchandise they receive—even though they ordered it before the Congress existed—"must be reshipped by your *own* direction;

and this direction you *must* give, under the penalty of being *gazetted*;—or ... stored at your *own risk*;—or, they must be sold under the direction of the committee." A merchant must pay to ship goods back to England or to store them if the committee so instructs. If or when the committee allows the goods to be sold, then they must be sold as the committee directs, and "the profit is to be applied to the relieving such poor inhabitants of the town of Boston as are immediate sufferers by the Boston Port-Bill." The merchant takes all of the risk and expense and receives none of the profit. If he balks, he is publicly denounced in the newspaper. Seabury chides and mocks those sympathetic to the Patriot cause: "Men who exclaim so violently for liberty and the rights of Englishmen ... voluntarily submit to such an abject state of slavery! ... *You*, who refuse submission to the Parliament, ... tamely give up your liberty and property to an illegal, tyrannical Congress."[53] This is in addition to the fact that those engaged in occupations related to trade, such as merchants, shipbuilders, sailors, ship owners, manufacturers and farmers who produce tradeable goods, and store owners, are prohibited by the Congress from making a living.

Seabury connects the illegality and illegitimacy of the Congress and of the committees with their oppressive dictates. Speaking to the merchants of New York, he asks: "What right had the *Congress* to give what did not belong to them? to give your money,—the profits arising from the sale of your goods,—without your consent?" He quickly answers his own question: "But I forget myself,—they first proclaimed themselves your representatives, and then of course they had an undoubted, legal, constitutional right to all your substance." As a result, he warns them, "your liberties and properties are now at the mercy of a body of men unchecked, uncontrouled by the civil power"; and "you are no longer your own masters:—you have subjected your business, your dealings, your mode of living, the conduct and regulation of your families, to *their* prudence and discretion." Reminding them again that the Congress is a "new authority ... subversive of the power of the legislature," he says of the trade boycott restrictions: "The laws of this government ... forbid us to disturb or hinder any person in the prosecution of his lawful business;—that is, in doing what the law permits to be done. ... But you have introduced a law of the congress, making that unlawful and impracticable which the laws of the province permit." Not only has the Congress imposed trade restrictions contravening the laws of New York (and the other colonies), but it has also authorized the committees to enforce those restrictions. The committees in turn have exceeded their original purpose and become a significant threat to liberty. Seabury calls the committee "a court of Inquisition, to decide, in the most arbitrary, tyrannical and unheard-of manner, upon the liberties and properties of your fellow-subjects, over whom you have no just or legal power."[54]

As the war raged on, many others besides Zubly suffered at the hands of the committees. Writing in 1779 to the president of the Continental Congress, Charles Inglis reminds John Jay that the Congress was convened simply to claim "redress of grievances." Because redress "has been repeatedly and amply offered," the British government is therefore "guiltless" of the consequences of war. Because they were not content with such redress, the members of the Congress "are the authors of all the calamities which overwhelm America" and their conduct, he says "is criminal in the extreme." In support of this serious charge, Inglis outlines the conduct that he describes as "criminal,"

> such as tarring and feathering, riding of men on rails by mobs and Committees, which mobs and committees were the principal fabricators and supporters of the congress in the beginning—such as chaining men together by the dozens, and driving them, like herds of cattle, into distant provinces, flinging them into loathsome jails, confiscating their estates, shooting them in swamps and woods as suspected tories, hanging them after a mock trial; and all this because they would not abjure their rightful Sovereign, and bear arms against him. You must be conscious that these methods were constantly practised by your Congress and their partizans [sic], that by these you gradually rose to your present usurped power . . . they were done in the true spirit of Machiavelism.[55]

In support of these charges, Inglis includes a footnote with details and particulars. The villains in these events are the committees, the henchmen carrying out these outrageous practices, but his primary point to Jay is that the Congress created the monsters and gave them free rein. Inglis contends that the Congress has lost all moral authority, and he consequently questions "whether a treaty of any kind should be held with the Congress—whether men, who have so much prostituted their usurped power, should ever be admitted to have any hand in the settlement of the colonies."[56]

What, then, should be done in response to the illegitimate and "illegal, tyrannical Congress" and "the arbitrary, illegal, and tyrannical procedure of the Committee of Correspondence?" Seabury announces that he will refuse "abject submission to your committee, or your delegates, or congress. I will not hold my rights and privileges on so precarious a tenure." He appeals to the legislature of New York to reassert their authority, take back their rightful place, and take more appropriate action in relation to England. He tells them: "To YOU, Gentlemen, the good people of this province look for relief: on YOU they have fixed their hopes: from YOU they expect deliverance from this intolerable state of slavery. They have chosen YOU to be the guardians of their rights and liberties." He urges them to "recur boldly to your good, old, legal and successful way of proceeding, by petition and remonstrance." As for the people in general, he urges them to "assemble yourselves together: tell your supervisor, that he has exceeded his commission:—That you will have no such Committees:—That you are Englishmen, and will maintain your rights and privileges, and will eat, and drink, and wear, whatever the public laws of your country permit, without asking leave of any illegal, tyrannical Congress or Committee on earth." Unfortunately for the Loyalist clergy, the committees and their extensive web of "spies and informers" could not be successfully opposed or dislodged.[57] They continued to harass the Loyalists and to enforce adherence to revolutionary edicts to the end of the conflict.

Conclusion

Although they were clergymen and not jurists or politicians, Loyalist ministers expressed great concern for legality and legitimate constitutional government and procedures. They were well-educated citizens, or more properly subjects, who were concerned about justice, rights, and the welfare of their congregants. They also had a great affinity for procedural and behavioral propriety; disobedience and defiance of authority really disturbed them. They firmly believed that the good of society required the stability provided by the traditional and constitutional features of the British governmental system—as well as by the colonial assemblies representing local interests. Ultimately, the Loyalist clergymen were Englishmen who greatly valued that identity and the institutions and rights that accompanied it.

Believing that all of the evidence was on their side, the Loyalist ministers were not hesitant to enter into any part of the legal discussion. By their analysis, the colonial charters supported the claims of the Crown and of the Parliament. As the supreme legislative authority of the British empire, Parliament had the right to tax all lands controlled by England—including the American colonies. This was also true given the inherent nature of the relationship between a colony and a parent country. The American colonists claimed to be Englishmen and loyal subjects of the Crown, so the relevant form of representation for Americans must be the English form. By that standard, the "no taxation without representation" slogan was meaningless. The colonists had no right to create continental congresses, their means of selection were illegal, and the congresses had no authority to contravene the constitutionally allowed and duly elected colonial legislatures. It follows that the Association agreed to by the First Continental Congress was invalid and the committees established to execute its edicts had no legal authority. In addition, those committees often consisted of the worst type of opportunists and partisans, and their arbitrary and tyrannical acts in violation of the rights of Englishmen vitiated any credibility or legitimacy that they might have gained over time. From the Loyalist perspective, the American colonies had descended from order and rule of law to anarchy and mob rule.

5 Rational Arguments Regarding the American Situation

> Happy for themselves if they are brought to think seriously at last, tho' it might have saved a world of trouble if they could have been induced to do so at first.
> —John Joachim Zubly

> I exerted myself to stem the torrent of popular clamor, to recall people to the use of their reason, and to retain them in their loyalty and allegiance.
> —Samuel Seabury

Loyalist ministers opposed rebellion or revolution on principle. In their view, both the Bible and reason dictated against resistance to authority. An observer might agree with them in principle but make exceptions in individual cases. Several of the Loyalist clergy themselves struggled with this temptation. When it came to the American situation, however, the Loyalist clergymen spoke with one voice in condemning the American Revolution. Most of them thought that the British government had made mistakes and that the Americans had reason to protest various parliamentary laws and ministerial actions, but none of them thought that rebellion was an appropriate or acceptable response. That, of course, is the basic ground for the collective name "Loyalist." This chapter addresses the Loyalist ministers' rational arguments against revolution in light of the American situation at the time: the relationship between Great Britain and the American colonies, manipulation of the public by troublemakers, insufficient efforts at conciliation, and the folly of an illegitimate congress.

American Situation

The first point that must be made—and is made repeatedly by the Loyalist clergy—is that the American colonies were English colonies and the American colonists were Englishmen. As Englishmen, Americans had a duty to obey the king and Parliament. Charles Inglis explains that the colonies were settled under charters granted by the kings of England and "the emigrants were as much subjects of the British Crown, as dependent on the supreme legislature of the empire, 'after,' as 'before,' their emigration." Thomas Bradbury Chandler declares: "I consider Great-Britain and her colonies . . . as but one body. . . . I consider them as constituting one great and illustrious family, to which I have the honour to belong." Samuel Seabury observes that all parties "profess the utmost loyalty to the King; the warmest affection to their fellow-subjects in England, Ireland, and the West-Indies." Jonathan Boucher asserts: "It is folly to imagine, that, as an Englishman, interested in the welfare of England, I am not equally interested in the welfare of America. I cannot dissociate the idea of a perfect sameness of interest between the two countries, as much as between a parent and a child." Even Swiss-born John Joachim Zubly says that "by descent or incorporation we are now all *Britons;* let *Britain's* interests be ever dear to us all" and "let us never fail to act the part of truly dutiful children. . . . May eastern and western *Britons* ever be more firmly united."[1]

These statements from the latter two commentators introduce a common theme among the Loyalists: a parent–child relationship between England and America. According to Boucher, the American colonies were not "lopped off the parent trunk" but "carefully transplanted here" and "assiduously and tenderly cherished by that Parent State." Zubly expresses concern that Americans would give anyone reason to question their loyalty to the king and "our sincere and firm attachment to our mother-country." Speaking of the king, he admonishes his audience to "always return a filial respect to the indulgence and tenderness of an affectionate parent." Inglis urges his fellow Americans to look upon Britain as "your parent state." He reminds them it has played the part of a parent; that it is "the state from which you originated—which protected and fostered you with tender care, and raised you to your late flourishing and envied condition." To the clergymen, the particular significance of this parent–child relationship is the obligations of the child (the American colonies). Seabury explains that

> the dependence of the colonies on the mother-country has ever been acknowledged. It is an impropriety of speech to talk of an independent

colony. The words *independency* and *colony*, convey contradictory ideas. ... As soon as a colony becomes independent on its parent state, it ceases to be any longer a colony. ... The British colonies make a part of the British empire. As parts of the body they must be subject to the general laws of the body.²

Chandler conveys the same idea, but he links it more closely to the familial authority relationship. He maintains that "some degree of respect ... [is] always due from inferiors to superiors, and especially from children to parents" and that "the refusal of this on any occasion ... [is] a violation of the general laws of society, to say nothing of the obligations of religion and morality." Since "Great-Britain bears ... a relation to these colonies, similar to that of a parent to children"; he asks "whether any parent can put up with such disrespectful and abusive treatment from children, as Great-Britain has lately received from her colonies?" He criticizes opposition to the power that "has cherished us in its bosom, and kindly protected us from our earliest infancy." Chandler questions whether Americans should have the privileges of children if they do not consider themselves under the authority of the parent: "What right the Americans have to plead the privilege of Englishmen, any more than the privilege of Dutchmen, if they are not in full subjection to the authority of *Great-Britain*, let those who can, shew."³ Dutchmen are not children of Great Britain, so they do not enjoy the privileges given by the England as a parent country. If the Americans are not willing to behave like children of Great Britain, then they should not enjoy—or claim—those privileges either.

As Chandler indicated, Englishmen must be fully subject to British authority. That is, identification with the king alone is not sufficient. Seabury explains that in "the Empire to which we belong, the supreme Authority is vested in the KING, the *Lords* and the *Commons* of the Realm, conjunctly called the PARLIAMENT; and to the Laws of this supreme Authority absolute Submission and Obedience are due, both upon the Principles of Religion, and of good Policy." The British king is an inseparable part of the British Parliament; an Englishman cannot reject the authority of Parliament and yet try to retain the king as his sovereign. Besides the inseparability issue, Seabury provides another reason: "The King of Great-Britain was placed on the throne by virtue of an act of Parliament: And he is King of America, by virtue of being King of Great-Britain. He is therefore King of America by act of Parliament. And if we disclaim that authority of Parliament which made him our King, we, in fact, reject him from being our King; for we disclaim that authority by which he is a King at all."⁴ According to Seabury, the colonists cannot claim to be only under the king's authority, and they cannot pick and choose which acts of Parliament that they will recognize as legitimate and which they will obey.

Chandler and Zubly specifically connect the necessity of subjection to the whole government with America's colonial status. Because the American colonies were settled under charters, Chandler says that "the Americans, with their own *free consent*, were originally placed under the absolute authority of the English Parliament;—that they never yet have been legally exempted from it;—and that they never can be properly exempted, but by the generous and friendly concessions of *Great-Britain*." He asks if the colonies are part of the "*British* community," are they not also "necessarily subject in all cases, to the jurisdiction of that legislative power which represents this community, or, in other words, to the *British* parliament?" To make the same point in reverse, he suggests that the supreme legislative authority must extend to "all the dominions" of a nation and that any place to which it does not extend cannot "justly be said to be a part of its dominions." In a 1769 sermon, Zubly points out that "the colonies in *America*, being settled upon lands discovered by the *English*, under charters from the crown of *England*, were always considered as a part of the *English* nation, and of the *British* empire, and looked upon as dependent upon *England*." Having established that, Zubly says: "All the inhabitants of the *British* empire together form the BRITISH NATION, and that the *British* Parliament is the supreme power and legislature in the British nation I never heard doubted."⁵

This comports with Boucher's remark in 1774 that "the supreme Power of the British Parliament over her Colonies, was ever till very lately, as universally acknowledg'd, by ourselves, as by our Fellow-Subjects in England." Chandler says the same in a 1774 pamphlet, adding that "many of us have solemnly sworn allegiance" to England, as all Church of England clergymen were required to do. Inglis accuses the Patriots of "spurn[ing] the most sacred obligations that subjects can be under to a Sovereign" and of violating oaths and compelling others to violate theirs. For the Loyalist clergymen, the only logical position was that all Englishmen living in the British empire were subject to the authority of the whole British government—including the parliament authorized to make laws for the empire. As Chandler summarizes, if the colonies—which originally belonged to Great Britain—are "not now to be regulated and governed by the authority of *Great Britain*," then they are not dependent on Great Britain, not part of its territories or dominions, not English, have no claim to "the privileges of Englishmen," and, "as they have never been legally discharged from the duty they owed it, they are rebels and apostates."[6]

Related to both the parent–child theme and the unique status of colonies is the theme of gratitude owed by Americans to Great Britain. As early as 1763—the end of the Seven Years' War—Boucher reminds his congregation that the "chief burden" of the war had been borne by "our mother country," that "*for us and our sakes* it was first entered into; and that our welfare has been principally consulted in the terms on which it has been concluded." He asks them to call to mind how they felt "when, not long since . . . you saw . . . your enemies at your very doors, ready to *swallow you up*." He then encourages them to be thankful and grateful to England. Samuel Andrews told his congregation that should "our Gratitude and Loyalty to the House of Hanover, our great Deliverer, prove ineffectual—then let us hang our Harps on the Willows and weep." In his response to Thomas Paine's claim in *Common Sense* that America would have flourished without British aid, Charles Inglis counters that America would have perished "as an infant without its proper food" without British aid and support. Even if they survived their "first difficulties," they would have been "seized" by a European power "in their infant state" if Great Britain had not "held out her protection." Responding to Paine's claim that England protected America for the sake of her own interest, Inglis asks: "Supposing this were true, where is the harm?" Either way, the British did protect them, and "it is a matter of little moment to us, what her motives were." He is certain that Paine is wrong about Britain's motives, however, and that it acted out of "affection and attachment" as well as interest. He urges his readers not to "undervalue" British protection because of speculation about motive.[7]

One way of undervaluing Britain's efforts on their behalf in the Seven Years' War is to overestimate America's role in the conflict. Boucher warns against any effort at moral equivalence, noting that Americans fought "to drive away an enemy from our own quarters," while the British "had but a remote interest" in the contest. They were involved chiefly because it concerned the Americans. The Americans, on the other hand, "were immediately interested, and must either have fought, or have given up our inheritance." Not only that, Boucher reminds his flock, but "they dismissed us *laden with silver and with gold*, for having lent only a feeble and very unequal aid to the avenging of our own quarrel." This alludes to the parliamentary grants made to reimburse the colonies for the sums that they advanced during the war against the French in North America. Seabury likewise tells his congregation that "Reason and common Sense will teach us to honor and esteem those from whom we receive Protection" and that Great Britain had "nursed [the colonies] with the greatest parental Tenderness, and protected and defended [them] with her choicest Blood and Treasure." Inglis also emphasizes that the colonies were "supported and protected at the expence of English blood and treasure."[8]

There is one fateful corollary to the matter of gratitude owed, particularly in the context of blood and treasure. As Boucher puts it, "Gratitude is a debt: and surely it is not a little that the Parent State is entitled to claim from us on the score of past benefits." The Loyalists stress the reciprocal nature of protection afforded by the government and the material and immaterial obligations of the protected. Partly in gratitude and partly as a matter of duty, the American colonists owed the British government subjection, obedience, and treasure. Seabury lays it out clearly and succinctly:

> Government implies, not only a power of making and enforcing *laws*, but defence and protection. Now protection implies tribute. Those that share in the protection of any government, are in reason and duty, bound to maintain and support the government that protects them: Otherwise they destroy their own protection; or else they throw an unjust burthen on their fellow-subjects, which they ought to bear in common with them. While therefore the colonies are under the British government, and share its protection, the British government has a right to raise, and they are in reason and duty bound to pay, a reasonable and proportionable part of the expence of its administration.[9]

In order to reciprocate for British protection—particularly during the war with France—the Loyalists argued that the colonies should not only give their obedience to the government but also give their treasure in the form of taxes to cover their fair share of Britain's expense on their behalf.

According to Seabury, Britain's economy and security depends so much on its navy and Americans benefit so greatly from its naval protection that "requesting us to bear a part of the expence, proportional to our ability, and to that protection and security which we receive from it" is certainly appropriate. The appropriate and logical context for an American contribution is therefore commerce and trade. Seabury argues that the British

Parliament has a right to regulate the commerce of its entire empire and that all parts of the empire must be subject to Parliament or else the trade of the whole cannot be regulated. As Zubly puts it, "When every branch of the legislature, and every member of the British empire, has a true regard to reciprocal duty, prerogative and privilege, the happiness of the whole is best likely to be secured and promoted."[10]

The problem, as the Loyalists see it, is that "no part of the empire has received so much from the Government, or contributed so little, as the British Colonies in North America." The people living in England paid much higher taxes than did Americans, a fact not lost on Zubly, who notes in 1769 that Americans "have hitherto been exempted from the taxes paid in England, which it must be owned are very heavy, by mere favour." Eventually the government decided that the Americans should assume a more reasonable share of the financial burden—at least covering a significant portion of the expense to defend them. Boucher imagines the British saying the following:

> You, therefore, are our tributaries; and we have the right to exercise dominion over you. . . . Unsupported by us, you never could have overcome all the dangers you had to encounter on your first settling here. . . . In consideration of your inability, we have hitherto forborne to levy any contributions on you: but you are now rich; and though even yet you cannot wholly remunerate us, you may pay back some portion of your debt. . . . You shall therefore now be taxed, and made to contribute to the common support.[11]

This is, by their account, only fair and a reasonable compensation for services rendered. Boucher admonishes his fellow Virginians: "Let us then, no longer disgrace ourselves, by illiberal, ungrateful Reproaches, by meanly ascribing, the most generous Conduct, to the most sordid Motives; we owe our Birth, our Progress, our Delivery to her; we still depend on her for Protection; we are surely able to bear some Part of the Expence of it; let us be willing to bear it." As the Revolution is in progress, Seabury says bluntly: "THE Pretences also for this Rebellion were frivilous [sic] and groundless.—Great-Britain asked nothing unreasonable; nothing but what a good Subject would have given unasked."[12]

The Loyalist clergymen could not understand why Americans rebelled. Indeed, the Patriots insisted even after the first battles of the Revolution that they were not seeking separation from Great Britain and did not intend to rebel. These are strange assurances from men who claimed legitimate grounds to rebel. Drawing parallels in 1775 with an event in the history of ancient Israel (recounted in Joshua 22), Boucher suggests that the Americans were not suspected of "a disposition to rebellion altogether without reason." According to him, the Americans had, like the two and one-half tribes in the biblical account, given "cause for suspicion" of "meditating a rebellion." Like them, the Americans need to explain how and why their actions do not signal a desire or intention to rebel. He calls on the Patriots to "make the same solemn appeal to Heaven" that the settlers of Gilead made: "that it is not *in rebellion* that our country is now set forth in hostile array." Boucher warns that "America is without excuse if [such an oath or pledge] be not made."[13]

From the perspective of the Loyalists, Americans had engaged in provocative actions and even initiated armed conflict despite living an almost idyllic life and enjoying great privileges. Chandler says: "Of all the subjects of Great Britain, those who reside in the American Colonies have been ... by far the happiest: surrounded with the blessings of peace, health, and never-failing plenty—enjoying the benefits of an equitable and free constitution—secured by the protection and patronage of the greatest maritime power in the world—and contributing, in but a small proportion, to the support of the necessary public expences." Boucher wants to teach Americans to "compare their happy Situation, with the Wretchedness of Nine Tenths of the Globe." To encourage that, he lists a number of blessings and good things that Americans enjoy:

> The general Diffusion of the Necessaries, the Conveniences and Pleasures of Life, among all Orders of People here; the certain Rewards of Industry, the innumerable Avenues to Wealth, the native, unsubdued Freedom of their Manners, and Conversation; the Spirit of Equality . . ., the entire Security of their Fortunes, Liberty, and Lives, the Equity, and Lenity, of their civil and criminal Justice, the Toleration of their religious Opinions, and Worship.[14]

Both of these men might be criticized for a pessimistic attitude toward change or for undue conservatism. Who is to say that Americans might not be better off independent from Great Britain? For them, however, such a criticism is missing the point. One cannot simply replace colonial status with independence; there must be a war in between. In order to justify the horrendous human and material toll taken by revolution, as well as to justify the precedents it sets, there must be some overwhelming and unavoidable reason—some unbearable oppression and tyranny. They did not believe that situation existed in the American colonies and, according to Seabury, the lack of it "enhances [the American Revolution's] Guilt to a Degree of Enormity not to be parralleled [sic] in History." Boucher likewise suggests that their folly and guilt are aggravated by "having chosen the happiest period in all your history for your revolt."[15]

Charles Inglis agrees with them and takes the argument directly to the president of the Continental Congress: "THE present rebellion is one of the most singular occurrences in the history of mankind.... Nations have been often plunged into civil war by the claims of pretenders to the regal authority, or by the imposition of enormous taxes, or other oppressions. But evidently these did not occasion the present rebellion; for no such claim, no such taxes or oppressions existed in America." Not only was there no basis for rebellion, but there "was not a more free or happy people on earth than the British colonists. Without any taxes, but for the support of their poor—as free from restraint of any kind as could consist with a state of society." In search of a parallel circumstance, Boucher quotes a speech by Spurius Servilius. Servilius spoke to the tribunes of Rome, but Boucher applies it to the Patriots: "You act contrary both to justice and piety . . . in not acknowledging the many great benefits you have received . . . and in resenting their refusal to grant some of your desires . . . from their regard to the advantage of the commonwealth."[16] Whether or not the parallel is precise, the quote echoes the Loyalist clergymen's criticism of the rebellion on both political and religious grounds and reflects British concern for the empire—not merely the interest of the Americans.

Having posited a profound incongruity between the general situation of the American colonies and rebellion against England, the Loyalist ministers also focus on the trivial nature of the Patriot complaints and claims of oppression. George Micklejohn argues that because of their representative system, it is particular "folly and contradiction" for Englishmen to oppose the laws passed by Parliament. But it is also irrational because of the nature of the laws themselves. In response to Patriot complaints about "the arbitrary proceedings of the British Parliament," Chandler replies that "if this [three-penny tax on tea] may be called a burden, so may the weight of an atom on the shoulders of a giant: besides, this burden may be easily avoided; for we have no occasion to purchase the tea, and unless we purchase it, we are under no obligations to pay the duty." The Loyalists zeroed in on the three-penny tea tax as symbolic of how trivial the charges of oppression were. Boucher mockingly reminds his congregation that the British government is now considered *"oppressive and severe"* "on account of an insignificant duty on tea, imposed by the British Parliament... which, we well know, two thirds of the people of America can never be called on to pay." He then asks: "Is it the part of an *understanding people*, of loyal subjects, or of good Christians, instantly to resist and rebel for a cause so trivial?" Chandler and Boucher emphasize that not only is the tax miniscule, but also that no one is compelled to pay it because no one must buy the tea. Whoever chooses to buy the tea essentially consents to pay the tax. Chandler calls the duty on tea *"de Lana Caprina"*—a piddling, worthless matter—and asks: "Can such behaviour on so slight a provocation, proceed from *dutiful and loyal subjects*?" That, one should remember, is what the Americans still claimed to be in 1774.[17]

The tea tax is a target for another reason: it was technically a duty, or an embedded tax on an imported commodity, not a direct tax. As a duty, it was an expression of Parliament's regulation of trade throughout the British empire. Even after rejecting Parliament's right to tax them internally, the Americans had recognized its right to tax them externally in order to regulate the empire's commerce. But it seemed to the Loyalists that whenever the Patriots agreed to a proper sphere of parliamentary action, they moved the goalpost and changed the rules as soon as Parliament in fact acted. Responding in 1774 to Patriot claims that Parliament had no right to "lay the duty" on tea, Chandler argues that "we have never proved that they have not" such a right and that "we ourselves have always believed and allowed that they have it, till the present occasion." He notes that whenever Parliament had exercised that power in the past, "we have submitted to their acts." Adding the moving boundary between acceptable and unacceptable parliamentary action to the aforementioned criticisms, Boucher asks:

> Shall we establish Distinctions, between internal, and external Taxation one Year, and laugh at them the next? Shall we confound Duties, with Taxes, and Regulations of Trade with Revenue Laws? ... Shall we refuse to obey the Tea Act, not as an oppressive Act, but as a dangerous, a sole Precedent of Taxation, when every Post-Day shews us a Precedent, which our Fore-Fathers submitted to, and which we still submit to, without murmuring? Shall we move Heaven, and Earth, against a trifling Duty, on a Luxury, unknown to nine Tenths of the Globe, unknown to our Ancestors! ... Which no Authority, no Necessity compels us to use?[18]

Are all taxes imposed by Parliament illegitimate, or just internal taxes? Must not an imperial power have the right to regulate its empire? Why, suddenly, are acts of Parliament that have been accepted for decades now unconstitutional and unbearable? And why rebel over a miniscule duty on a luxury item that no one is compelled to buy?

The Patriot argument concerning the duty on tea is that it, and other duties, establish precedents, so that "if Parliament has a right to take from us one penny, without our consent, it has a right to strip us of our whole property, and to make us absolute slaves." Chandler points out that precedents for regulating the trade of the colonies "are not wanting. Every reign since the settlement of the Colonies has produced them." He reminds his readers that they are daily paying duties because of legislation passed before it became fashionable to protest. He also suggests that this "is the first time that a sovereign power has been in want of *precedents*, to justify its making laws to govern any part of its dominions." He appeals again to the fact that the supreme legislature of Great Britain has the power to make laws for all British dominions. It needs no precedents. Regarding the argument that if they can take a penny, they can take all property, Chandler retorts: "Altho' so great a man as Mr. Locke was the father of it, it appears to me to be weak and sophistical. A right to do what is reasonable, implies not a right to do what is unreasonable." As to the question of consent, he again argues that "unless you consent to the tax, you are not to pay the duty. You may refuse it, if you please, without incurring any penalty, or considerable inconvenience." Chandler adds that because the colonies have "peculiar views and interests" and do not agree on matters of commerce, nothing could be put in place if their consent is necessary. Therefore, Great Britain must regulate trade for the whole empire and, if not, "she had better relinquish at once her claim of authority over the colonies; after which they cannot expect to enjoy her protection."[19]

Chandler expounds further on the issue of consent. When the Patriots complain that "if we are to be bound by laws to which we have never consented, we have not the rights of Englishmen," Chandler replies that "it never was, nor can it be, the right of Englishmen to be exempted from the authority of an English or British Parliament." It is not consenting to laws enacted by the British Parliament that distinguishes a British subject from a foreigner but being bound by those laws. "So long as a man resides within any dominions, he is a subject of it, and is obligated to submit to its laws, as far as they concern him, whether he approves of them or not." He appeals to the example of "the Minority, where there is a division, whose votes are overruled by the major part; for the law necessarily passes, not only without, but contrary to, their consent." In addition, "there are millions of people residing in England, who have no votes in elections, and are never consulted about the expediency of laws." They give no other consent to the laws to which they must submit "than what is implied in their freely residing within the jurisdiction and protection of Parliament. In this sense, the Americans ... consent to be governed by the British laws." Chandler further contends that the original settlers of America knew that they would be under the authority of Parliament without the opportunity to send representatives. "*On these terms they willingly settled here;* and they have always enjoyed every advantage which they originally expected to receive, and which was contracted for in their stipulation with the Crown, and they can have no justification to complain on this account."[20]

Chandler makes one other argument concerning the desire of the Patriots to be exempted "from the authority of parliament, with regard to taxation." He challenges them "to prove, that this privilege had been properly granted to them, either in the original establishment of the colonies or by some legal subsequent act. A point of this nature must be proved by clear *facts*, and not by metaphysical arguments, taken from the abstract nature of Englishmen, and of such Englishmen too as refuse submission to the English laws." He notes that Parliament "has always exercised the authority which is now contested" and that it "would have gone far towards securing" the Patriot position if they "could have made it appear, either by apparent facts, or conclusive arguments, that the parliament was mistaken." "If after that the parliament would have still persisted in its claim, we might have appealed to the world for its invalidity; and none of us would have had *scruples of conscience*, to prevent our joining in a general association to recover by a vigorous effort, a right that was rendered unquestionable. But the [Continental] Congress has neither proved the right, nor attempted to prove it." Appeals to natural rights are of no avail in this dispute because "the privileges enjoyed by virtue of the *English* constitution of government are ... *political* privileges," so "the natural right of the *Americans*" cannot entitle them to "the political privileges of *Englishmen*, any more than to the political privileges of *Dutchmen*."[21]

Ministers also emphasize other aspects of the American colonial situation in relation to the genesis of the rebellion. Samuel Andrews is among those who spotlight the role of "dissenting" ministers—that is, clergymen from non-Anglican churches. He warns his Church of England brethren in

1770 that they "have a plentiful Crop of Misery to gather in, if we credit the Sermons and Declarations of the multiformed Sects of Protestant-protesting Associators, who have assumed a self-constituted Power of nullifying Acts of Parliament and the Statutes of this Colony." Andrews sees rebellion on the horizon as early as 1770, largely advanced by the Patriot preachers. Boucher also points to the dissenting clergy. He speaks of them traveling the length of America for years, "disseminating, as They go along, their mischievous Tenets." After talking about the preponderancy of Presbyterianism in America, he says: "Early Prejudices, fostered by Education, & confirmed by Religion, all conspire to cherish Republicanism. Their Schools, Academies or Colleges seem, in general, to have been instituted but for that End." According to him, the schools, colleges, and churches of the dissenters "openly teach & inculcate Principles subversive of all good Government." Boucher is so convinced of this influence that he refers to northern schools as "Seminaries of Sedition" and suggests that if the Americans win a war with England, the result would be a "Triumphancy of the Saints" (meaning dissenters). In short, Boucher puts much of the blame on the "republican Spirit (every where so fostered by Dissenters) that has long been busy in undermining the Constitution both here & there."[22]

Charles Inglis casts a wider net, identifying multiple sources for the potentially revolutionary ideas that had taken root in America. He writes the following to the president of the Continental Congress:

> As matters were situated in America, some such convulsion as the present was unavoidable, sooner or later. . . . Deep rooted republicanism, democratic, levelling principles, ever unfriendly to monarchy, had spread their baneful influence far and wide. Actuated by these, your adherents were disposed to revolt: The ambition, artifice, and duplicity of the Congress did the rest. From these combined causes sprung this most detestable rebellion; neither of which singly had been adequate to such an effect. . . . The particulars which some have falsly [sic] assigned as causes of the rebellion, were no more than circumstances that hastened matters to a crisis.[23]

Inglis, then, attributes the rebellion to a combination of causes and makes it more intentional and deliberate. Republican levelers spread their antimonarchical gospel, which plowed the ground, and the ill-intentioned Continental Congress planted the seeds. In a footnote, he identifies "the particulars" that had been "falsely assigned as causes of the rebellion."

These include: "*the three penny duty on tea, some acts of parliament which were complained of here, and have been mostly repealed, the opposition to government by the minority, on the part of Britain; and on this side of the Atlantic, the practice of smuggling, the hopes of defrauding creditors in Britain, and an apprehension in the colonists that they would be taxed beyond their due proportion, &c.*" Boucher agrees that the Stamp Act and the duty on tea merely brought "the present Disorders in America" to light. But he argues that there is "a Principle of Revolt in all Colonies; and in Those of G. Britain, which may be said to have been planted in Imperfection, more than in any others." As a result either of Inglis's deeper causes or "particulars" or of Boucher's principle of revolt, the Americans "waged war against that state which gave them existence, which always cherished them with parental tenderness, and raised them to their late flourishing condition."[24]

Errors by Great Britain

The Loyalist ministers were not blind apologists for the British government. They did not like being called Tories, as that too closely aligned them with British politics. They called themselves Loyalists. Some scholars have used the term "Whig-Loyalist"[25] when referring to a number of them in order to reflect their seemingly inconsistent loyalism. It is offered, for example, as an apt description of John Joachim Zubly, who was enough of a Whig to be selected a member of the Continental Congress but balked at the point of rebellion. Some may find the composite term useful, but it is probably more accurate to simply call them Loyalists and to explain that theirs was not an uncritical loyalty. The fact that they were willing to be critical of actual British excesses arguably contributes significantly to their credibility.

A few examples should suffice to demonstrate that the Loyalist ministers looked critically on the acts of the Parliament and shared many of the concerns of their fellow Americans. Boucher refers to "this terrible Stamp Act" and declares that it is "in every Sense, oppressive, impolitic & illegal." As a result, in his view, the "best & dearest Rights" of Americans "have been mercilessly invaded by Parliament." He is also critical of the Royal Proclamation of 1763 limiting colonial expansion westward, calling it "very impolitic, as well as unjust." Zubly refers to the Stamp Act as "this unhappy act" and suggests that if it had not been repealed, "the year 1765 must have been the fatal year from which the loss of American liberty must have been dated." According to Zubly, "inconsiderate measures, framed on the other side of the atlantic, are the cause of all our mischiefs." Inglis says of the fateful mission that precipitated the first shots of the Revolution that "the expedition to Lexington was rash and ill-judged" and that he "disapprove[s] the design of it." Chandler is even critical of Parliament's taxing policy on some of the grounds claimed by the Patriots. He declares "honestly and candidly" that "the policy of some of the late acts" had been wrong and that "we do not enjoy all the privileges of Englishmen, while we give no kind of consent to the laws that govern us;—and, that it is time that we were exempted, in a regular way, from parliamentary taxation, on some generous and equitable plan." He sees some of the laws as "violations of . . . constitutional liberty" and charges that "silent submission" to them would have "a dangerous tendency" and that continuation of them "would be productive of evil."[26] Chandler regularly lobbies for an American constitution specifying rights and the scope of parliamentary authority, particularly in the area of taxation.

It is not just specific legislation that angers Boucher, however. He also excoriates Parliament for being "unaccountably ignorant" of a proper means of taxing the Americans and of the present state of the colonies. Complaining about the "Strange Inattention of the Mother Country to these [colonies]," he blames them for "suffering a strange refractory Spirit to grow up, which, ere long, will work her irremediable Woe." According to Boucher, even the best-intentioned efforts of the British government contributed directly to the ultimate separation: "Their Improvement & Aggrandisement have been chiefly aim'd at . . . never reflecting, that every Accession of Strength & opulence to Them, whilst govern'd as they have hitherto been, was, in Effect, advancing them still nearer to Independency." More important, though, were the many errors in governing the colonies—the "strange, wild, wavering & unsettled Systems of Colony Administration."[27] But who is responsible for the hapless administration of the American colonies and for the offensive policies of the British government toward them?

The Loyalist clergy often place the blame squarely on the king's government ministers—the British bureaucracy. Zubly urges his congregation to pray against the king's "evil counsellors" and, after insisting that Americans do not want separation from Great Britain, says that "what America detests as the greatest evil, a British ministry has taken the greatest pains to effect." Indeed, the king's ministers have "wasted British blood and treasure to alienate America and Great-Britain." Zubly implies or assumes bad motives on the part of the ministers, while Boucher is undecided as to whether they are wicked or merely incompetent. The one thing that is clear to him is that Britain's "whole conduct, indeed has been ... utterly devoid of counsel." The king, of course, depends on his ministers for counsel. In a sermon using the dispute between Abram and Lot as a picture of the quarrel between England and America, Boucher blames the "herdsmen"—the representatives—of each for inititating and sustaining a conflict that neither primary party wanted. The ministers seemed to have a knack for taking just the wrong action—for doing "both too much and too little." They had been too hostile to reconciliation but were unwilling to forcefully compel obedience. As a consequence, "every step they have taken, since the dispute began, has, through their folly, or our perverseness, or both, tended only to widen the breach." England, he argues, is "chargeable with a thousand errors in her management of the Colonies," but the one thing she cannot be rightfully charged with is governing them too oppressively or with too much firmness. Ironically, he notes, "it is solely on a charge of injustice, and rigour and oppression, that our herdsmen have stirred up this *strife*." There is plenty of blame to go around; the Americans are equally at fault for their inappropriate responses. As Boucher says: "It is by no means my intention to attempt to vindicate the herdsmen either of America or Great Britain." It is clear, though, that it is primarily the king's "herdsmen" who are responsible for Great Britain's errors.[28]

Particularly concerning and disconcerting for the Loyalists is the fact that America had "long and often experienced [England's] justice and her generosity," but "through the degeneracy, or the imperfection, of all political wisdom and principles, she now seems to us no longer just or generous." Boucher urgently reminds his congregants that "the ministers of government, and government itself, however nearly connected, are distinct: ministers may be unwise and unjust, and, as such, may not deserve support; but the constitution of government, as long as it exists, is to be regarded as infallible and irresistible." He acknowledges that "however possible it may seem to be in theory to oppose the ministers of government, and at the same time to support government, the history both of the mother country and her colonies shews, that, in practice, it is always difficult, if not impossible." This is one of the great frustrations of the Loyalist clergymen as they desperately try to stem the revolutionary tide. They must convince their flocks that it is appropriate to protest against the excesses and injustices of persons in government and to demand justice, but not to attack government or authority itself. This particularly applies to government ministers—bureaucrats—but it also applies to the legislature. Boucher sums up the Loyalist position regarding errors made by the British government:

> That some of the measures of the British Parliament have been injudicious, and perhaps injurious, it's [sic] staunchest friends will not be so hardy as to deny: but we have been taught to magnify their errors, and to exaggerate our wrongs; and to seek redress, not as heretofore by petitioning and remonstrating, but by resisting and rebelling. No government on earth is infallible. Perfection is not in human nature; and should no more be expected from aggregate bodies, than from individuals.[29]

King George

Although we ought not to expect perfection from any individual or any body, the Loyalist clergymen are nearly willing to expect it from George III. They recognize errors made by Parliament and by the king's ministers, but not by George himself. Not only do they preach the duty to obey and submit to kings in general but they also particularly put forward George as a preeminent and specially worthy king. In a sermon preached before the start of hostilities, Zubly refers to George as "the best of kings" and as "our great and good King, the friend of mankind, and the father of his people." He further suggests that "no king can have a better title to the hearts of those over whom he rules." He urges Americans in particular to pay George "every possible demonstration of loyalty and affection." Zubly's tune does not change in the first year of the armed conflict. In a 1775 sermon to the Second Provincial Congress of Georgia, he recommends appeals to the king with this glowing commendation: "By our law the king can do no wrong, but of his present Majesty, who is universally known to be adorned with many social virtues, may we not justly conclude that he would not do any wrong, even though he could."[30] Such glowing praise of George III was not unusual in the early days of the Revolution—even though blood had been spilled. It was not until the Declaration of Independence that George became a target for criticism by Americans.

Some of the Loyalist clergy held and urged a high view of King George well into the conflict. Referring to British kings in general in a sermon to British troops in America, Seabury admonishes the soldiers (and American readers of the published version) that "the highest Honor and Respect must be due" to the king or "the *Sacred Person of our* ROYAL SOVEREIGN." But Seabury singles out George III for special praise. He wants his audience to add to the normal obligations due to the king "those arising from the amiable, unexceptionable Character of our present most gracious Sovereign" and to "pay him all that Respect, Duty and Affection, which both his exalted Station and eminent Virtues, entitle him to." Not shying away from hyperbole, Seabury gushes that George III "probably surpasses, any who filled the Throne before him." He urges the soldiers and readers to offer thanksgiving and praise to God for "raising up, and fixing on the Throne, a Monarch so illustrious for all human and royal Virtues." This sermon was preached in 1777, so Seabury's sentiments are by this time a tough sell to the general American public.[31]

In the same year, Inglis refers to George as "our gracious Sovereign" and praises his "unparalleled Lenity" in dealing with the rebellious Americans and restraining his troops and ships "from acting offensively, even after Hostilities had been commenced on the Part of the Rebels." He contends that George used force only when every other alternative had been exhausted. In a later message, near the end of the Revolution, Inglis still maintains that there is no better king in the world at the time, and few equivalent kings at any time. He argues that George's ambition is to preserve rights and to provide happiness; that he is "a shining Example of Religion and Virtue"; and that he is a patron of science and the liberal arts who "unites the private Virtues of the Christian and Citizen with the more splendid Virtues and Accomplishments of the Monarch." He ends the accolade by proclaiming that George "adds Lustre to the Throne he fills!"[32] The Loyalist preachers are hesitant to ascribe any blame to King George III himself. The parliament of which he is a part and which cannot pass any legislation without his signature makes errors. The members of the king's cabinet and bureaucracy make errors. But George himself does not. It is perhaps in this regard that the Loyalist clergymen most resemble Tories.

Troublemakers

According to the Loyalist clergy, then, Americans enjoying a nearly idyllic life rebelled against their mother country. They did so on the basis of a few errors on the part of the British government that, while legitimate grievances, were relatively minor, and the worst of which were repealed. The question remains: why would a child take up arms against its parent over relatively insignificant offenses? For the Loyalist ministers, the answer is plain and simple: the people of America were deluded and led astray by rabble-rousing troublemakers who had rebellion and independence in mind from the beginning. Perhaps no other single subject is so widely and roundly criticized or draws so much ire in the writings of the Loyalist clergymen.

Several types of troublemakers emerge from the Loyalists' denunciations. There are those who inculcate "a general persuasion that government is neither sacred nor inviolable" in principle. They find "fault with almost every thing that is established." They take advantage of man's "very common propensity, to *think evil of dignities*" and to believe in "visionary Ideas of Perfection, which never were, nor ever will be found, either in publick or in private Life." These men lead others to "think less and less of the whole of our excellent Constitution, by incessantly inveighing against some of it's [sic] parts." As a consequence, we become discontent with excellence and "foolishly grasp at perfection." It is a foolish attempt because man, by his nature, is not capable of perfection. In order to make others dissatisfied with good government, these troublemakers "exaggerate and aggravate all the little circumstances on which [the dispute] was pretended to be founded." Boucher complains that "we are taught to exaggerate all the errors and the failings of our Parent State." He maintains that "no satisfactory evidence has yet been produced, to prove that the injuries we have received from our Parent State are so great as they are represented to be" or that her intentions toward America are unfriendly and hostile. Assuming that the British government "under which till now you have lived happily" has suddenly become "*oppressive and severe*," how, he asks his flock, did you make that discovery? The answer he offers is that most Americans did not make the discovery themselves but "are acquainted with these oppressions only from the report of others."[33] If things are as bad as is claimed, why cannot everyone see that without being told? Boucher's point, of course, is that though the British government has made errors, those errors have not risen to the level of real oppression; rather, troublemakers have labored to convince them that they are oppressed.

Due to human nature, the people will be generally discontent with government. The multitude will always be ready to follow one who says they are not governed as they ought to be. This, argues Boucher, is clearly true in America. What is needed is someone to "excite" or activate popular discontent. And "in every society there always have been, and too probably there always will be, men of restless and ambitious minds; who are never long satisfied with any system of government, or with any administration;

because it is hardly possible for any government, or for any administration, to distinguish with their favours every man who may conceive himself to be entitled to distinction." America is no exception. It has self-interested, ambitious men who cannot be satisfied, whom Boucher alternately calls "*firebrands*," "*wrathful men*," "*pestilent fellows*," "*movers of sedition*," and "*perturbed spirits*." They are always "ready to *stir up strife*; ready either to blow the coals of contention, or to add fuel to a flame already kindled." They constantly keep passions heated "by haranguing perpetually on the abuses of government" and dwell "with unnatural satisfaction on the dark side of the picture." They excel in "putting bad interpretations upon the acts of Government" and "ill constructions upon public measures." They are "enemies to peace" and "will find occasions of quarrelling even . . . with brethren." They are "demagogues, who enflame you" and infer that because government has once done wrong, it will always do wrong. "Kingdoms are shaken and overturned" as a result of their efforts and nations fall into rebellion and civil war. Americans have fallen prey to such men and it is they who have led the rush to armed conflict with the mother country.[34]

Other than being too-willing dupes, the American people are not to blame. They have been deceived by "Crafty designing Knaves, turbulent Demagogues, . . . and Impostors in Patriotism" who broached "Doctrines unknown to the Constitution, under the Name of constitutional Principles." Rumors and lies are "the general forerunners of revolutions" and the American people, though well-meaning, were fooled by them. "Attending more to what seemed expedient, than to what they should have known was their duty, many swallowed the bait that was so artfully thrown out to lure them to their destruction." That bait was largely fed to them from handbills, pamphlets, and newspapers, which Boucher calls "shallow and turbid Sources" and which he blames for biasing and misleading the public. He bemoans the fact that bold assertions on the part of the Patriots were taken as demonstrations or proofs in these media. In a footnote added to a sermon years after it was delivered, Boucher says, "It neither is, nor ever was, my opinion, that the people of America, properly so called, were generally favourable to the revolt." In a begrudging testimony to the effective efforts of these troublemakers, he concludes: "Nor let it be thought an improbable circumstance, that a whole people should have been made so materially to contribute to an event, of which a very large number of them totally disapproved."[35]

In addition to their role in deluding and misleading the people, troublemakers engaged in militant and violent actions to provoke a response that would drive the colonies away from the arms of Great Britain and into open conflict with her. The most famous of these troublemakers were the so-called Sons of Liberty. If Bostonians had allowed the East India Company tea to be landed and stored, they could simply have refused to buy it in order to avoid paying the duty, and their dispute over the three-penny duty would have been conducted legally. "But this peaceable conduct comported not with the intemperate, fiery zeal of the *Sons of Liberty*." These "artful men" took advantage of the opportunity to excite conflict with England. Instead of peaceful conduct, "every violent measure has been pursued." Seabury severely questions the motives of those involved in the Tea Party, alleging: "The present commotions were first excited, not by patriotism, but the selfishness of those merchants who had engrossed the tea-trade with Holland. All was quiet till *they* were alarmed by the design of sending the tea belonging to the East-India company, to be sold in the colonies. Then began the cry of liberty."[36]

Seabury points to other examples of militant actions with less than pure motives. The radicals spread a false alarm of a supposed attack on Boston that resulted in thousands of Americans marching to its defense. This ruse served two purposes: it convinced the radicals in Boston that other colonists "were ready to join them in their most extravagant schemes,—to rush headlong with them down the precipice of rebellion. It served also to inflame the congress, and to prepare the way for another Boston manœvre." That other maneuver was the announcement of the Suffolk Resolves, in which "the authority of the government of Great-Britain was denied, the courts of justice shut up, his Majesty's counsellors . . . declared to be 'obstinate and incorrigible enemies to their country.' The command of the militia taken from the King, and lodged in the people; with several other positions and declarations equally seditious and rebellious." As the radicals anticipated—and counted on—Britain responded somewhat harshly. Using sympathy for the suffering Bostonians as a wedge, the radicals pulled the other colonies in. In getting the Congress to approve them, the radicals made "those rebellious resolves" the act of all of the American colonies and thereby achieved their goal of widening the scope of the conflict.[37]

Not content with that, the Congress passed its famous or infamous resolution of nonimportation, nonexportation, and nonconsumption. Seabury argues that the "undoubted design" of the resolution is to cause "clamours, discord, confusion, mobs, riots, insurrections, rebellions, in Great-Britain,

Ireland, and the West-Indies." Ultimately, it is "to force them all to join their clamours with ours." But, Seabury asks, where is the justice in punishing the manufacturers in these countries? What about the ruin and death that may result? He lays the blame squarely on "the ill-projected, ill-conducted, abominable scheme of some of the colonists, to form a republican government independent of Great-Britain, [which] cannot otherwise succeed." In other words, these troublemakers are ruthless and careless in the pursuit of their goals. Seabury goes so far as to suggest that they do not have "the spirit of humanity."[38]

Like Boucher, Seabury believes that a majority of Americans disapprove of the tactics of the troublemakers. "If we except the worshippers of the congress, the universal opinion is, that the destroying of the tea at Boston, was a flagrant act of injustice, and deserving of correction: and that the refusal of the town to pay for it, is foolish and unjustifiable." Even if the cause is just, he argues, "violent and illegal measures, even in the most necessary struggles for liberty, can never be justified, till all legal and moderate ones have failed." The big problem is that the demands of the radicals have risen to the point that "no honest man in England, can abet or support us in them." To sum up his opinion of the troublemakers, Seabury addresses them with a tongue-in-cheek suggestion of a tax that would pay off the English national debt: "A moderate tax of four pence a hundred, upon all the fibs, falsehoods and misrepresentations of you and your party, in England and America."[39]

In his public letters to presidents of the Congress in the midst of the Revolution, Inglis seems to pick up where Seabury's caustic and direct criticism leaves off. Inglis bars no holds and pulls no punches. Using sitting president Henry Laurens as a foil for the Patriots in general, he accuses the radicals of seducing "thousands who utterly disapproved" of their actions or of compelling them with violence to support their cause; and he stresses that those thousands are suffering as a result. In addition, he charges that multitudes "have fallen victims" to the "ambition and cruelty" of these troublemakers and that their victims' "blood cries vengeance" against them. Inglis tells John Jay that he went astray because of "connections with bad, unprincipled men" and "entered indeed with reluctance into the detestable schemes of the babel builders of Congress." He then sarcastically congratulates Jay: "You now figure among the foremost in the *glorious* work of rebellion, and ruining your country." Writing to the troublemakers through Jay, Inglis charges: "You made Europe and America ring with mournful accounts of British cruelties; and yet in truth most of them were purely fictitious; others were exaggerated; and the rest were such as you yourselves made necessary, or that are unavoidable in time of war." He adds that they "appointed *a Committee of Grievances* to arrange and record the virulent tales that were sent in by every seditious, republican zealot, however groundless." The result of these efforts is that the "artifices of inordinate ambition, seconded by the simplicity of the multitude, have been an over match for the dictates of truth, the lessons of experience and history, the remonstrances of conscience, and duty to mankind."[40] Truth and duty had fallen by the wayside.

As one can see, two of Inglis's themes are the personal ambition of the troublemakers and their assault on truth in order to scare the people into supporting the cause. In the midst of the war, he blames the devastation of America on "the Discontent of those who were goaded on by Ambition to rise above their Fellows." The Loyalist ministers do not see grand principles or concern for the rights of either Englishmen or mankind in those who stirred the revolutionary pot. From their perspective, the leaders of the rebellion were self-interested and frustrated by their inability to rise within the confines of the British system. In an open letter to the people of North America, Inglis contends: "Republicans, smugglers, debtors and men of desperate fortunes, were the principal promoters of this unnatural rebellion. If to these be added a very few individuals who were stimulated by ambition to figure at the head of a new empire, and cared not what the consequences would be, provided only they obtained their ends, I am confident the list will contain the sum total of those who were active and zealous for independency." He makes a firm distinction between those who set the Revolution in motion and those who are merely participating in it. "Necessity and compulsion, it is true, drew in many to join these afterwards; others were imposed on by specious falshoods [sic], and thereby seduced from their allegiance and interest; but these only acted a subordinate part, and were not initiated into the grand mysteries of state." Inglis makes it clear that he understands that "there were many of you, my countrymen, I doubt not, who engaged in it with upright, sincere intentions."[41]

As for the people as a whole, they were fooled. Inglis says that "many well meaning people were duped" by promises of empire, abolished taxes, and "freedom seated on her peerless throne." He calls them "our deluded Countrymen" and concludes that "however criminal some of them have been; certain it is that Deception held up her false Mirror, and represented Things in a distorted Light to many more; and under the Influence of this Error, they act with misguided Zeal." "Imaginary Dangers were pretended" to incite the fears of the people. In particular, the propagandists of rebellion imputed to the king "Designs which had not the least Foundation in Truth." Inglis gives examples of such false designs: "It was affirmed that a Plan had been formed to enslave the Colonies—that Popery was to be universally established . . . —an Act of Parliament was forged and printed in the News-Papers, in which, among other Extravagancies, the *tenth Child* through all the Colonies was assigned to the King or parochial Clergyman, I forget which; and such was the Credulity of People that this Act was believed to be genuine, &c. &c."[42] These threats seem ludicrous in hindsight, but the common people in the 1700s were much less sophisticated and much more trusting—or gullible. These counterfeit plans were the more effective because they fed on some of the greatest fears of the people.

In an effort to address the propaganda of the period directly, Inglis wrote a pamphlet responding to Thomas Paine's wildly popular and influential *Common Sense*. In it, Inglis charges that Paine "leaves no method untried, which the most experienced practitioner in the art of deceiving could invent, to persuade any people to a measure, which was against their inclinations and interest, that was both disagreeable and destructive." He explains that Paine's "main attack, is upon the passions of his readers." Furthermore, "every thing that falls in with his own scheme, or that he happens to dislike, is represented in the most aggravated light, and with the most distorted features."[43] That is an apt description of how the Loyalists viewed most of the Patriot pre-Revolution literature.

New Yorker Thomas Bradbury Chandler focuses much of his attention specifically on the New England troublemakers. He shares the view held by many that the New Englanders—particularly the Bostonians—are largely to blame for the crisis in general and for the war. He argues in 1774 that the first settlers of New England were "thorough-paced *Republicans*" and that they have been waiting for the "confusions of the present time . . . to afford a favorable opportunity" to "*erect the Republic.*" In his view, "the *Rubicon* has been passed, and there can be no thought of retreating. They have drawn the sword, with an aim to plunge it into the bowels of our ancient and venerable Constitution." The Rubicon was crossed with the Boston Tea Party. The Sons of Liberty were determined to force the issue and, if you will, make such a splash that the British could not afford to respond with lenience and still maintain control over Massachusetts. Chandler is not surprised by their attempt to force the issue, asking when "the *sons of liberty* . . . ever *willingly* allowed to others the liberty of thinking and acting for themselves." From the perspective of the Loyalists, the Boston Sons of Liberty, like the radicals in other areas, were determined to do whatever it takes to move toward rebellion and independence.⁴⁴

Chandler spills a lot of ink addressing the Tea Party itself as well as the situation in Boston under the resultant Coercive Acts. For his part, he approves of South Carolina's protest of the Tea Act: they agreed not to purchase the tea. This was an insult to the government, but one that could be "overlooked." The troublemakers did not want a response that could be excused or borne but one that the government would find "unsufferable." Not only was their action "criminal," "of the highest insolence towards government," and "atrocious," but "it was very notorious, that the intention of the perpetrators was, by this example, to lead and excite others . . . to the same wanton excess of riot and licentiousness." This was an act designed to stir the pot and inspire others to take violent, destructive actions against British rule. It was meant to bring a harsh response that would serve the propaganda needs of the radicals. After offering explanations of why the Coercive Acts are not unjust or excessive but rather proper and restrained punishment for violent criminal destruction of property and insubordination, Chandler expresses an expectation that "our political incendiaries will go on in their own way, and still contend, that these acts are tyrannical and arbitrary, and threaten the destruction of American liberty." They will do that because they are "under the undue influence of prejudice and passion" and "put the very worst constructions upon, and assign the very worst motives for, all the proceedings of the British Parliament." They have an agenda and to advance it they need the people to feel oppressed and threatened.⁴⁵

The Tea Party was not the end of their militancy. Chandler notes that "the SELECT MEN and the COMMITTEE of CORRESPONDENCE have proclaimed the King's troops to be public ENEMIES," and he presents a report from the governor of "continual acts of hostility" from these "rebellious Republicans" and "hair-brained fanaticks": "Orders, says he, are given to prevent all supplies for English troops: Straw purchased for their use is daily burnt, vessels with bricks sunk, carts with wood overturned, and thus even the King's property is destroyed in every manner in which it can be effected." Given their actions and their character, Chandler wonders why anyone would pay any attention to these "interested, designing men . . . who court popularity." He asks whether those who have "urged on a greater evil, in order to avoid a less" are "in reality, whatever they may have intended, friends to their country." He calls them "obstinate, hot-headed Zealots" and fellows who specialize in "blustering and bellowings at town meetings." Although he tries to innoculate his readers against the "sophistry" and "insidious arts" of these men, Chandler is nonetheless certain that they have been markedly successful in manipulating the people. Writing in 1774, he says that "the present confusion of the Colonies has been occasioned by misinformations and false alarms."[46]

In a couple of 1774 pamphlets, Chandler addresses and answers a number of examples of misinformation. To show the language in newspapers by which Americans had been "poisoned" against the government, he transcribes a section of a story about sending aide to Boston, which, according to the newspaper article, "ought to be supported at the expence of the last mite, and even the last drop of blood in North-America, for their noble stand against the oppression and tyranny of a miserable, corrupt, debauched, and almost bankrumpt [sic] administration, devoid of sense, humanity, and every principle superior to that of meer brutes; an administration, compared with whom a common highway robber is almost a saint." If one combines this type of reporting with the fact that most newspapers were closed to the Loyalist perspective, one begins to understand Chandler's concerns and something of the effectiveness of the Patriot propaganda machine. As another example of Patriot misinformation, Chandler points to the official papers of the First Continental Congress, which claim that Roman Catholicism, instead of being tolerated in Canada as stipulated by the 1763 peace treaty, is established by the Quebec Act. Chandler reprints portions of the treaty of surrender, the treaty of peace, and "the Act *for more effectual provision*, &c." in order to prove that, contrary to the fear-mongering, "the act of Parliament allows them no more than, the *free exercise of their religion, without being molested*, in the public use of it, and ... *entire liberty* in religious matters." That, as he reassures his readers, is far from establishment. In fact, the legislation specifically makes provision "for the *encouragement of the Protestant Religion*, and for the maintenance and *support of a Protestant Clergy* within the said province."[47] Contrary to the reports of the radicals, provision was made for the establishment of Protestantism with merely toleration for Catholicism.

Chandler argues in 1774 that if the Americans acted moderately, the tea duty would likely be repealed, as the Stamp Act was. But given the provocative messaging and actions of the troublemakers, he complains that "our conduct now is so wild and distracted—our tumults and disorders are carried to so unreasonable and unwarrantable a length—nay, such a spirit of rebellion has broke forth among us, and such a determined enmity against the *supremacy* of *Great Britain* now predominates in the Colonies, that we have hardly a single friend remaining in England." In other words, the radicals had alienated those in Parliament who had been willing to argue the American case and to seek conciliation. A year later, Chandler sums up the effect of the troublemakers' efforts: "If the greatest Enemies of British-America had been employed to contrive the ruin of the colonies, they could not have proposed a more effectual scheme for the purpose, than that we should be led on to provoke the resentment, and engage the power, of Great-Britain, by acts of hostility and rebellion." Chandler's observation here comes after the fateful events at Lexington and Concord, the grounds for which were set up by the earlier false stories of British attacks and atrocities. "That a forcible opposition to the King's troops, when imployed [sic] to protect the King's civil officers in the execution of the British laws within the British dominions, is an act of hostility against Great-Britain, is surely too plain to require proof. The laws of England have made it *treason*, which is the highest and most unpardonable of all crimes relating to the state."[48] From his perspective and that of the other Loyalist ministers, the colonies were driven to this result by design.

Conciliation

If there is a subject that occupies the Loyalist ministers as much as their criticism of the troublemakers, it is their arguments in favor of conciliation. In many ways, these two subjects are opposite images and discussion of the one leads reflexively to the other. Conciliation is the enemy of provocation and vice versa. Consequently, the radicals were not at all interested in conciliation but only in driving the move toward rebellion and independence. The Loyalists, on the other hand, desperately promote conciliation in pursuit of reconciliation with England. They excoriated the radicals for failing to offer conciliation, for responding to the British government in an improper and disrespectful fashion, and for rejecting conciliatory British overtures.

Using the strife between Abram and Lot (Genesis 13) as a picture of the American conflict with Great Britain, Boucher places the blame squarely on the "herdsmen"—that is, the radicals in America and the king's ministers in England. Because Lot was younger, a dependent of Abram, and "under infinite obligations to him," it was Lot's place to make the first moves toward reconciliation, but he did not. Instead, "with all the meekness and magnanimity of a man who is truly great, he [Abram] came forward to his nephew with a CONCILIATORY PROPOSITION." In the contemporary strife, it was the place of the dependent colonists to humbly seek reconciliation, but when they did not, the British government offered conciliation. The Americans, like Lot, listened too much to "the peevish remonstrances" of their "herdsmen," the troublemakers. Again drawing a parallel between the two, Boucher suggests that, like the reaction of the American radicals to British offers, "I can even suppose that the overture made by Abram, towards a reconciliation, was interpreted into a concession extorted from fear: and in that view it was easy to improve it into an argument with him and his herdsmen for keeping up the breach, and even becoming more violent." Boucher concludes his sermon by wishing that "some wise and good men, uncontrouled by the interested herdsmen, would arise," take the matter "out of the hands of factious herdsmen," and "make common cause" between the two relations.[49]

Seabury declares that one who wants reconciliation with Great Britain is a "*real* friend to America" and that "the government at home [England] ... would embrace us with the arms of friendship; they would press us to their bosoms, to their hearts, would we give them a fair opportunity." "It is our duty to make some proposals of accomodation [sic] with our parent country: And they ought to be reasonable ones. . . . But if we expect . . . to force *her* to concede every thing, while we will concede nothing:—If we are determined to proceed as we have done," then things will only get worse. He warns that "we are rushing into a war with our parent state, without offering the least concession; without even deigning to propose an accomodation [sic]."[50]

In 1776, Charles Inglis focuses on the need for conciliatory efforts despite the hostilities at Lexington. According to him, peace and reconciliation are as equally desirable after "that unfortunate day" as before it. Only "some tribes of savages" would "ever lose sight of argument and negociation [sic], to terminate such disputes." From his perspective, "a reconciliation and constitutional union with Great-Britain" with appropriately adapted laws is "what every honest American should earnestly wish for." Responding to Paine's denial that reconciliation is a duty, Inglis answers that, irrespective of the duty of subjects of the king, if "what would promote our happiness and interest, to mention nothing else, be a duty, then Reconciliation is our duty." Inglis also answers Paine's challenge to anyone to "shew a single advantage that this country can reap by being connected with Great-Britain."[51] In response, Inglis outlines seven great advantages of reconciliation with Great Britain[52] and concludes his case by stating: "These advantages are not imaginary but real. They are such as we have already experienced; and such as we may derive from a connection with Great-Britain for ages to come."[53]

Not only had the Americans failed to pursue reconciliation by making any concessions but they had also approached and responded to the British improperly and disrespectfully—in a manner calculated, or at least doomed, to fail. Boucher admonishes them for "having *asked amiss*" when dealing with the British. "You asked with arms in your hands. This was as impolitic, as it was undutiful." In a letter to the Continental Congress, he tells the members that their role is to "propose, with the Modesty of Subjects, some practicable Plan of Accommodation" and "to obey." He urges them not to "assemble with the Passions and Language of a common Town Meeting, to sit in Judgment, like some foreign Imperial Power on the Decrees of a British Legislature." He warns that doing so will have the effect of "exasperating and provoking" the leaders of England and of "seducing" Americans from their allegiance, "inflaming their Passions, and exciting them to popular Tumults, and Insurrections."[54]

Boucher points out that the Stamp Act was repealed by Parliament when American complaints were presented properly and with respect, and he bemoans the fact that the contemporary leadership has "profited so little by so excellent an example." To them he says, "You ought to have aimed at the obtaining the same thing by persuasion, and not by violence. . . . You do not consider; but are agitated by your demagogues . . . and provoked to rage, and will not suffer the commonwealth to enjoy the least quiet and tranquillity [sic]." In his best-known sermon, he concludes this argument: "If you think the duty of threepence a pound upon tea, laid on by the British Parliament, a grievance, it is your duty to instruct your members to take all the constitutional means in their power to obtain redress: if those means fail of success, you cannot but be sorry and grieved; but you will better bear your disappointment, by being able to reflect that it was not owing to any misconduct of your own."[55]

Seabury argues for regulating their exchanges with Great Britain by "prudence and probability of success." But, he complains: "Some people have got a strange way of complaining, petitioning, and remonstrating, in a manner that they know must fail, and then they make a great noise about the disregard with which their applications are treated." Like Boucher, he notes the success of "proper" American petitions in getting the Stamp Act and the Townshend Acts repealed. He challenges opponents to name an instance of a petition being treated with contempt or neglect "unless you construe the not granting a petition, a contempt of it," and he urges continued use of such petitions because America's friends in Parliament recommend them as "the most decent and probable means of succeeding." "But by the hasty resolves and violent proceedings of the Congress, we have effectually prevented them from appearing in our behalf: and . . . we have, by our haughty demands of independency on the supreme legislature of the nation, detached most of them from our interest, and forced them to take part against us."[56] America's supporters in Parliament could not present or support disrespectful and uncivil demands.

Seabury's statement about "hasty resolves and violent proceedings of the Congress" refers to their attempts to pressure the Irish and West Indians to join in rebellion and "excite tumults and seditions in Great Britain and Quebec by inflammatory addresses to the people," and to their adoption of the Suffolk Resolves, of which Seabury is particularly critical and disdainful. He says that they

> all tend, under cover of strong and lamentable cries about liberty, and the rights of Englishmen, to degrade and contravene the authority of the British parliament over the British dominions. . . . They all tend to raise jealousies, to excite animosities, to foment discords between us and our mother country. Not a word of peace and reconciliation,— not even a soothing expression:—No concessions are offered on our part,—nor even a possibility of their treating with us left. The parliament must give up their whole authority,—repeal all the acts, in a lump, which the Congress have found fault with, and trust, for the future, to our humour, to pay them just so much submission as we shall think convenient.[57]

He further says of the Suffolk Resolves that all who want reconciliation with Great Britain, good government, and happiness for their children "must condemn and abhor them." His condemnation does not come without the suggestion of another solution to the sufferings of the Boston poor: pay for the property (tea) they destroyed, and "thereby qualify themselves to have their port opened" as well as meeting the demands of "bare justice."[58]

Inglis is confident as late as 1776 that if the Americans show "a disposition to treat or negociate [sic] in earnest . . . and if once properly begun, there is a moral certainty that this unhappy dispute will be settled to the mutual satisfaction and interest of both countries." He in fact argues for "a Reconciliation with Great-Britain, on solid, constitutional principles, excluding all parliamentary taxation" and is convinced it could be achieved by a proper approach to the mother country.[59] After laying out a few concessions on which America "should insist,"[60] he concludes that "there is every reason to believe that [Great Britain] will enter on such a treaty . . . and that she will listen to reasonable proposals. It is her interest to do so."[61] The problem was obstruction by radicals who did not want reconciliation—even with the removal of taxation.

Chandler's sole focus regarding the matter of conciliation is on the tone and spirit of the American response. He is concerned that regardless of who is right or wrong in the dispute, "our behavior has been such as every government must and will think intolerable." According to Chandler, "subjects may complain and remonstrate against them in a respectful manner," but they are not to behave "undutifully" and "much more not to behave insolently and rebelliously." He argues that the protests against the Stamp Act and the Townshend Acts were successful largely because the American approach was "comparatively moderate," and consequently, "we had a large body of friends in England to support us." Since that time, however, "every indulgence or concession granted to the colonies operates against the authority of parliament, as for every inch given from a principle of generosity, an ell [forty-five inches] is demanded as matter of right." The colonists will seemingly never be satisfied short of "an absolute renunciation of all claim of authority or jurisdiction, in the British parliament." That, of course, is an unreasonable demand that cannot be agreed to. Another problem is the assumption that Great Britain's motives have been altogether wrong and those of the colonies altogether right. Chandler does not consider this "a mark either of wisdom or candour."[62]

Perhaps the biggest obstacle to conciliation from Chandler's point of view is the provocative actions of the Continental Congress. Instead of "respectful representation, or remonstrance, and petition," and instead of appealing to "the King *and* parliament," they appealed to "the inhabitants of the Colonies, with a particular view to the disaffected part of them,—to the *people* of Great-Britain,—and, as very 'sincere and affectionate friends,' to the Papists in Canada." "Instead of exhorting the inhabitants of the Colonies . . . to return immediately to their duty, to behave themselves peaceably, . . . not . . . to meddle with matters out of their line, . . . they set them all up for politicians and patriots, inflame their minds with resentment against their lawful superiors, and animate them to rebellion." Chandler suggests a "dutiful and respectful application to the *King, Lords and Commons* of Great-Britain" that is "duly expressive, of loyalty to the King" as the only possible starting point that could bring positive results. He reports that the Congress opened with "a very worthy and respectable member" offering a plan drawn up in "the cool hours of leisure and retirement" that reflected "candour and moderation" and "a due regard to the dignity and honour of Great-Britain," but that the radicals torpedoed it.[63]

Along with the attitude adjustment, Chandler twice lists a number of concessions that the Americans should be willing to make, once in 1774 and again in 1775. In both instances, he suggests the same concessions. First, they should confess that unjustified "tumultuous and disorderly" acts had been done due to a "mistaken zeal for liberty" and should beg forgiveness for those acts. Second, they should profess "loyalty and allegiance to the King in the strongest terms; and express our willingness to acknowledge the supremacy of Great Britain in all cases, excepting those of taxation." Third, they should thoroughly disavow interest in independence and declare that they see their security and happiness as being dependent on the "protection and mild superintendency" of Great Britain. Fourth, they should promise "to raise annually" enough money for the government to function. After listing these concessions, he concludes with an appropriate summary statement of his primary concern: "In short, propose and say whatever you may think proper; only be careful that your addresses be dutiful, your requests reasonable, and your offers generous."[64] One should note that Chandler exempts taxation from their willingness to accede to Parliament, but he urges assurances that appropriate revenue to meet the need will be raised by the colonial assemblies.

Given the disrespectful behavior of the Congress, Chandler is pessimistic about the chances of properly approaching the king and Parliament in collective negotiations. He refers to the other colonies (besides his own New York) as "sisters" who have for some time "been in an ill humour" and lately been "deluded and debauched." They "go on like a parcel of saucy and impudent hussies, threatning [sic] and abusing her [mother England]." An "amicable conference" between them has been proposed, but "they swear and protest, that they will not exchange a single word with her in that way; but that they will stab the *old hag* to the heart, or starve her to death, but they will force her to a submission." As a result of these circumstances, Chandler makes a bold suggestion: he urges the New York assembly "to do what ought to be done by every province on the continent; that is to prepare and transmit proper addresses to the King, Lords and Commons of Great-Britain." Because of the inexcusable approach taken by the Congress, he encourages the rightful representatives of the people in the individual colonies to make another, better effort. He is sure that requests from the legally recognized assembly would be received and regarded.[65]

Just before the outbreak of hostilities, in an attempt to find a peaceful settlement, Parliament passed the Conciliatory Resolution of 1775 and sent it to the individual colonies. After the Congress had rejected it on behalf of the colonies, Boucher responds by suggesting that the royal governors and ministers of the king had made many overtures and "above all" Parliament had passed the resolution. He says that in it "they invited and even solicited you to an accommodation almost on your own terms." He recognizes that good men might disagree about the terms offered, but dissatisfaction with the terms does not merit the American response. "Even admitting that the proposition was 'unreasonable,' and such an one as you ought not to have acceded to, still it was an overture of peace, and made by the Parent State." At the least it might have been the basis for further negotiation and diplomacy. He suggests to his flock that it was not unreasonable, however, and that their "own untutored and unbiassed judgments" told them that it was quite reasonable until the troublemakers helped them "discover" that it was bad. Boucher emphasizes that England had made repeated overtures of peace and accommodation which were either ignored or roundly rejected.[66]

Inglis is similarly critical of the Americans' repeated spurnings of British reconciliation proposals. He declares: "A redress of grievances was all that the American Congress claimed at first. This redress has been repeatedly and amply offered by Government: Government is therefore guiltless of whatever consequences may attend the war." But under the influence of the radicals, the American Congress had increased their claims and appeared to be determined to offend rather than to conciliate. Inglis complains to the president of the Congress that he "shut the door against all future accommodation" by "contemptuously" rejecting very "liberal overtures of accommodation" with "the grossest insults." He also criticizes President Laurens for keeping a British offer of conciliation from the people. Essentially charging him with hypocrisy, Inglis reminds Laurens that according to his "system" (republicanism), "the people are the fountain of all authority and power," so their elected representatives in the colonial assemblies ought to have had their "say" in the acceptance or rejection of the proposals. Inglis further complains to subsequent president John Jay: "Had the rebellion originated from real grievances, a redress of those grievances, repeatedly offered on the part of government, had long since composed our troubles. Ample security against taxation was held out, an accommodation proffered; you contemptuously rejected both." In fact, "when every thing, except absolute independence, was allowed—when even the substance of that was granted, and nothing but the bare name was witheld [sic]: Yet your Congress turned a deaf ear to all those proposals, and contemptuously rejected the offers of peace."[67] The troublemaking radicals held sway.

Perhaps because he supported the Whig cause up to the point of rebellion and war, Zubly's entire focus when it comes to conciliation is on Patriot rejection of British peace overtures. He emphasizes the critically important fact that "there may be a just cause for complaint where yet there is no cause of war." That is precisely Zubly's own position. In his "Helvetius" essays, Zubly quotes Hugo Grotius and Emmerich de Vattel in pursuit of standards for determining what is a just war. He indicts the Americans for violating a number of those standards, including rushing into war when they had not exhausted "every possible method and hope of obtaining redress" and there remained a "possibility to avoid or prevent it." Zubly also cites a number of historical examples in which peoples did not rebel despite greater provocation than the Americans had suffered and despite, in contrast to the Americans, having a real cause for rebellion. He considers war to be a great evil—and civil war doubly so. Consequently, before one enters into the evils of war, one must be absolutely certain that the cause is valid, just, and unavoidable. If one is not certain, "it is our duty to forbear." Above all, every power must be open to reconciliation. Zubly chides the Americans for not being so, as the Staten Island Peace Conference demonstrated. "The respectful reception given to the Delegates from Congress (Franklin, Adams, Rutledge) and the most generous offer made by the King's Commissioner, sufficiently evince Great Britain's desire of a reconciliation, and the haughtiness and stubborn inflexibility of a Franklin and Adams clearly point out what was their original design."[68]

Zubly warns his American newspaper audience: "If a nation will not hearken to or receive any proposals of peace they renounce human nature, and offend against mankind at large." "Is it not a most notorious fact that Great Britain not only repealed every law and grievance complained of, but also made the most generous offers to Congress, and each state separately, and that those offers have been treated with a scorn and contempt which would be deemed intolerable between private individuals, and with an insult that violates the laws of all civilized nations?" He urges them to remember that "God resisteth the proud, himself is at war with them and those whom neither sense, reason, nor religion, can humble." In his last statement regarding conciliation, Zubly declares: "All this complication of guilt hangs over the heads of the late or present governors of any of the states ever since they rejected Britain's too favourable offers; . . . it falls heaviest upon that worst set of bad men (clergy or laity) who have been the principal authors and fomenters."[69] Zubly left the Patriot camp before such a doom could fall upon him.

In his "Alarm" to the New York legislature, Seabury provides an effective Loyalist summary of the American response to Great Britain's overtures of conciliation:

> The unhappy contention we have entered into with our parent state, would inevitably be attended with many disagreeable circumstances, with many and great inconveniences to us, even were it conducted on our part, with *propriety* and *moderation*. What then must be the case, when all proper and moderate measures are *rejected*? When not even the *appearance* of decency is regarded? When nothing seems to be consulted, but how to perplex, irritate, and affront, the *British Ministry, Parliament, Nation and King*? When every scheme that tends to *peace*, is branded with *ignominy*; as being the machination of slavery! When nothing is called FREEDOM but SEDITION! Nothing LIBERTY but REBELLION![70]

In the end, Seabury makes the same recommendation as did Chandler; he urges the New York legislature to pursue reconciliation with Great Britain themselves on behalf of the people of New York. He asks them "to make the best terms that we can, for ourselves." He labels this "the most prudent course" and suggests that it will "save *this province*, and probably the *whole continent*, from *desolation and destruction*." He explains that all "the Colonies in *New-England*, and *some* to the *southward*, have run head-long, under the influence of the Congress, into such measures, as evidently *tend* to a war against our *mother-country*, and our *gracious Sovereign*." Seabury goes one step further than Chandler, however. He suggests that New York could become "the mediatrix with Great-Britain, for all the *other* Colonies, and to prevent the rage of slaughter, and the effusion of human blood."[71] Cooler heads must prevail; some authoritative body in America must step forward and conciliate. The logical body for the task is the legislature of the colony with the greatest Loyalist presence and sentiment.

Congress

As the Loyalist ministers saw it, advocates for conciliation were forced to seek some representative body other than the Continental Congress to treat with England because it was "doubtless unequal to the great Business" and America was rapidly running into civil war under its leadership. The actions of the Congress led Inglis, for example, to conclude that "the Congress—and the Congress *only*—are chargeable, before God and the world, with all the calamities that are suffered by America." Inglis also warns of a problem related to the improper tone and language in Congress's dealings with the British. He accuses the Congress of a "mean rusticity" and "dishonourable breach of public faith" and asks whether their lack of respect, civility, and decorum "will inspire the European states with much ardor to accept of an alliance with you."[72]

He suggests that the response of the Congress to England has poisoned the well for future potential dealings with other kings and governments. Congress has established a less than favorable reputation abroad. Boucher and Inglis criticize the Congress to some extent, but Chandler and Seabury do so more extensively. Given that presses were not available to them after 1775, when they speak of Congress, they refer to the First Continental Congress.

Chandler's primary criticism is that the Congress does not represent the majority of the American people and has not expressed the will of the people in its words or its actions. Chandler claims that the "greatest part of this province" and "a very great part of the Americans are not their *constituents* in any sense at all, as they never voted for them, nor ever signified any approbation of their acting in behalf, and in the name, of the colonies." So even if their decisions bind "their *constituents*," that number is relatively small.[73] A discussion of the process by which the delegates to Congress were chosen can be found in the chapter on legal arguments. The Loyalists believed that as few as one person in one hundred participated in choosing the members of Congress.

Not only does the Congress not properly represent the people themselves but it also has not properly represented their wishes. According to Chandler, their "proper business" was "to procure for the American colonies relief from parliamentary taxation" and to produce "a happy reconciliation" with Great Britain. He points to the "*printed resolves* from all parts of the country" which contained instructions for the delegates from their colonial assemblies. He contends that they are more reliable representations of "the general opinion, even of the most dissatisfied part of the colonies" than "the passionate *verbal declarations of a few.*" Those resolutions charged the delegates to do what is "prudent and lawful" and also indicated "that subjection and obedience were due from us to Great-Britain, in most cases. Her general supremacy over the Colonies was then acknowledged." "In most of those resolves, the *loyalty* of the people is warmly asserted," so, he argues, "the Congress must have known, that it was no part of their business to concert measures that were inconsistent with the loyalty professed, or with the subordination acknowledged to be due to the mother country."[74]

But the Congress did take actions inconsistent with loyalty and subordination to England. They "were *disposed* to enter into a league offensive and defensive, with its *worst enemies* the New-England and other Presbyterian Republicans," they "hastily and eagerly published . . . their cordial approbation of the *Suffolk Resolves* for erecting an *Independent Government* in *New-England;* and recommended to the Americans the support of those measures *with united efforts.*" They also used the "force of threatenings" regarding New England's use of force, as the Congress declared: "RESOLVED, That this Congress do APPROVE of the opposition made by the Inhabitants of the Massachusetts-Bay, to the execution of the late acts of parliament: and if the same shall be attempted to be carried into execution by force, in such case ALL AMERICA OUGHT TO SUPPORT THEM IN THEIR OPPOSITION." After quoting a letter from a cabinet member, Chandler further complains that they "have rejected the only way, which they had been told would be likely to succeed, and have adopted that specific mode of conduct which they had been told would not succeed, but would bring down upon them and their adherents *severity* and *chastisement,* and *render their case desperate.*" Finally, he notes that Congress repeatedly says that "there are many other *infringements and violations of their rights*" that they are passing over for now. From this, Chandler concludes, "Great-Britain will naturally judge, that granting even all that they demand *at present* will be no security for the future peaceable demeanor of the Colonies."[75]

From all of this, Chandler argues that "the views of the Congress are thus immoderate" and that "the whole tenor of their proceedings was calculated to increase the evil, which they were sent to remove." Chandler summarizes Congress's neglect of its commission:

> On the review, it appears, that instead of promoting, they have counter-acted, the design of their appointment; that they have

altogether neglected the work they were sent upon; that the powers delegated to them by their constituents, for the good of the colonies, were prostituted to the purposes of private ambition; and that all their proceedings as far as we can judge, were instigated and directed by the New-England republicans, to the utmost confusion of the Colonies, the disgrace of their constituents, and their own infamy.[76]

In light of all of this, Chandler decides that "it has become necessary to *inquire*, previously to our entering into more particular disputes, *how far the colonies are bound to abide by, and to execute the decisions of, the late Congress?*" His baseline for making that determination is that "if they either departed from their commission, or if their commission was unlawful in any degree, so far their proceedings can lay no obligation upon any of their constituents." Given those criteria, he determines that all that Congress has done "in the way of hostility against Great-Britain . . . was uncommissioned and unauthorized, and cannot be binding even upon their constituents." Furthermore, regarding the use of threats, "what they had no right nor power to do, they had no right to *threaten* that they would do; and . . . we are no more obliged to adopt the language of their threatenings, than to execute their projects of hostility." The Congress engaged in "such a breach of the trust reposed in them" that their constituents cannot be considered bound by it; "on the contrary, they are under the strongest ties, both of duty and interest, to give them no countenance." Consequently, Chandler draws this grave conclusion: "We manifestly owe them no obedience at all; we owe them no respect as a body: Much less are we bound to plunge ourselves headlong into that abyss of misery and destruction which they have opened."[77]

Seabury makes some of the same charges and claims as does Chandler, but his emphasis is on the imperious—even tyrannical—nature of congressional rule. Like Chandler, Seabury questions the legitimacy of the Congress. He claims that less than "a hundredth part of the people of this province . . . had any vote in sending the Delegates" from New York and that the "manner in which they were chosen was subversive of all law, and of the very constitution of the province." Because of their unrepresentative and unconstitutional nature, "they were only a popular assembly, without check or controul, and therefore unqualified to make laws, or to pass ordinances." In response to those who argue that the delegates cannot be charged with exceeding the limits of their authority because the people did not give them any "fixed boundary," Seabury alleges that less than one in a hundred approved of the idea of even having a congress, so they obviously did not bother "to *circumscribe* them, when they did not chuse [*sic*] to have any thing to do with them." He suggests that those who did approve of the Congress expected it to accommodate and conciliate, not to "revile and trample on the authority of Parliament, and make our breach with the parent state a thousand times more irreparable than it was before." From his perspective, the Congress "are broken up without ever attempting [accommodation]: they have taken no one step that tended to peace: they have gone from bad to worse, and have either ignorantly misunderstood, carelessly neglected, or basely betrayed the interests of all the Colonies." Accommodation could hardly be expected, however, because their disposition was "suspicious, jealous, parsimonious, stingy, contracted," and their "mode" "certainly deficient, both in point of prudence and efficacy."[78]

Instead of conciliating and making accommodation, the Congress approved the "mad proceedings of the people of Boston," wrote "inflammatory addresses," and exercised "*an assumed power of legislation*." Their "productions" are "positive assertions, without proof; declamations, without argument; and railing, without modesty." Seabury says that he writes "not to *please* or *amuse*, but to *convince* my countrymen and fellow-subjects of the evil tendency of the measures of the Congress, and to give all the obstruction in my power to their being carried into execution." In pursuit of that obstruction, Seabury levels blistering verbal attacks on the Congress, its decrees, and its supporters. In so doing, he says that his "business is to detect and expose the false, arbitrary, and tyrannical PRINCIPLES upon which the Congress acted, and to point out their fatal tendency to the interests and liberties of the colonies." He regularly speaks of tyranny in conjunction with the Congress and often sarcastically turns the hyperbolic language of the Patriots back on them.[79]

For example, in an attempt to get the public to realize the implications of the policy established by "Our sovereign Lords and Masters, the High and Mighty Delegates, in Grand Continental Congress assembled," Seabury warns that committees will be chosen

> to inspect the conduct of the inhabitants, and see whether they violate the Association.—Among other things, Whether they drink any Tea or wine in their families, . . . or wear any British or Irish manufactures; or use any English molasses, &c. . . . If they do, their names are to be published in the Gazette. . . . —In plain English,—They shall be

considered as Out-laws, unworthy of the protection of civil society, and delivered over to the vengeance of a lawless, outrageous mob, to be *tarred, feathered, hanged, drawn, quartered, and burnt.*—O rare American Freedom![80]

This is an exaggeration, of course, but not by much. Actual enforcement of the nonconsumption agreement reached by the Congress would require searches with some level of invasiveness, though known or suspected Loyalists would no doubt be those targeted. The Association agreement specifically calls for the publication of the names of violators in the newspapers and the punishments mentioned here—with the exception of drawing and quartering—had already become all too common in mob assaults on anyone whose support for the Patriot cause was less than enthusiastic. Seabury's own response to the prospect of such searches is twofold. In a well-known statement, he declares: "If I must be enslaved, let it be by a King at least, and not by a parcel of upstart lawless Committee-men. If I must be devoured, let me be devoured by the jaws of a lion, and not *gnawed* to death by rats and vermin." He then prods his audience: "Do as you please: . . . open your doors to them,—let them examine your tea-cannisters, and molasses-jugs, and your wives and daughters petty-coats,—bow, and cringe, and tremble, and quake,—fall down and worship our sovereign Lord the Mob." But he warns potential investigators that "my house is my castle" and if a committee man does not leave, "a good hiccory [sic] cudgel shall teach him better manners."[81]

In another example of his sarcastic twist on their rhetoric, he says: "For you know, gentlemen, that representation and taxation go together. God and nature hath joined them.—But how, on this principle, you will keep your money out of the harpy-claws of the congress, I cannot conceive. They have shewn you already what they can do: And power is apt to be encroaching." Using the language of the Association, he mocks the requirement that a merchant be "willing" to give his profits to the Boston poor "whether he *will or not;* and at the same time to oblige him to be *willing* to do so, even *against his will.*" Still trying to raise concern in the people, Seabury cautions: "I don't see how a man can act *freely* upon *compulsion.* . . . Unwilling or not, he must be *willing,*—or the dread of the GAZETTE shall make him so." He also makes use of an absurd example to highlight the injustice of the congressional policy. For any man who has already ordered goods that arrive after the operative date of the policy, "he will be in the state of a man, who being condemned to be hanged, by a law made after his pretended crime was committed, was yet . . . obliged to hang himself; or at least, obliged, freely and willingly to give directions to somebody else to perform the friendly office for him." To add sarcastic insult to injury, Seabury suggests that this "smells most confoundedly strong of passive obedience and non-resistance."[82] The Patriots famously refused passive obedience and rejected the concept of nonresistance to British law as irrational and a violation of rights.

Seabury taunts supporters of the Congress with other inconsistencies. He asks them: "You that spurned at the thought of holding your rights on the precarious tenure of the will of a British ministry . . . or of a British Parliament, can you submit to hold them on as precarious a tenure, the will of a New-York committee, of a continental congress?" He continues: "You have blustered, and bellowed, and swaggered, and bragged, that no British Parliament should dispose of a penny of your money without your leave, and now you suffer yourselves to be bullied by a Congress, and cowed by a COMMITTEE, and through fear of the Gazette, are obliged to open your pocket." "There is not one of you that will dare to act contrary to the laws of the congress." To those who argue that the colonial assemblies are "useless" if Parliament has supreme authority, Seabury retorts: "Virginia and Massachusetts madmen, met at Philadelphia, have made laws for the province of New-York, and have rendered our Assembly useless." The Congress has already effectively made the colonial assemblies useless. To those who claim that their honor is engaged because they sent delegates to the Congress and "promised to abide by, and observe all their determinations and laws," Seabury answers that their honor was "previously engaged to the government under which you live, before you promised to abide by the determinations of the congress." Furthermore: "You had no right to make a promise implicitly to obey all their regulations, before you knew what they were, and whether they would interfere with the public laws of the government, or not. And you are so far from being bound in honour to obey any determinations of the congress, which interfere with the laws of the government, that you are really bound in honour to oppose them." He also admonishes them that there is no honor in punishing people with mob violence or for trade that the laws of the province permit. He consequently concludes that they are not obliged by honor to obey the regulations of the Congress or to enforce them.[83]

Seabury's caustic use of Patriot rhetoric against the Congress reaches a pinnacle with his references to "that abject slavery and cruel oppression which the tyranny of the late Congress has brought upon us." In the view of the Loyalists, the rebels too loosely referred to "liberty" and cavalierly and irresponsibly exploited the word "slavery." In the midst of his criticism of the Congress, Seabury maintains that

> liberty is a very good thing, and slavery a very bad thing. But then I must think that liberty under a *King, Lords* and *Commons* is as good as liberty under a republican Congress: And that slavery under a republican Congress is as bad, at least, as slavery under a *King, Lords* and *Commons*: And upon the whole, that *liberty* under the supreme authority and protection of Great-Britain, is infinitely preferable to *slavery* under an American Congress.

It is difficult to imagine a statement more calculated to tweak the sensibilities of the Patriots or more representative of the persecuted Loyalists.[84]

As might be expected, Seabury received a lot of criticism for canvassing (that is, strongly criticizing) the Congress. He claims that he writes "from a principle of conscience, from a sense of duty, from a love of liberty, of *order*, of *good* government, and of *America* my native country." He reminds his critics that it has always been "the privilege of Englishmen to canvass freely, the proceedings of every branch of the legislature." He notes that this is "one of the grand pillars which support our present happy constitution" and suggests hypocrisy on the part of his critics. Did the Congress not officially criticize Parliament? "Does not every pidler [sic] in politics, who calls himself a *son of liberty*, take the licence of censuring and condemning the conduct of the *King*, the *Lords*, and the *Commons*, the supreme sovereign authority of the whole British Empire?" Given their partisan criticism, he accuses his opponents of "endeavouring to intimidate your countrymen from exercising this Right with regard to the Congress."[85] It is worth noting that extant publications critical of the Congress are relatively rare after 1775 because the Patriots were effective in their efforts to silence opposition.

Returning to the theme of hypocrisy and double standards, Seabury ramps up his rhetoric in demanding his right to speak out against the Congress: "The Congress . . . was founded in sedition; its decisions are supported by tyranny; and is it *presumption* to controvert its *authority?*" The Patriots call those who "dare to speak against the *Congress*" "*restless spirits*" and "enemies to the natural rights of mankind." But those who "traduce and slander the sovereign authority of the nation; contravene and trample under foot the laws of their country" are called "friends to America, and to the natural rights of mankind." For Seabury, this is both a serious problem in and of itself and a display of their partisan intellectual dishonesty.[86]

Seabury addresses one other pro-Congress argument: "that these [committee] men are contending for our rights; that they are defending our liberties; and though they act against law, yet that the necessity of the times will justify them." He asks whether interferences in personal business are "the rights, is this the liberty, these men are contending for." Regarding the "necessity of the times," Seabury asks: "Who induced this necessity? Who involved the province in discord, anarchy and confusion? These very men. They created that necessity, which they now plead in their own justification."[87]

At the conclusion of their criticism of Congress, Chandler and Seabury ultimately offer the same solution: renounce or ignore the Congress and go back to living under the proper constitutional authority—the colonial assembly. This was their solution to the conciliation issue, and it is their solution to the "tyranny" imposed by congressional resolutions. Chandler says: "If we regard the Congress at all, we shall bitterly repent it. But if we have recourse to our legal representatives, allow them their due honour and influence, and under their direction pursue only *prudent* and *constitutional* measures, it will undoubtedly prove, in a more proper sense than the word has commonly been used in, the *salvation* of this province." His call to action is to "withdraw ourselves immediately from within the *vortex* of the Congress," "disband our Committees," and "let us scorn to yield any obedience but to the laws and to lawful authority." He urges an immediate end to "any violent methods, till mild and safe ones shall have been fairly tried." Fundamentally, "we must rescue our necks from the *yoke* of the Congress, and our legs and arms from the *fetters* of Committees. This is the bondage we have most reason to dread, as it is equally oppressive and disgraceful." If, he argues, the present representatives in the assembly "refuse to act a worthy part," it must be borne until replacements can be legally elected.[88]

Referring to the New York legislature, Seabury asks: "Have your representatives neglected your interests? . . . Given up your liberties? . . . Betrayed your rights? . . . Shown any *disposition* to do these things?—If not, why are they neglected? Why are they treated as though they were not worthy to be trusted?" Having directed the merchants of New York back to their constitutional representatives, Seabury warns: "We have no right to procede [sic] to such violent means of redress as the congress have directed, and you are executing, till the legal and constitutional applications of our Assembly have failed." At the end of his "Free Thoughts" pamphlet, Seabury urges the people in general to "renounce all dependence on Congresses, and Committees. They have neglected, or betrayed your interests. Turn then your eyes to your *constitutional* representatives. They are the true, and legal, and have been hitherto, the faithful defenders of your rights, and liberties. . . . Address yourselves to them. They are the proper persons to obtain redress of any grievances that you can justly complain of."[89] Chandler ends two of his pamphlets with harsh criticisms of Congress. At the end of "The American Querist," he suggests ominously that the Congress will be "answerable . . . both in this world and the next, for THE FATE OF THE COLONIES." But Chandler saves his most biting and severe comments about the Congress for the end of "What Think Ye of Congress Now?" Ironically, after apologizing for speaking too harshly of the Congress, he proceeds to call it "hideous and detestable [sic]," to add that he "abhors" it, and to declare it to be "a *mad, blind* monster!"[90] Not all of the Loyalist ministers would use such hyperbole, but most would agree with the sentiment. The exception is John Joachim Zubly, who not only did not oppose the idea of a Congress but also served in the Second Continental Congress until suspicion arose that he was not sufficiently committed to the Patriot cause. That suspicion sprang from his opposition to taking the step of rebellion. He remained relatively comfortable with the cause up to that point.

Conclusion

In their attempt to persuade their fellow American colonists to support a legal and peaceful settlement to the dispute with Great Britain, Loyalist clergymen appealed to rational arguments based on their view of the American situation. That view began with the fact that the overwhelming majority of American colonists were Englishmen by birth and by affirmation, and they consequently were naturally subject to the British Parliament and the king of England. Their colonial charters were issued by the English king, and the relationship between the "mother country" and the colonies was a parent-child relationship, in which the child owed subjection, obedience, and respect to the parent. They further argued that the idea of recognizing the authority of the king while rejecting the authority of Parliament was foolhardy and irrational as well as illegal. In addition to law, reason told them that the British king was an inseparable part of the British Parliament. An Englishman must be fully subject to British authority. The very status of "colony" made no sense apart from subjection to the constitutional authority of the mother country.

Apart from their rational obligations as Englishmen, as a colony, and as a child, however, the Loyalist ministers emphasized the reciprocal nature of protection afforded by the government and the material and immaterial obligations of the protected. Great Britain had in fact protected their frontier during war and protected their merchant vessels in commerce. It had afforded them countless benefits and reason demanded a significant degree of gratitude on their part, as well as a reasonable amount of compensation. That said, they were not blind apologists for the British government. They recognized substantial errors made by the government, particularly by the king's often corrupt or incompetent ministers. They agreed with the Patriots that some measures, such as the Stamp Act, went beyond a reasonable expectation of compensation, and others exhibited excessive control or even violated constitutional liberties. But they insisted that criticism and demands for justice could and should be made civilly and without attacking the government's authority.

In their view, such a civil and reasonable response was not forthcoming from the colonists because of the work of rabble-rousing troublemakers who were determined for their own gain to manipulate the people into rebellion and pursuit of independence. The people as a whole were victims of ambitious, self-interested demagogues who distorted or deliberately withheld the truth. Largely because of the efforts and influence of these agitators, the colonists did not respond to the British government in a proper or respectful fashion, but their rude and arrogant tone displayed a militant and contemptuous spirit. They rejected many British overtures of conciliation and refused to compromise on anything. They responded to British offers with further provocations in place of conciliation.

According to the Loyalist writers, the responsibility and blame for the improper responses lay at the feet of the First Continental Congress. The Congress was dominated by the troublemakers; historians often refer to them as "the radicals." They argued that the Congress did not in fact represent the majority of Americans and did not accurately represent the will of the people in its words or actions. Not only did the Congress act immoderately, but it also acted in violation of the commission and instructions given to its delegates. The Loyalists tried to show their audience that the Congress was the body acting tyrannically and urged their readers to renounce the Congress and to return to living under the colonial assembly. In their view, the actions taken by the Congress and its functionaries were, by any rational standard, disastrous and would lead America to ruin.

6 Rational Arguments Based on Colonial Actions

> Let us then like men of sense, sit down calmly and count the cost.
>
> —*Thomas Bradbury Chandler*

For better or for worse, the American colonies stood on the bank of the Rubicon in 1775 and early 1776. The Loyalist ministers thought it was for the worse. Actions were taken and contemplated by the Continental Congress and by Parliament that, in the view of the Loyalist clergy, held dire consequences. They believed that by drawing public attention to the "tyrannical" actions of the Congress and its enforcement agencies and by raising the specter of war and its inherent calamities, they could still stem the tide of rebellion and independence. This chapter addresses the Loyalist ministers' rational arguments against revolution in light of the actions of the American colonies and the prospects for the future after war and potential separation.

The Three "Nons"

The best-known action of the First Continental Congress was also arguably the most controversial. The Congress agreed to impose a policy of nonimportation, nonexportation, and nonconsumption. British goods would not be imported into America, American goods would not be exported to Great Britain, and British goods would not be consumed by Americans. It was, of course, designed to put economic pressure on Great Britain to change its policies toward America. The Loyalist ministers express severe doubts and concerns about the policy.

They believe, as a starting point, that the extent to which Great Britain is dependent on trade with the American colonies is overestimated. Jonathan Boucher contends that the number of British manufactured goods imported into America "is very inconsiderable, compared with the Opinions about it, that are so industriously circulated thro' all the Colonies, and so generally received." He asks, "Can we seriously believe, that this Wealth, and Power, is derived almost entirely, from her North-American Colonies? Can we . . . reasonably hope, to starve into Compliance, so great, and so powerful a Nation? Shall we punish ourselves, like froward Children, who refuse to eat, when they are Hungry, that they may vex their indulgent Mothers? . . . We may teize [vex or annoy] the Mother Country, we cannot ruin her."[1] Also arguing that the scheme will not work, Thomas Bradbury Chandler claims that "the non-importation in question, while it would cause a total stagnation of our commerce, would produce no more than a partial stagnation of hers; and consequently would not place her in a situation so distressing, as it would place us. Her trade is not confined to her American Colonies." Samuel Seabury agrees: "Her wealth is great. Her people enterprizing, and persevering in their attempts to extend and enlarge and protect her trade. The total loss of our trade would be felt only for a time. Her merchants would turn their attention another way." He recognizes that America is important to England, "but if we estimate it so high as to suppose that Great Britain could not subsist without us, or could not subsist in a happy and flourishing state, we deceive ourselves with fancied notions of our own consequence."[2]

The likelihood that Great Britain will not be sufficiently affected by the policy is far from the only concern of the Loyalists. Boucher and Seabury question the inherent justice of the policy. Both are bothered by forced restrictions on people's livelihoods that contravene laws made by constitutional authorities. According to Boucher: "A Combination to Ruin, or to obstruct the Trade of a fellow Citizen . . . adopted in Passion, prosecuted by . . . Innuendoes, Insinuations, Threatnings [sic], and publicly signed, by large Numbers of leading Men, would I presume, be a manifest Violation, of the Laws of God and Man, and would on Conviction, be severely punished in every Court of Justice in the Universe." As one can see, he is also distressed by the prospect of enforcement by committees. After this statement, he expresses concern about overruling laws passed by the assembly. Speaking of those hampered by this decree from a legally unrecognized body, Seabury argues: "In importing the goods he has transgressed no law of God, of nature, nor of the province. On the contrary, the laws of God, of nature, and of the province, forbid you to molest him in the prosecution of his business. But you are introducing a regulation of the congress superior to the laws of God, of nature, and of the province:—A regulation that supersedes and vacates them all." Like Boucher, he also bemoans the enforcement mechanisms. He complains that "our very mode of living is made subject to their inspection," calls the nonconsumption agreement "slavish," and warns that under the committees, "the tyranny of a mob, is the *freedom* of America."[3]

Boucher stresses that many Americans across the country oppose the scheme, "some of them from Opinion, others from Interest, and many from down-right Necessity." This introduces what is perhaps the primary concern: the inevitable suffering of many Americans. Boucher urges his fellow Virginians not to cooperate with "the high menacing Resolves." He implores them not to subject "Thousands of your Fellow Citizens, to the cruel Alternative, of involving themselves, their Wives, and Children, in Indigence, and Wretchedness; or of being publicly branded, and pointed out by the frantic Multitude, as Apostates, and Traitors to their Country." Herein lies a significant problem with the plan: violators will be subjected to public disgrace and suspicion, but for many who intend no political statement, their livelihood will compel them to breach the agreement. Using terminology that he hopes those sympathetic to the Patriot cause will understand, Boucher says: "There are Thousands of honest industrious Families, who have no Resources, but in the Consequences of Exportation, and Importation. Shall we levy a Tax, upon these innocent Citizens, a Tax unheard of, disproportionate, a Tax, never suggested by the most inhuman Tyrant? A Tax, to the Amount of their daily Bread?"[4] Is it fair or wise to essentially impose a 100 percent tax on some by shutting down their means of income in order to protest a miniscule duty on tea that no one is forced to pay? Pointing to the claims of those suffering under the Boston Port Bill, he asks, "Shall we multiply these Calamities, ten Thousand Fold?"[5]

Also invoking the hyperbolic number "ten thousand" to describe the extent of the danger to average Americans, Chandler argues that "a remedy of this kind is ten thousand times worse than the disease. It is, for the wisdom of it, like cutting off an arm, in order to get rid of a small sore in one of the fingers." He opposes the policy because "it will greatly distress a country which I love; and that it will not answer the purpose." It will not work and it will cause great hardship. Chandler and Seabury address the hardship in both general and specific terms. Americans had tried a nonimportation scheme before, and Chandler notes that while it proved that it did not endanger "*animal* life," it showed that "*civilized* life . . . which is necessary to the happiness of all but savages, depended, in no small degree, upon our importations from *Great-Britain*." In other words, the survival of Americans would not be jeopardized, but their quality of life or standard of living will be severely compromised. He notes that "more than a hundred thousand American dram-drinkers" will be affected by the loss of the molasses trade and an inability to make rum. More importantly, "every family upon this Continent" will be "distressed" by the lack of available sugar. "We engage to deprive ourselves of the comforts of life, to become as poor as dogs, and to live like savages, if the Parliament will not consent to give up its authority."[6]

Seabury warns that "our very mode of living is made subject to their inspection." Seabury asks the merchants of New York: "Are you sure that your non-importation, non-exportation, non-consumption schemes, will not draw the resentment of the British parliament on *you*, as well as on *Boston*?" Chandler has the same concern and fully expects England to shut down all of the American ports in response to the plan. He advises his readers to consider this prospect: "If the operation of such an act upon the single town of Boston only, has brought so much distress upon so many of its inhabitants, that all America has been obliged to contribute to their relief; we may judge in what manner we shall be affected by the shutting up of this port, while all the neighboring ports will be in the same condition, and our poor will have no prospect of assistance from any of the other Colonies."[7]

Having laid out the general threat, they focus on and address specific groups and the peril facing each. Their goal is to mobilize virtually every element of society against the scheme. Everyone can see that there will be negative effects for some merchants and those in the shipping industry. Regarding the shipping industry, Seabury warns that "our sailors, ship-carpenters, carmen, sail-makers, riggers, miners, smelters, forge-men, and workers in bar-iron, &c. would be immediately out of employ." Chandler widens the affected circle by disclosing the effects of the loss of the molasses and sugar trade and by concluding that "all that live by this commerce would be thrown out of employ." To really make an impact with their argument and persuade the vast majority of Americans to oppose the plan, Chandler and Seabury stress the disastrous effects for farmers. Chandler relates the plight of those other workers to harmful effects for farmers: "It is their farms, as all other resources will fail, that must support all the abovementioned thousands of distressed people. Who must furnish them with food? None can do it, but, the FARMERS. Who must supply them with cloathing [sic]? The FARMERS. Who must shelter many of them in their houses? The FARMERS. And can they expect pay for all this? Alas! those poor creatures will have nothing to make payment with." Seabury grabs their attention by beginning his discussion with the claim that "should their whole plan be carried fully into execution, the laborious, necessary and numerous *body of* FARMERS would soon be reduced to distress and beggary."⁸

To explain why the scheme would be so painful for farmers, he addresses specific crop exports and trading partners, in particular Ireland and the West Indies. Seabury suggests that Canada could supply Ireland and "at a much more reasonable rate." Canada, Georgia (under British control), Florida, and Nova Scotia could supply the West Indies. He says that "all these countries would be enriched by our folly, and would laugh at it." He warns that "the loss to the farmers of this province would be immense" and that "the loss of [the sale of your feed] for one year would be of more damage to you, than paying the three-penny duty on tea for twenty." The West Indians could get food from Canada, and "the Irish can do just as well with their linens, upon their hands, as we can with our flax seed upon ours. . . . We should suffer as much for the want of their linens, as they would for the want of our flaxseed." He then identifies alternative sources of flax seed that the Irish could use. Seabury calls Ireland "another victim, devoted by the Congress to the infernal Gods, to render them propitious to sedition and rebellion," but he cautions that "the Americans can neither force them into rebellion, nor starve them to death." To add insult to injury for the farmers, Seabury argues that congressional policy has made it nearly "an absolute necessity" that they will lose the sale of their feed the next year, and the consequence will be "that we must sell our feed at the oil-mills in New-York, just at the price the manufacturers shall please to give us." Ultimately, the prices farmers can get for their produce will be so low that it will not be worth their while to raise more than they can consume. This in turn means that they will not be able to pay their debts or even their interest payments, and consequently, they will lose their farms. He sarcastically declares to the farmers: "Glorious effect of Non-exportation!" and asks them, "When the Congress adopted this cursed scheme, did they in the least consider your interest?"⁹

Speaking of prices, while the prices farmers can get for their goods will be low, the prices they must pay for their own needs will increase dramatically. Discussing the "advanced prices of goods, which will, not only probably, but necessarily, follow, as soon as the non-importation from Great Britain, &c. shall take effect," Seabury appeals to the law of supply and demand. He notes that demand always increases in proportion to scarcity and scarcity of goods will, of course, be a result of the nonimportation scheme. Prices will increase, but to what extent? "Who is to judge what a reasonable profit is? Why, the merchants." Will the merchants show patriotic restraint?

"Not to raise the price of a commodity when it is scarce, and in demand, is contrary to the principles and practice of merchants." To support his claim, he points to the rise in prices during the nonimportation agreement that had been tried years earlier. He says that it is inevitable that the scheme "must raise the prices of goods; not only now, but probably for some years to come." This leads to yet another problem; it is not just the shipping industry and farmers who will suffer. "If the Non-importation agreement continues any length of time, the wealthy merchants will grow enormously rich, the merchant with a small capital will probably fail." There will not be enough trade to keep everyone busy and those with greater means will be the survivors. "These inferior merchants are of great consequence to the community: they keep down the price of goods, and prevent it becoming excessive.... But the wealthy merchant can wait for a better price, without hurting his estate or credit." As further evidence that prices will increase, Seabury mentions that they are already increasing in anticipation of the agreement going into effect.[10]

In addition to Ireland and the West Indies seeking new trade partners to meet their needs, Great Britain will as well. America has provided a ready market for British goods, a mutually beneficial situation for both. But Britain is better equipped to deal with a severing of their commerce. Seabury spends several paragraphs explaining why the colonies will not be able to clothe themselves with their own manufactures or feed themselves with their own produce. At the end of the discussion, he further explains that "the American market hath hitherto had the preference in England. They looked out for no vent for those articles which we wanted. Should their trade with us fail, very small concessions to Portugal, Russia, Turkey, &c. would open a vent for all they could send." Not only will England seek other trade partners but also the nonimportation agreement will probably "induce the Parliament to block up our ports and prevent our trade intirely [sic]. It would certainly be good policy in the government to do so." "If then we stop our imports, the benefit of our trade is in a manner lost to her, and she would find but little additional disadvantage, should she stop our trade with all the world." Because of Great Britain's great navy, and because the colonies are still under her authority, she "can embarrass our trade in the Mediterranean with Spain, Holland &c. . . . for whatever regulations she should make, would effectually be enforced, by the same Navy that she keeps in readiness to protect her own trade." Knowing that the nonimportation scheme cannot last forever, she can also "raise immense revenues, by laying duties in England, Ireland, and the West-Indies." This is likely to raise resentment against America on the part of the Irish and West Indians.[11]

The clergymen point to several other detrimental effects of the congressional policy. "We have no trade but under the protection of Great-Britain. . . . We have no influence abroad, no ambassadors, no consuls, no fleet to protect our ships in passing the seas, nor our merchants and people in foreign countries." Americans will not be able to import critical medicines; there is great inconsistency in what products or goods are and are not allowed; it encourages and works to the advantage of smugglers. Because British regulations had restrained their particular interests and forced them to cooperate with one another, with the removal of that regulation, "the colonies will probably be soon at variance with each other." The American economy will suffer as a result of "the want of the money, of which we have been lately drained, in order to pamper the Boston fanaticks." Though the policy is designed to create unrest in England and other colonies, there will be "twenty mobs and riots in our own country, before one would happen in Britain or Ireland." Because different classes or groups of people will blame one another as being "the authors of this general calamity," the result will be "quarrels, and riots, and disturbances, and acts of violence, amongst ourselves." Finally, the policy is doomed to fail; Americans will eventually have to give in and submit to England's authority. At that point, "she will have a right to establish new and less favourable terms for us. . . . So that this non-importation project, instead of relieving us from parliamentary taxation, will in the end, naturally and almost necessarily, cause it to fall upon us with more than double weight."[12]

In sum, the Loyalist ministers see the "non" scheme as causing shrinking land values, unemployment, and crime. "To undertake such a frantic adventure, must be the business only of fools or fanaticks." "It is highly probable that [the measures of Congress] will not succeed; and that they are not founded in good policy, but in arrant folly." When their disastrous effects are experienced, "we should then tast [sic] the sweets of *natural* liberty, and see the *natural* rights of mankind exemplified in dreadful instances." "We should then have reason and leisure enough to repent of our folly, and lament that infatuation, which tempted us to *grasp* at the mere *shadow* of civil freedom, while we lost its real *substance*."[13]

Not every Loyalist minister published lengthy polemic public pamphlets in opposition to the policies of the Congress. Many fled, and many others suffered quietly. John Sayre provides an example of a clergyman who was more meek than militant but who stood his ground firmly in defiance of the committee overseeing his community. He demonstrates what is intended to be a biblical response to the congressional mandate. As a prominent member of the community, Sayre was approached and "requested" (expected) to subscribe to (approve of) the continental association carrying out the "non" scheme. In a letter to the committee, Sayre walks through the parts of the association agreement and firmly but gently declines each. In each part, Sayre bases his decision to decline firmly on Scripture and his identity as a Christian.

After some introductory contextual remarks, he addresses the first part of the paper. He reports that the "first clause contains a recital of some of those things which are commonly charged against the Mother Country, as unconstitutional (and therefore unwarrantable) exertions of power on her part; and of the resolutions of the United Colonies, on their part; to resist by force of arms, the measures prescribed by the Parent State, and to die or be free." Sayre responds that he is "a servant (though unworthy) of the Gospel of Christ" and that II Corinthians 10:4 teaches him that the weapons of a Christian are not "carnal" but "spiritual." Therefore, he will not take up any carnal arms. He continues by quoting Philippians 4:11 in order to explain that God requires him to be content though God "should bring me into a state even of slavery itself." Because of that, he reasons, "I dare not, therefore, resolve that I will be free; because I am sensible that many better men than myself have, by the Providence of God, been brought into a state of bondage, and that I ought not to complain, if I should be made partaker of the same affliction."[14]

The second clause requires one to resolve "faithfully to observe and comply with" the Continental Association (the "non" agreement) "without any equivocation or mental reservation." But there is one part of the association with which Sayre says he "dare not promise to comply" because his conscience will not permit it. That part prohibits anyone from aiding or providing hospitality to any who refuse to be bound by the association agreement. Under the agreement, anyone who violates the policy is boycotted themselves and to be treated as an outcast. Sayre responds that the "Saviour of the world, whose servant I am, hath commanded me to feed the hungry, and give drink to the thirsty; to clothe the naked; to take in the stranger or traveller [Matthew 25:35–40]; to give to him that asketh of me, and not to turn away from him that would borrow of me [Matthew 5:42]." In that way, he explains that he cannot abide by the association's restriction.

Anticipating what an opponent might say, Sayre stresses that it does not matter if a person is an enemy because "our Lord hath expressly, and that too in an especial manner, commanded me to extend my kind offices to mine enemies as such [Luke 6:35]."[15]

"The remainder of it," says Sayre, "commenceth with a declaration, that we notice and gratefully acknowledge the Divine interpositions, in favour of all our warlike enterprizes, crowning them with most unparalleled success." At this point, Sayre takes his boldest step by questioning the virtue of the Revolution. He suggests that he cannot properly judge whether the Revolution is good or not, "for history, sacred and prophane [sic], furnisheth us with many instances, in which we shall all agree in saying, that the most unjust cause did not always meet an overthrow, nor the most just prosper." He adds that there are "sundry prophecies yet to be fulfilled, which declare, that the potentates of the earth shall have power to make war against the saints, and to overcome them." This is an astounding statement to put into writing and shows Sayre's courage. He suggests that the Revolution might be a "war against the saints"—that God might be against the Revolution as a device of Satan to thwart God's plan. He adds that he sees "the present unnatural war" as a judgment by God on both sides.[16]

Having placed some potentially incriminating evidence on the page, Sayre concludes by attempting to assure the committee that he is a friend and not a threat. He surmises that "the design of this Association is to make a discrimination between the friends of America and its liberties, and the enemies of both." He vows that he is "a sincere friend to both" America and its liberties. To convince them that he is no threat, he assures them that "I am no politician; am not connected with politicians as such, and never will be either." In other words, he will not be politically active or a vocal Loyalist. In conclusion, to dissuade them from publicly acting against him, he politely says that "advertising me as an enemy to my country" would be a violation of the ninth commandment against bearing false witness. Although Sayre tries to convince the committee that he is no threat and attempts to fly under their radar, he is eventually forced to flee Fairfield and winds up in New York city at the end of the war.[17]

Hypocrisy and "Un-American" Treatment

Sayre was brought to the attention of the committees and ultimately forced to flee because people—especially clergymen—were not allowed by the Patriots to be neutral and nonpolitical. They were forced to take sides, and if loyal or insufficiently patriotic, they were harassed and persecuted in various ways ranging from verbal abuse to assault, confiscation of property to exile, imprisonment to death. Along the way, Loyalists were denied freedom of speech, freedom of the press, freedom of religion, due process of law, and other rights.

Loyalist ministers scolded, lectured, and at times taunted the Patriots for hypocrisy when it came to civil and natural rights. It is common knowledge that much of the argument for the American cause was couched in terms of rights—English and/or natural rights. From the perspective and experience of the Loyalists, the Patriots were far worse violators of rights than were the British. More importantly, they ruthlessly and routinely violated nearly every right that they demanded for themselves. To the Loyalists, the Patriots' practice disqualified them from making rights claims, and perhaps from having their own rights recognized. They certainly lost any moral ground for such claims. To use a biblical metaphor, the Loyalist ministers essentially asked the Patriots to remove the log from their own eyes before complaining to England about splinters.

Samuel Andrews argues that "no Reason can be assigned why the People, who claim the greatest Liberties for themselves, should at the same time . . . deprive others of their civil, natural, and religious Liberties:—but so it is." Drawing on I Peter 2:16, Andrews says: "We have Reason to fear that they are using Liberty for a Cloak of Maliciousness, and not as Subjects to their King elect [Christ], whose Laws as little please, as those of George, our rightful King." Charles Inglis took the argument directly to the president of the Continental Congress, John Jay. In his letter to Jay, he calls the actions of the Congress "a mockery of the Supreme Being" and "a mockery of men." They are the latter because "the security of their rights and liberties was the ostensible object held up; yet measures were pursued which must necessarily subvert both, as hath actually happened." In an ultimate insult, Inglis declares: "There is more liberty in Turkey than in the dominions of the Congress." This was as severe an insult as one could give, as in America at that time, "the Turk" was an idiom for tyranny. In support of his extreme claim, Inglis asks: "Can liberty exist where every man who differs in sentiment from you, is not only precluded from the common rights of citizens, but is also liable to imprisonment, confiscation and death?"[18] This was not an exaggeration and therefore was an effective argument.

Jonathan Boucher took the argument one step higher—to George Washington. In August 1775, Boucher wrote a scorching letter to his longtime friend. He wrote to inform him that their friendship was over—not because of their political disagreements or finding themselves on opposite sides of a huge conflict, but because Washington had not acted to quell violations of the rights of Loyalists. Boucher begins the hypocrisy charge: "No Tory has yet in a single instance misused or injured a Whig merely for being a Whig. . . . How contrary all this is to all that liberty which Whigs for ever are so forward to profess, needs not be insisted on: it is so contrary to all justice and honour, that were there no other reasons to determine me against it, . . . I would not be a Whig, because their principles, at least as I see them exemplified in practice, lead so directly to all that is mean and unmanly." Boucher wants to know: where is the celebrated Whig concern for rights? After acknowledging that not all Whigs, including Washington, are "tyrants," Boucher nonetheless complains that Washington has not discouraged others from persecuting "fellow-subjects on the score of their political creeds." Implying that the same cannot be said for Washington on this score, Boucher declares that "it is impossible I should sometimes avow one kind of principles and sometimes another. I have at least the merit of consistency." Turning to the personal, he says: "You cannot say that I deserved to be run down, vilified, and injured in the manner which you know has fallen to my lot, merely because I cannot bring myself to think on some political points just as you and your party would have me think. And yet you have borne to look on, at least as an unconcerned spectator, if not an abettor, whilst like the poor frogs in the fable, I have in a manner been petted to death." Boucher ends with a dagger: "You are no longer worthy of my friendship; a man of honour can no longer without dishonour be connected with you."[19]

Inglis elsewhere claims that civil liberty was "the ostensible Object" of the Patriot appeal, but was in reality simply "the Bait that was flung out to catch the Populace at large & engage them in the Rebellion." Other ministers similarly leveled charges of hypocrisy against the Patriots. Samuel Seabury, upon being personally denied fundamental rights by the rebels, calls his situation "a high infringement of the liberty for which the virtuous sons of America are now nobly struggling." He then points out that what happened to him at the hands of the Patriots was exactly the same as a "great grievance justly complained of by the people of America." Richard Mansfield notes that "they have made a Law with a very severe Penalty for only speaking disrespectfully of the Continental Congress while at the same time, it is thought, not only allowable but commendable, and even meritorious, to bestow upon the King and the two Houses of Parliament the Epithets of

Tyrant and Ministerial Butchers." Loyalist lawyer Daniel Leonard thought it "astonishing" "that those, who are in pursuit of liberty, should ever suffer arbitrary power, in such an hideous form and squalid hue, to get a footing among them." The 1781 Loyalist "Declaration of Dependence" accused the Congress of a number of inconsistencies, among them: "We find them contending for liberty of speech, and at the same time controlling the press, by means of a mob, and persecuting everyone who ventures to hint his disapprobation of their proceedings."[20]

The most severe aspect of the Loyalist clergy's charge of hypocrisy against the Patriots was their claim of tyranny on the part of those ostensibly fighting against tyranny. The threat and the imposition of tyranny was a common theme for the Loyalist ministers. It was, in their view, a tyranny in terms of effect and substance; but perhaps more importantly, it was a tyranny in legal terms. Not only did the rebels engage in tyrannical practices but they also had no legal authority to rule or to make the oppressive decrees in the first place. The Patriots denied rights to political opponents, gave preferential treatment and graft to cronies, demanded support for their cause and punished any who refused such support, ran roughshod over personal conviction, imprisoned and executed people for mere expressions of disagreement with their cause, and even tried to legislate the thoughts of the people. They did all of this, said the Loyalist ministers, on their own authority, without legal sanction, and often by the manipulation and implementation of mob violence. That is arguably the definition of tyranny.

Loyalists in general and Loyalist clergy in particular questioned or denied the legal authority of those bodies and officials making oppressive laws and acting as tribunals to punish Loyalists or suspected Loyalists. They focused particularly on the Continental Congresses, the provincial congresses and conventions, and the committees of various types created by those congresses. In April 1775, a "numerous body" of New Yorkers met in what became known as the White Plains Protest. Several of their leaders were clergymen, including, most prominently, Samuel Seabury. Their declaration reflects the general Loyalist sentiment: "We . . . declare our honest abhorrence of all unlawful Congresses and committees, and that we are determined, at the hazard of our lives and properties, to support the King and Constitution; and that we acknowledge no representatives but the General Assembly."[21]

Jonathan Boucher, as he did with most issues, addressed the question of authority head on. In his "Quæres Addressed to the People of Maryland," he asks: "What is tyranny but the assumption and exercise of power without any authority?" In the context of a dozen other questions related to injustices taking place in Maryland, the question is not academic but rather directed to their particular situation. In his "Farewell Sermon," he accuses those cooperating with the Patriots of "persecuting such of their brethren as give offence, not against the laws either of God or man, but against the decrees of persons invested with no constitutional jurisdiction over any of us." He then urges his parishioners to be "undictated to, and uncontrolled by, men who are your superiors only in confidence and self-sufficiency," but not in legal authority. The power of the committees was such that Boucher concludes that "it is better to have the meanest Committee-Man your Friend, than the best & most powerful Governor." He contends that the power of those committees, conventions, and Congresses stems not from right or legitimate authority, but from their backing "by regiments, battalions and armies." As in all tyrannies, they had established "might, as the only criterion of right." When brought before a committee himself, he stuck to his principles and "protest[ed] against their having any authority over [him]." For his part, Seabury urged the New York legislature to assert itself and its authority to give the people "deliverance from the tyranny of the *Congress* and *Committees*."[22]

The worst treatment often fell on the clergy, and "they were marked for closer restraint and subjected to sharper trials and persecutions" than others. This was at least partly because the revolutionaries "crafted an explicit link between Anglicanism and British oppression and imbued the Anglican Church with much greater authority than it actually exercised in the colonies." Charles Inglis reported that those Loyalist ministers who were "in the Hands of the Rebels are subject to the most mortifying Insults, & Persecution."[23]

Though threatened, assaulted, proscribed, and even kidnapped, Loyalist ministers were undeterred and continued to criticize the Patriot regime, although they often wrote under pseudonyms. Boucher explains that in some provinces, Loyalists dared not "declare Themselves" because they would "fall an easy Prey to the Committees, & the Independent Companies, who, on the first appearance of a Suspicion only of their Defection, as it would be called, wou'd be sure to fall on Them." John Joachim Zubly alleges: "Every man that was suspected of thinking became a suspected person, and to think differently from people that did not think at all was a crime which exposed to every species of insult, suffering, and injustice." Inglis agrees and charges that "every mouth was closed" and "every hand arrested" that would support the opposition. He says that the "iron scourge of tyranny" restrained any and all voices of opposition and "the people were not permitted to deliberate impartially about them, or to act as they chose. The privilege of speaking or writing their sentiments, or acting according to their judgement, is reserved for [the Congress's] warm partizans [sic] only."[24]

Inglis refers to Loyalists "groaning in Bondage, under the Iron Scourge of Persecution and Oppression" and reassures a Loyalist corps that they had taken up the sword to "defend your Families, your Lives, Liberties and Property—to secure to yourselves and Posterity, that Inheritance of constitutional Freedom, to which you were born: And all this against the Violence of usurped Power, which would deny you even the Right of Judgment or Choice." But it is Samuel Seabury who perhaps best sums up the view of the Loyalist ministers regarding the extent of the tyranny imposed on the Americans by the Congress and the committees: "The state to which the GRAND CONGRESS, and the *subordinate Committees*, have reduced the colonies, is *really deplorable*. They have introduced a *system* of the most *oppressive tyranny* that can possibly be imagined;—a *tyranny*, not only over the *actions*, but over the *words, thoughts, and wills*, of the *good people of this province*. People have been threatened with the *vengeance of a mob*, for speaking in support of *order* and *good government*." Theirs was a tyranny over words, thoughts, and wills. Seabury appeals to the language of the Association resolution passed by the Congress in support of this claim: "They not only oblige people to *pay* the tax assessed on their goods for the benefit of the Boston poor, but they also oblige them to say, that they are *willing* to do it."[25]

Loyalist ministers also complained about large-scale property confiscation and banishment, with the latter affecting one-fourth of all Anglican clergy in America as well as some non-Anglicans such as Zubly. It is important to remember that these men committed no crime. They were not punished for espionage or sabotage but simply for maintaining loyalty to the legal established government and for disagreeing with the rebels. Some states made refusal of an oath of allegiance to the Patriot cause a sufficient cause for banishment. In the case of Church of England clergymen, they had taken a solemn oath of allegiance to the king—an oath that most took seriously. In response to the Patriot argument that colonies "have a right to follow their own judgment" in deciding whether to rebel, Jonathan Boucher reasoned that by the same token, individuals must have a similar right. He asks: "On what principle then are the thousands of unfortunate persons, who are shocked at the guilt of violating their oaths of allegiance, and therefore refuse to subscribe to the wild notions which are now so industriously circulated, subjected to have their estates confiscated, and their persons proscribed?" Charles Inglis similarly complains that the ministers did not "draw this Treatment on themselves by any Imprudence, but for adhering to their Duty, which gave Offence to some furious Demagogues, who raised Mobs to persecute them on that very Account."[26]

In an open letter to Continental Congress president John Jay in the midst of the Revolution, Inglis accuses Jay and the Congress of using Machiavellian tactics—with two exceptions. He notes that Machiavelli warned "usurpers" to avoid being hated by declining to take people's property and by resisting the urge to engage in regular cruelties. "That Congress have not observed the caution here recommended on those two points, is evident from the number of confiscations and executions which we are daily advertised of in your own news-papers." The Congress had been even more cruel and ruthless than Machiavelli advised. In a footnote supporting this charge, Inglis claims that about 300 Bostonians had been banished, about 400 estates in Massachusetts, 1,000 in New Jersey, and 300 in Pennsylvania had been confiscated and sold, and that "several hundreds" of people had been hanged "for the CRIME of loyalty." He then suggests that "any candid person may now judge whether my assertion is true"; that is, whether "*there is remarkable conformity between the conduct of your Congress and the rules laid down by Machiavel [sic] in his Prince.*" In an effort to shame Jay into changing the policy, Inglis says: "In this light you are viewed by Loyalists; in this light you are, and will be viewed by the unprejudiced, virtuous part of mankind, who really know you." He concludes the letter by recounting the unhappy end of a Machiavellian hero, Cesare Borgia, and warns: "Providence, for its own vindication, and in compassion to poor mortals, frequently exhibits such examples of justice as a warning to others."[27] Neither Jay nor the Congress heeded the warning.

As leaders in the community and potential voices against the revolutionary cause, Loyalist clergymen were also special targets for physical assaults to make an example of them and to intimidate them into silence. The key spokesmen addressed this issue as well in making their case against the Revolution and the Patriots. In a 1775 sermon, Jonathan Boucher shows his contempt for those who used physical assaults in place of reasoned arguments: "I [lack] spirits to enter on any such discussions with those persons among us, who, settling controverted points with their hands rather than with their tongues, demonstrate with tar and feathers, fetch arguments from prisons, and confute by confiscation and exile." Chandler similarly mocks the reprehensible methods of the Patriots by suggesting aristocratic titles for Patriot "nobles": "The Viscounts may consist of Heroes that are famed for their exploits in *tarring and feathering;* and the Barons ... of those, whose merit has been signalized in burning such Pamphlets as they were unable to answer."[28] The Loyalist ministers believed that virtually every biblical, legal, and rational argument was on their side and that the Patriots had to resort to intimidation and violence against defenseless civilians in order to achieve their desired results. In their view, the Patriots expended tremendous effort to silence their opposition because they could not win an open argument.

In addition to the persecution already discussed, many Loyalist ministers suffered imprisonment or at least house arrest or forced confinement to a small area. In his open letter to John Jay, Charles Inglis emphasizes that these clergymen were imprisoned for "undeviating loyalty, ... unshaken attachment to principle, to the dictates of conscience, and to the interest of their country, which would do honour to any people, in any place, or at any period. They have literally FORSAKEN ALL, that they might adhere to these." He chides Jay: "They had what you *cannot* have, the testimony of a good conscience to support them." In an open letter to the people of America, Inglis explains that "protestant clergymen, who will not *perjure* themselves to support the Congress, are banished, imprisoned, and otherwise cruelly persecuted." He was arguing that they were prisoners of conscience—what we would today refer to as political dissidents. In the vast majority of cases, they had committed no crimes—and were not even accused of any. They were not detained for physically aiding the enemy or for espionage but merely for holding—and sometimes expressing—unpopular political views in favor of the legal government or for refusing to actively participate in a rebellion against the legal government.

In his report to Richard Hind in 1776, Inglis summarizes imprisonment experiences in the early war years. Speaking specifically of the clergy, Inglis reports:

> Some have been carried Prisoners by armed Mobs into distant Provinces, where they were detained in close Confinement for several Weeks, & much insulted, without any Crime being even alleged against them. Some have been flung into Jails by Committees, for frivolous Suspicions of Plots, of which even their Persecutors afterwards

acquitted them. Some who were obliged to fly their Own Province to save their Lives, have been taken Prisoners, sent back, & are threatened to be tried for their Lives because they fled from Danger.[29]

There was, of course, one consequence more severe than imprisonment that was suffered by a significant number of Loyalist clergymen: death.

The total number of Loyalist ministers who died during or as a result of the American Revolution is unknown. Records are incomplete or missing. Records for Church of England ministers are the best available. Reliable sources indicate that about 20 percent of the Church of England ministers in America in 1775 did not survive the war. Some, of course, died of natural causes, but the deaths of many were directly or indirectly caused by their treatment as Loyalists. In one of his letters to John Jay, Charles Inglis claims that "many hundreds" of Loyalists—not all ministers, of course—lost their lives by the "severities" visited upon them via imprisonment and banishment. He also attributes some to hanging. John Joachim Zubly also addresses the deaths of Loyalists during the conflict: "Too great a number have fallen a sacrifice to the desperate fury and cruelty of those who were not satisfied to sport away the lives of their fellow creatures in military service, but would also enjoy the triumph of wickedness in consigning better men than themselves to an ignominious death. The infamy rests not upon the martyr, but upon the unrighteous judge." He identifies those unrighteous judges as "their present or late factious rulers"—in other words, the leaders of the rebellion.[30]

In that same newspaper essay, Zubly makes a powerful, scorching indictment of the Patriots. Addressing them directly, he warns:

> The penalty due to obstinate rebellion in this life is a trifle not to be mentioned with what you must expect when all the ghosts of the slain, every drop of innocent blood you spilt, every act of violence and injustice which you concurred in or committed, all the confederates of your crime who you have forced or seduced, every injured widow's groans, and every orphan's tear, whom you have ruined, the spoils of the honest and innocent whom you have robbed, every friendly warning which you rejected, will at once arise in judgment against you, and render you as compleatly [sic] miserable as you have rendered yourselves distinguishingly wicked.

Regarding this sentence, Janice Potter-MacKinnon and Robert Calhoon suggest: "No single sentence in all of the loyalist press dealt so comprehensively with the nature and impact of the Revolution."³¹ According to the Loyalist ministers, the Patriots were willing to pay any price, including denial of basic human, English, and American rights and the deadly horrors of war.

In addition to physical and economic mistreatment at the hands of the Patriots, Loyalist ministers suffered the loss of every civil right associated with Americanism and every right the Patriots were supposedly fighting the British to obtain or guarantee. Freedom of religion is, of course, one of the most important American freedoms, and one for which the United States is particularly known. Because of their occupation and their priorities, it was also of preeminent interest to the Loyalist ministers. Religious issues were a part of the dispute between the American colonies (New England in particular) and Great Britain. Many Patriots were concerned about a perceived plan by the British to promote Roman Catholicism in America. That complaint did not make its way into the Declaration of Independence's catalog of royal offenses because the Americans were appealing for French help and did not want to alienate their potential Catholic allies, but it was a significant cause of the Revolution for some. There was also a prominent religious dispute between the New England colonies and the Anglican church in America. Church of England clergymen lobbied passionately for the establishment of an American Anglican bishop. Leaders of dissenting (non-Anglican) churches, primarily in New England, fought hard to keep it from being approved. This argument caused a lot of bad blood between dissenting pastors and Anglican priests, which was further exacerbated and expanded by their political differences.

The coming of the Revolution provided an opportunity for the religious dissenters to silence their theological opponents under the auspices of silencing their political opponents. The result was extremely consequential in the war of ideas because the Loyalist pulpits—like the Patriot pulpits—were an important source of popular support for their side. The Patriots were not willing to allow people to hear both sides of the argument and then make up their own minds. All preaching that mentioned the king in anything but critical terms was shut down, and churches that refused to toe the Patriot line were shut up. Whether through intimidation and threats or vandalism and burnings, doors were chained and churches closed. In some cases, to add insult to injury, former Loyalist churches were turned into field hospitals or stables. In addition to silencing the voices of Loyalist ministers by taking away their pulpits, the Patriots zealously embarked on a campaign to prevent the publication of all Loyalist pamphlets and published sermons, to destroy them if they succeeded in being printed, and to destroy any printing presses made available to Loyalist pamphleteers and sermonizers. Not surprisingly, those voices of Loyalist clergymen that were able to penetrate the blackout (for a time) complained bitterly about the denial of their religious freedom.

In his *Reminiscences*, Jonathan Boucher reports that he was "set down as a Government-man." "It was an obvious policy in the insurgents to get rid of such men, and accordingly I was soon marked as a man not to be endured." Before long, he was "restrained from preaching" and moved to another parish. His reputation preceded him to Queen Anne's parish, and the "violent patriots" there arranged a "most unpleasant reception." In fact, "the very first Sunday I found the church doors shut against me; and not many Sundays after a turbulent fellow had paid eight dollars for so many loads of stones to drive me and my friends from the church by force." Although there were threats on his life if he entered the pulpit on a particular Sunday, he determined to do so. Concerned friends physically restrained him to protect him from a sniper's bullet. The company assigned to intimidate or eliminate him thought that their task was accomplished, but the next Sunday he showed up to preach his "Farewell Sermon." In it, Boucher questions why he was not allowed to preach from his "own pulpit" what he had "intended for your edification and your comfort" the Sunday before. He also rhetorically asks why he "was suffered to be treated with such unmerited insult and indignity as I believe has seldom been experienced by persons of my calling in any civilized and Christian country." He tells the congregation that he has been told that he can no longer preach unless he quits praying for the king, but he explains that he cannot comply with that demand. Shortly after, he left for England.[32]

Some of the ministers anticipated such a loss of religious freedom. Chandler, writing before the Revolution, issues a solemn warning of great threat to religious liberty in a rebellion and in an independent America. He suggests that the "principal conductors of the rebellion, would naturally have the principal authority in the republic," and that, given their record, they would be "oppressive" and "tyrannical." He sees the New Englanders as the "principal conductors" of the coming rebellion. All, he says, would have to submit "to the republican zealots and bigots of New-England; whose tender mercies, when they had power in their hands, have been ever cruel, towards all that presumed to differ from them in matters either of religion or government." Although this is a bit overstated, the New England colonies did not in fact have a history of allowing religious freedom for those who disagreed with them. After a long discussion of future persecution against the Church of England by Presbyterians if the rebellion is successful, Chandler warns: "Nor will it fare better with the *Friends*, or people called *Quakers*." He reminds readers of the history of such persecution and admonishes Quakers: "You can never wish to have your necks again encumbered with that *Presbyterian* yoke of bondage, which neither you nor your fathers were able to bear." He then reminds Baptists: "The *Baptists* have never had fair quarter allowed them by the demagogues of *New-England*; and they are perpetually complaining, from year to year, of the acts of oppression and violence with which they are harassed by them."[33]

Chandler argues that even those seemingly within the Presbyterian camp would be endangered: "Nor can the moderate part of the *Presbyterians*, and *Congregationalists* themselves, have any prospect of continuing free from molestation under their government. Nothing can be more odious to bigots, than generosity and candour; or more intolerable in the opinion of the furious, than moderation and meekness." One might point to the establishment of Rhode Island by moderates expelled from Massachusetts in support of Chandler's point. He then argues that such persecution has occurred and that moderates have been treated "as if they had been Mahometans and Heathens." Chandler sums up his warning: "In a word: no order or denomination of men amongst us would enjoy liberty or safety, if subjected to the fiery genius of a New-England Republican Government; the little finger of which we should soon experience to be heavier than the loins of Parliament."[34] Chandler wrote this prediction of oppressive rule in 1774, before the armed conflict began. One could argue that events during the Revolution proved him right in the short run, though not regarding the eventual independent United States. One could also argue that it did not become true of the United States because the New Englanders did not have the dominance over the new regime that Chandler anticipated.

As the Loyalist clergymen of the Church of England in America saw it, assaults on their religious liberty were grounded in hard feelings resulting from the fight over an Episcopal bishop and competitive desires to dominate the American religious landscape. These factors—in addition to their own support for rebellion—made New England pastors natural allies with Whig political leaders and co-conspirators in efforts to silence Loyalist ministers and to close Anglican churches. Both religious and political ideas that the Presbyterians disliked could be quashed by making impossible demands on religious speech and practice, removing offending ministers, and/or closing churches. The primary demand was for Church of England clergymen to omit prayers for the king from their liturgy. To impose changes in a denomination's liturgy and to regulate the substance of public prayers was, of course, a fundamental violation of their religious freedom. It was particularly obnoxious because ministers of the Church of England took a solemn oath to pray for the king and royal family, so they were asked to violate an oath that most considered to be sacred. Most considered this prohibition "an intolerable mutilation" of the liturgy.[35] Rather than obey such an order, a majority of Anglican clergy closed their churches.

In a letter near the end of 1776, Inglis explains the dilemma faced by these ministers: "To officiate publickly, & not pray for the King & Royal Family according to the Liturgy, was against their Duty & Oath, as well as Dictates of their Consciences; & yet to use the Prayers for the King & Royal Family, would have drawn inevitable Destruction on them." Inglis concludes that the only solution was to "suspend the public Exercise of their Function, & shut up their Churches." He expresses amazement that in New York, New Jersey, and the New England colonies, Anglican clergymen "all fell upon the same Method of shutting up their Churches" without consulting each other. Inglis was pleased that nearly all the Anglican churches in these colonies and in Pennsylvania closed rather than accede to the unconscionable demand.[36]

In an interesting contrast to the church closures, one of the "charges" against Samuel Seabury when he was carried into captivity was that he had "neglected to open his church on the day of the Continental Fast."[37] One could be forced to close one's church and one could be held accountable for not opening it to serve the Patriot's purpose. When it came to matters of religious liberty, the Patriots felt free to control a church's liturgy; to intimidate, threaten, and assault clergymen because of what they said in services; to prevent those who disagreed with them from speaking publicly and from printing and disseminating their contrary ideas; and to force the closure of churches that did not support their cause. The Patriots eliminated the need to win a war of ideas by denying the opposition all its weapons. A critical element of their assault on religious freedom was their assault on freedom of speech and the press.

In a letter to George Washington, Jonathan Boucher complains about the tactics of the Patriots. Boucher expresses the prevailing view of the Loyalists: "The true plan in such cases [disagreements over politics] is for each party to defend his own side as well as he can by fair argument, and also, if possible, to convince his adversary; but everything that savours of, or but approaches to, coercion or compulsion is persecution and tyranny. It is on this ground that I complain of you and those with whom you side." Chandler essentially challenges the theoretical manhood of the Patriots and accuses them of using censorship to cover the inadequacies of their ideas. Chandler asks whether there can be "a greater proof of bigotry, either in religion or politics, than an obstinate resolution to hear or see nothing that is offered on the subject in question, by persons who are supposed to be of different sentiments." Is not "such a resolution . . . proof, that a man is *conscious* of the *weakness* of his cause, and *afraid* of the force of those arguments which may be offered against him?" Finally, is not the inevitable conclusion that there are "many of the colonists, who, by refusing to hear or see what is offered on the side of government, betray the abovementioned consciousness and fear?"[38] If the Patriots believed that their ideas were true, then they must not have believed that the truth will ultimately prevail. In addition to disallowing praying for the king, the Patriots made every effort to prevent any ideas of which they did not approve from being preached, published, or simply spoken in public.

In January 1776, the Continental Congress urged the states to shut down "all speech or writing against the states or Congress" in order to "prevent 'honest and well-meaning but misinformed people' from being 'deceived and drawn into erroneous opinion.'" Of course, a fundamental hallmark of a free society is freedom of speech and press, and the competition of ideas by which people can weigh opinions and make up their own minds. In 1777 and 1778, laws were passed to further constrict freedom of speech. One must not "affirm that the King or Parliament of Great Britain had any authority" over America—not even "under the pretense of prayer." Laws prohibited criticism of the continental currency—especially the worthless paper money—and all humor directed toward the Patriot cause was "hushed." Finally, "in preaching or praying, in public or in private discourse, no one was to be allowed to discourage people from supporting the Declaration of Independence."[39]

The Patriot assault on freedom of the press was, of course, related to their attacks on freedom of speech, but it was arguably more consequential in the long run because printed materials could reach a much larger and wider audience over a longer period of time. Chandler again puts his finger on the central issue:

> One of the most sacred and invaluable rights of Englishmen, and consequently of the inhabitants of his Majesty's American colonies, is *the liberty of the press*. . . . *The liberty of the press* is so essential to the well-being of society in general, that the late *Congress*, in their *Address to the inhabitants of* QUEBEC, mention it as one of those "rights, without which a people cannot be free and happy. . . ." They complain that the King's "*profligate* ministry," are endeavouring to wrest it from us, and declare their resolution not to resign it but with their latest breath.

Not only is freedom of the press an essential freedom but also the Continental Congress affirmed it as such just before denying it to the Loyalists. Chandler continues: "It is a pity" that the Congress "did not place some guard for the security of a right, which was deemed by them so essential to the freedom and happiness of Americans." He makes the undeniable charge that "*the Sons of Liberty*, are perpetually running counter to the [expressed] sentiments of the *Congress*, in striving to intimidate writers, and printers, and readers, and speakers, and thinkers, on the side of government." Chandler then combines a jab at the Patriots for their apparent inability to answer Loyalist pamphlets with grave and effective criticism of the serious practice of burning Loyalist publications: "One of their ways of confuting pamphlets . . . is by fire and faggot. This proceeds from the same bigotry, and is dictated by the same spirit, which commonly disgraced the dark ages preceding the Reformation."[40] In other words, because they cannot win the argument on the merit of their ideas, they must prevent people from hearing the other side; the result is ignorance.

At this point in his argument, Chandler warns of a danger and expresses a fear that is shared by Inglis. Chandler suggests that if the Sons of Liberty, whom he calls "Sons of Licentiousness," gain the power that they seek and if they discover who certain writers are, "there is reason to believe, that the *writers and their writings* would be both consumed together in the same fire." To show that this is a present, not remote, possibility, he cites "*Holt, in his Journal of November* 24" as reporting that a mob burned a pamphlet "'as it *was thought the* AUTHOR DESERVED *to be treated . . . committed to the flames!*'" This was not an isolated incident. Inglis reported that when his response to Paine's *Common Sense* was advertised for sale, a mob surrounded the printer's house, condemned the pamphlet, and burned all copies of it. Inglis ends his account with his opinion that if they had known that he was the author, he "probably would have shared the same fate as his pamphlet." A similar threat faced the unknown author A. W. Farmer (Samuel Seabury). Copies of his pamphlets were burned and in some cases "tarred, feathered, and nailed to the whipping-post, as an indication of the treatment which their author would receive if he were detected."[41]

Van Tyne observes: "Speaking or writing favorably of Great Britain had its price." One price paid by the writers among the Loyalist ministers was that both the fact that they wrote in opposition to the Patriot cause and the content of the writings became potential charges against them. Much effort was expended to try to discover who wrote offending pamphlets; the authors used pseudonyms largely to avoid persecution. The use of pseudonyms or pen names in political writing was a common practice in eighteenth-century America, but normally it was done so that readers could interact with expressed ideas without being influenced by their personal opinion of the author. Loyalist ministers often wrote under a false name for safety's sake. Inglis explains that he wrote his response to Paine's *Common Sense* at "the Risque not only of my Liberty, but of my Life." When the ironically named Sons of *Liberty* denied him freedom of the press by burning all of the copies of his response, he republished it in Philadelphia, whereupon it was "laid to my Charge, & swelled the Catalogue of my Political Transgressions. In short, I was in the utmost Danger; & it is to the over-ruling Hand of Providence that I attribute my Deliverance & Safety." Other publications added to his "heavy load of guilt" and list of "specific Crimes," including a 1777 letter to the SPG and a 1777 sermon to a Loyalist corps. One of the charges made by the mob against Samuel Peters was "writing articles for the New London newspaper that contained 'a doctrine destructive to the liberties of America'"; and one of the charges against Seabury when held captive in Connecticut was that he had "written pamphlets and newspapers against the liberties of America."[42]

It is worth mentioning again that many of the Loyalist ministers were not blind apologists for the British government and that they expressed agreement in writing with some of the grievances that spawned the American Revolution. The monumental difference between them and the Patriots was that they wanted to redress grievances against the British government peacefully and legally. In addition, they wanted to use their constitutional rights to freedom of speech and the press to persuade their fellow Americans to join them in that peaceful, legal course. For a brief time, they used "polemical writing employing the same medium of highly charged pamphlets that served Whig politicians so well";[43] but they may have been too effective, too persuasive. They only had a brief time, however. The Patriots felt the need to violate the British constitution and their own claim to venerate freedom in order to silence opposition to their cause. Extant published sermons and pamphlets by Loyalist ministers are extremely rare after 1775 and almost nonexistent after 1777 because these ministers were not allowed to preach, presses were not allowed to print their materials, and any sermons or pamphlets that were printed were destroyed whenever found.

In his "Quæres Addressed to the People of Maryland," Jonathan Boucher asks two pertinent questions regarding the suppression of speech and press. First: "On what principles either of justice or common sense, or even of the common ideas of liberty, are the people of this Province, or any individuals thereof, to be restrained from debating on and questioning any public measures, where they are not restrained either by the laws of God or the laws of this land?" Second: "What liberty can the people of this Province be said to enjoy . . . when they no longer have a free press; when the ministers of the Word of God are dictated to and controlled in their holy function and when even the freedom of private debate is overawed by Committee-censures and the denunciation of tar and feathers?"[44]

In *The Political Thought of the American Revolution*, Clinton Rossiter hails the revolutionary Americans' celebration of "that firmest Barrier of English Liberty, THE TRIAL BY JURIES," and he explains that for them, the "right to a jury trial was generally considered to cover all other procedural rights, including 'that great bulwark and palladium of English liberty,' habeas corpus." Rossiter quotes John Adams rhapsodizing at length on the glories of due process of law and its guarantees that a man "can lie under the imputation of no guilt, be subjected to no punishment, lose none of his property" except by the judgment of his peers "who have no end to serve by punishing him" and according to established rules and laws.[45] The Loyalist ministers could only wish that more Patriots had read Adams's words and taken them to heart or that they were as committed to due process for others as they were for themselves.

There are numerous examples of Loyalist ministers who were denied due process of law. Among them, Charles Inglis talks about being identified as "*notoriously disaffected*—an Imputation which had flung others into Jail without any other Crime." John Joachim Zubly was outraged by his treatment by Patriot authorities. He was arrested by a self-appointed body for refusing to take an oath of allegiance to the same Continental Congress of which he had been a member. Declared "an enemy of the state" after a "perfunctory" hearing, the cash-poor revolutionary government in Georgia confiscated his estate and banished him. During his "hearing," Zubly took an oath regarding his innocence and testimony. When that oath was ignored, Zubly writes that "never is the violation of an oath more horrible in itself, or more pernicious to the community, than when it is disregarded by judges, jurors, or evidences, in a court of justice." At that time and in that place, the solemn oath of a gentleman was routinely accepted as strong, if not decisive, evidence. Zubly became an outspoken critic of "self-appointed agents of the people who violated natural and constitutional rights with greater impunity than the British."[46]

Aside from his illegal capture, Samuel Seabury complained about a number of due process violations. He noted that he was a citizen of New York but was "judged by the laws of Connecticut," to which he owed no obedience. He was "deprived of the benefit of those evidences which may be necessary for the vindication of his innocence." He was not given a jury of his peers but "judged by strangers to him, to his character." He was imprisoned illegally. The regulations of the Congress stipulated that he be judged in and by New York. He was charged with signing the White Plains protest, but he pointed out that it simply supported the measures taken by the New York general assembly—the representatives of the people. He was singled out among the more than 300 signers of the document, and because it had taken place eight months earlier, he was denied the right to a speedy trial. The provincial congress of New York had already investigated the fact that he had neglected to open his church on an appointed fast day. Speaking of himself in the third person, Seabury says that "he conceives it to be *cruel, abitrary* [sic], and in the highest degree *unjust*, after his supposed offense has been examined before the proper tribunal, to be dragged like a felon seventy miles from home, and again impeached of the same crime. At this rate of proceeding, should he be acquitted at New Haven, he may be forced seventy miles farther, and so on without end." In other words, he was denied double jeopardy protection. Finally, he argues that nothing he had done was "so repugnant to the regulations of the Congress, as the conduct of those people who in an arbitrary and hostile manner forced him from his house, and have kept him now four weeks a prisoner." Seabury also tried to shame the Connecticut general assembly into releasing him, saying that he was "confident that the supreme legislative authority in this colony will not permit him to be treated in a manner so destructive to that liberty for which they are now contending."[47] Seabury was eventually released, but it took an unusual request from the provincial congress of New York—a benefit that most sufferers for loyalism did not enjoy.

A final example, Jonathan Boucher, took a different, more immediate, and direct approach to protesting violations of due process. Boucher's "supposed inimicality to America" brought him into conflict with the Patriot authorities. He complained about his accusers, "a Papist and two Presbyterians," who might be expected to be prejudiced against him for religious reasons; and he argued that the charges against him were, "as is usual, much exaggerated." When he was brought before the provincial committee in Annapolis, he "protest[ed] against their having any authority over [him]." Where Boucher differs from most, however, is that he appealed directly to the mob. He apparently won them over and reports that the crowd "bawled out aloud" on his behalf and he was "accordingly acquitted." On yet another occasion, when surrounded by a mob, he again addressed "the surrounding multitude" rather than his "particular opponents" and first "excepted against" the Presbyterian leader of the mob "as an improper judge of . . . a minister of the Church of England, to all of whom he was well known to bear a rooted enmity." He then impeached the character of the other leader who had a "private quarrel" with him and offered "to settle with him this moment, as a man of honour ought to settle private differences." The other man "complained of my artifice, and declared he would not be my dupe and let me get off so. The people attributed this to his being afraid of me; and so . . . I again got off."[48] Like Seabury, Boucher was able to get away from serious punishment despite suffering violations of due process. Most were not so fortunate or so charismatic.

In 1774, Seabury declares: "We have so long paid attention to sophistical declamations about liberty and property, the power of government, and the rights of the people, the force of laws and the benefit of the constitution, that we have very little of any of them left among us: And if we continue to support and imitate the mad schemes of our eastern neighbours [New England], . . . in a very short time, we shall have none at all." A year later, Chandler says of the people of New York: "They have been witnesses of a long train of such infamous abuses of, and insults upon, true constitutional Liberty, as they think are unsufferable."[49] Little did these men know, but the abuses of their liberty and the restrictions of their rights were just beginning. As mob rule always does, the suppression and oppression of those who disagreed with the Patriot cause brought out the worst in human nature.

Jonathan Boucher addresses the nascent ill treatment of Loyalists in his

"Farewell Sermon" in 1775: "The literal import of the word *persecution* is the being made to suffer undeservedly: and therefore, though coercion, rigour and severity may sometimes perhaps be inflicted without blame, persecution never can." Persecution—there was no other word for what the Loyalists had begun to experience and for what they would suffer for the next eight years of revolution at the hands of those who held strongly to a differing political view. Boucher then directly addresses "those persons in the community, who, either through passion and prejudice, or through mistaken principles of policy, pursue with such unrelenting rigour those of their brethren who cannot adopt or even approve of all their measures." He admonishes them that "for one party to persecute another, merely because of a difference of opinion, is a crime," and he appeals to their sense of shame: "A good cause should disdain the aid of so unworthy an ally as Persecution." In the spirit of Roger Williams, Boucher reminds his congregation that "no man was ever made a convert to any opinion by compulsion" and that the most coercion can accomplish is to "make men seem to acquiesce, whether they really do or no, merely in the hope of being permitted to be safe."[50]

Perhaps because it was so early in the conflict, and perhaps because Boucher wished to believe the best about his fellow Americans, he appears to proceed under the assumption that the Patriots were trying to persuade Loyalists. If it was not already apparent, it soon became clear that the primary goal of the Patriots was to silence the Loyalists, not convert them. What was already clear to Boucher was the hypocrisy and inconsistency of the Patriots' denial of liberty to the Loyalists: "How contrary all this is to all that liberty which Whigs for ever are so forward to profess." In the middle of the war, Seabury blasts the Patriots for "treading under Foot the Dictates of Humanity and the Rights of their Fellow Subjects" and for "introducing the most horrid Oppression and Tyranny." Late in the war, in his open letter to the people of America, Inglis offers as a contrast the liberty offered by Britain: "Her constitution insures real, substantial liberty to every subject—all are under the protection of equal laws—none are exposed to the caprice of arbitrary will—the property and person, the civil and religious liberties of every man are perfectly secure."[51]

It is important to note Boucher's concession that "coercion, rigour and severity may sometimes perhaps be inflicted without blame." A case might be made for some of the actions, tactics, and methods practiced by the Patriots as a means by which a government might need to protect itself against insurrection or rebellion. One might point to Abraham Lincoln's actions at the start of the Civil War or to the Constitution's provision for suspension of the writ of habeas corpus, or even to the passage of the Patriot Act after the September 11, 2001, terrorist attack on America. That argument might be made to excuse some of the British army's excesses in putting down the revolt. Such an argument for the Americans breaks down, however, when one remembers that the Patriots were not the government protecting itself against rebels—they *were* the rebels. They were not Lincoln putting down an insurrection—they were the insurrectionists. They were not Congress and the president giving law enforcement agencies tools to prevent violence and vandalism—they were the ones committing violence and vandalism. The Patriots were not the legal authority, but an extralegal, self-appointed power. Furthermore, in these other examples, the government acted to protect itself from acts, not words. Unlike the Patriots, the governments in these other cases did not use their power to silence opposing viewpoints or to shut down churches or control liturgy or forbid law-abiding preachers to preach. Whatever one's view of the Revolution, it is difficult to put on a friendly gloss or make excuse for the oppressive actions taken by the Patriots against the Loyalist ministers.

A statement by Seabury to a group of Loyalists who eventually volunteered as provincial soldiers summarizes well the Loyalist position: "How we have been oppressed and harrassed by Congresses, Committees and Banditties of armed Men, none of you can be ignorant. The cruel Effects of their lawless Tyranny many of you yet feel in the Distress of your Families, the Destruction of your Property, the Imprisonment of your Friends, and the Banishment of your Persons from your formerly peaceful and quiet Dwellings.—These are the *proper*, the *genuine* Fruits of Rebellion."[52] As upset as the Loyalist ministers were about their treatment at the hands of the Patriots—and the hypocrisy of the Patriots in crying for liberty while denying it to Loyalists—the crux of their argument and the theme that united them was, of course, opposition to the Revolution itself.

The Revolution

Most of the Loyalist clergymen opposed the Continental Congresses in principle, opposed their inaction with regard to conciliation, opposed their actions in imposing the three "nons," and opposed creating the oppressive committee system. Ultimately, though, *all* of them opposed the movement by Congress toward independence and rebellion. All of them opposed the Declaration of Independence and the armed confrontations supported by

Congress that resulted in the war. Although some have been described as Whig-Loyalists for adhering to Whig ideas and defending Patriot actions throughout much of the period, they all drew the line at taking up arms against Great Britain and seeking to separate from it. Furthermore, all took the side of the British and hoped and prayed for British victory once the fighting began. They joined Boucher in fully expecting a British victory: "War is an appeal to God: those, therefore, who engage in an unjust war, appeal to God in an unjust cause: and hence it is natural and rational to expect that God should take part against them, and award the victory to that party which has the most justice on it's [sic] side."[53] In their view, the side with the most justice clearly was Great Britain.

The Patriots, of course, thought that justice was on their side. As they envisioned the situation, they were not rebelling but merely defending themselves against tyranny and unjust treatment. The Loyalist ministers would have none of that. In his sermon on Joshua 22, delivered at the very beginning of the conflict in 1775, Boucher argues that like the Israelite tribes beyond the Jordan, Americans had taken provocative actions that should reasonably be interpreted as rebellion. He contends that "these *wars and rumours of wars*, at least on the part of the Parent State, are justified by our conduct. The altar that we have erected, or are about to erect, we choose indeed to call an altar of Liberty: but, whatever it's [sic] name be, it's [sic] object too clearly is to counteract and resist, if not directly to deny, the supremacy of the Mother Country." Unlike the innocent trans-Jordan tribes, the intention of the American "altar" has not been misinterpreted. Rather, he says, "our principle in setting it up at all, is to declare ourselves, in some sense, and to some degree, a separate and independent people; whereas, to have done so would, in their estimation, have been *rebellion*." In the American case, then, it is clearly an act of rebellion. Boucher explains that "to say that rebellion is not rebellion, is no more in my power than it is to *call bitter sweet, and sweet bitter*" (Isaiah 5:20).[54]

For the Loyalist ministers, professions of loyalty to the king and claims of legal injustices done by Parliament do not remove the stain of rebellion. "The question wherein Rebellion consists can never be agitated with apparently greater disadvantage than in a time when opposite parties struggle to the utmost to fix or ward off the odious appellation." For his part, Chandler argues that "all violent opposition to lawful authority partakes of the nature of rebellion." He warns "all reasonable Americans" that "the time cannot be distant, in which both you and they ['New-England fanaticks'] will be legally proclaimed *Rebels* and *Traitors*—they as principals, and you as their abettors. You may still profess yourselves to be his *Majesty's most dutiful and loyal subjects*, as you did in your late RESOLVES, . . . but this will not skreen [sic] you from vengeance." He believes that "the grievances in question, supposing them to be real, are, at most, no more than a just ground for decent remonstrance, but not a sufficient reason for forcible resistance." In his discussion of what constitutes just causes for war, Zubly concludes: "What may justify a war against a different nation may not even be a plausible pretence for taking up arms against our own sovereign." "The case is far different in subjects taking up arms against their prince. What may justify independent established powers subjects cannot make use of even as a plea." Even if the claims of the Patriots are true, "very great evils and just complaints grow small and unworthy of the resentment they might otherwise deserve, where the evils produced by an intestine war for redress are thrown into the opposite scale of the balance."[55] The potential horrors of civil war far outweigh any of the Patriot complaints—many of which Zubly shares.

Chandler also warns that whether or not the colonies consider themselves under the authority of England, "it is certain that Great-Britain claims a jurisdiction over the colonies *as a part of its realm*, and will consider the same actions to be *treason* here which are *treason* in England; and there can be no doubt but that a war levied against the King by any of *his subjects*, whether in Europe or America, will be treated as equally criminal." In order to drive that point home and to link it with specific American actions, Chandler quotes several sections of the Suffolk Resolves, followed by this summary of its main points:

> First, a DECLARATION OF INDEPENDENCY . . . asserting that *no obedience is due* from them to any *acts of Parliaments*, which they disapprove of. *Secondly*, an EDICT, to shut up the courts of justice. . . . *Thirdly*, a PROSCRIPTION, of all that do not resign their commissions held under the authority aforesaid, as *obstinate and incorrigible enemies*. . . . *Fourthly*, a PROCLAMATION, that officers be forthwith appointed by the people, to supersede those that are appointed by the Crown. *Fifthly*, an ORDER, issued to their own officers and people to *arm* themselves, and *learn the art of war*, to qualify them to fight against their LAWFUL SOVEREIGN. And, *Sixthly*, a DECREE, for seizing and throwing into confinement . . . every person in the province who is thought worthy of confidence by the crown [as hostages to trade].[56]

Chandler's conclusion from these provocative, criminal, and arguably treasonable acts is: "If all this does not amount to an open revolt and rebellion, I have always mistaken the meaning of the word." The treasonous and rebellious nature of the Suffolk Resolves is not confined to Suffolk County because by officially approving them, "the Congress have, in reality, given their sanction to the rebellion that has begun in the county of *Suffolk*." Seabury is similarly displeased with the situation created by the Congress's action: "This is the wretched state to which your adored Congress have reduced us. . . . No alternative is left us, but either to renounce their measures, or to plunge head-long into rebellion and civil war." He refers to the impending conflict as "the worst kind of war—a civil war . . . founded on rebellion." In the midst of the Revolution, Seabury calls those who "have excited, and still support and carry on, the present Rebellion" wicked and criminal. Looking back on the start of the conflict five years later, Zubly suggests that the Patriots knew all along what they were really doing: "It was the universal and professed maxim of that day, '*if we succeed it will be called a Revolution, and deemed a Rebellion if we miscarry*.'"[57]

If successful, it would be called a revolution—but would it be successful? The Loyalist clergymen disagree somewhat about the role of the people in the coming conflict, but their analysis appears to change over time. In 1774, Chandler says of some Americans that "there is too much reason to believe, that our minds are unprincipled, and our hearts disposed for rebellion. Ever since the reduction of *Canada*, we have been bloated with a vain opinion of our own power and importance." However, he does not think that this applies to a majority of Americans. On the contrary, he argues that many Loyalists will fight for the king if it comes to civil war and that Loyalists will constitute a "formidable" force. Not only that but "it is morally certain that, in the day of trial, a large majority of the Americans will heartily unite with the King's troops, in reducing *America* to order."[58] Chandler was wrong, of course, perhaps underestimating the combined power of propaganda and intimidation.

Boucher makes similar claims in 1774, but by 1775, he recognizes the impact of the manipulation of the public. In 1774, he affirms "on as good evidence as the case admits of, that the people of America do not desire a separation: and that a very large number (we think, a majority) do now, and ever will, regard a revolt from Great Britain as the greatest evil and heaviest calamity that can possibly befal [sic] us." By 1775, however, Boucher sees a different spirit among the people and offers a couple of reasons for the new reality. First, he claims that mankind "have everywhere and always been prone to be refractory, and to oppose power," and that this is "more especially the case with those parts of the community that are at a distance from the seat of government, such as colonies." He even suggests that "a principle of revolt seems to be interwoven" in "the very frame" of colonies. This was true in the days of ancient Israel, and it is true in the eighteenth-century American colonies. By Boucher's account, the minds of the colonists are "very generally unsettled and ill-disposed towards the government." Second, he believes that "an evil spirit of discontent, clamour, and refractoriness, seems to have gone forth among us; disposing us to object to, and quarrel with, every thing that has been long established." In 1775, he expresses an expectation that a sizable portion of the American colonists will join the fight with those who take part in the revolution in pursuit of their own interest. He reminds his congregation that the battle for the support of the people is critical because the people are "always of the greatest weight in all violent revolutions."[59] Boucher's optimism concerning the battle for the hearts and minds of the people turned to pessimism between 1774 and 1775.

The War

There is no disagreement at any time among the Loyalist clergy as to the outcome of a war between Great Britain and its colonies in America. From their earliest writings to their last, they all think it inevitable that the mother country will prevail, and they also think that "a rebellion of the Colonies, whether it should prove successful or unsuccessful, would necessarily terminate in ruin and destruction." This, they believe, is another exceedingly important reason not to go to war to begin with. In addition to all of the theoretical, biblical, and legal arguments, it will not work from a practical perspective. In 1775, Boucher is confident that the colonists will either be defeated or "defeat themselves," adding: "One of which, I think, there is little Hazard in declaring must be the Case." He later identifies as a potential cause of self-defeat "the Principles of Disunion, which . . . prevail in the confederated Colonies." As for being defeated, Boucher warns before the war of "the uncertain Events of a War, against all Odds, against Invasions from Canada, Incursions of Savages, Revolt of Slaves, multiplied Fleets and Armies, a War which must begin where Wars commonly end, in the Ruin of our Trade, in the Surrender of our Ports and Capitals, in the Misery of Thousands." He warns that it is foolhardy to fight over "political Problems, Distinctions, Refinements . . . lest while we deny the Mother Country, every

Mode, every Right of Taxation, we give her the Rights of Conquest."[60] Whatever the current grievances, things will be much worse when America is conquered—and Boucher thought that conquest to be inevitable.

In pamphlets written during the first two years of war, Chandler states what the Loyalists thought obvious: "The strongest must conquer." He offers a recent historical example to support the idea that Britain is the strongest. During the Seven Years' War, "the colonies were unable to withstand the militia of *Canada*, supported by a few regiments of regular troops from *France*," as many "authentic documents of that period" show. He concludes: "There is no room to doubt but such an army as was employed in the reduction of Canada would be more than sufficient for the conquest of all the disaffected American Colonies." This is demonstrably true because the colonies "are open and accessible on every quarter, and have not a single fortress to cover them; and they are without military stores, without magazines, and without the skill that is necessary for supporting an army."[61] At the beginning of the conflict, all evidence did point toward a British victory, and there was every reason for Loyalists to be confident in that seemingly inevitable outcome.

In early 1776, just before the announcement of the Declaration of Independence, Charles Inglis cautions that "Britain has not exerted her power." He argues that England has plenty of power but has held back to seek accommodation. "But as soon as we declare for Independency, every prospect of this kind must vanish. Ruthless war, with all its aggravated horrors, will ravage our once happy land—our sea-coasts and ports will be ruined, and our ships taken. Torrents of blood will be spilt, and thousands reduced to beggary and wretchedness."[62]

Late in the war, the Loyalists were no less confident. They simply could not believe that the often demonstrated power of the British army and navy could be defeated by colonials. They chose rather to believe that England had been withholding its might out of reticence to crush their wayward countrymen. In a letter to the people of America late in the war, Inglis tries to discourage false hopes and to explain why the rebellion had not already been put down. Toward that end, he declares: "Independency is UNATTAINABLE. Britain is *determined* to assert her just claim to her American colonies, and she is able to carry her determination and claim into execution." He claims that "she will contend as earnestly for her American colonies, as she would for any county in England, were it invaded." In response to the claim that the prolongation of the conflict indicates that the Americans had a chance to succeed, Inglis explains away such evidence: "Britain is slow in her operations at the beginning of every war, and often unsuccessful. The freedom of her constitution subjects her to this inconvenience." What appears at first to be a weakness makes her stronger in the long run. "That Freedom, from which embarrassments arise at first, enables her, when thoroughly roused, to exert a vigour which the dastard sons of servitude can neither attain nor withstand."[63] In other words, it is hard for a constitutional monarchy to decide to go to war and to mobilize for war, but her record shows that once she does, Britain ultimately prevails.

Inglis makes a similar argument directly to the president of the Congress. Speaking of England's ability to prevail, Inglis asserts: "Never at any period was her commerce more flourishing, her wealth greater, her fleets so formidable, or her armies more gallant or numerous. Your deceit and specious pretences indeed divided her councils for a time; and this, with the mild spirit of her government, has protracted your usurpation beyond all rational expectation." Again, the delay in crushing the rebels is attributed to the British form of government, in particular the support for the Americans in Parliament. But now, Inglis ominously proclaims: "The strength of Britain will be no longer shackled or restrained; and when let loose, you will find her lenity, not your own resources or power, prevented this most detestable and wanton rebellion from being long since crushed." The only concern on this account comes from Boucher, who expresses concern in 1776 that the British acting too slowly and with too little force will "tempt the Rebels to continue in Arms."[64] It did.

It seemed obvious to Loyalist clergymen that there were a number of reasons that the deck was stacked against the Americans and in favor of England. Seabury, Chandler, and Inglis express wonder at how a colonial military force would be paid and supplied. Seabury suggests that the colonies do not have the resources "to pay, to cloath [sic], arm, feed" the number of soldiers necessary to fight the Revolution. Given the Patriots' aversion to taxation, he also asks: "Who are to levy the taxes necessary to defray the expence of these articles?" Chandler suggests that American soldiers would not be "punctually paid," that their view of and response to authority would make military discipline impossible, and that it would be impossible to feed a large enough army. Inglis argues that American paper currency is the primary financial support for the rebellion and declares its credit to be "irretrievably lost." Furthermore, "France cannot, Holland or Spain will not lend you money."[65]

Inglis also highlights problems with recruitment and morale. America is "thinned of its inhabitants. *Seventy thousand men*, and those generally the most useful and industrious [Loyalists] are already swept away." "Those that remain, are harrassed [sic] with perpetual musters, and called from their necessary labour to attend the operations of war." After several years of war, "the first enthusiastic zeal for revolt . . . is subsided, even among your partizans [sic]." Very few are now willing to enlist "even for a few months." Those that do enlist are attracted by "exorbitant premiums" and "artful falsehoods—such as accounts of victories never obtained—public rejoicings for those victories—great and good news from Europe, altogether fictitious—loans, fleets and armies coming over, which never had an existence, &c. &c." In addition, the "yoke" of the Congress and its heavy-handed policies has been "galling" and its "tyranny" "detested by the colonists." The end result is that in the army, "distrust and disaffection prevail." Another problem for soldiers and military morale is that "altho' they compel you to be enrolled as militia, and this subjects you to all the penalties of rebellion; yet they will not redeem you from captivity, nor exchange you. . . . They oblige you to take arms against your rightful Sovereign; yet you must expect no relief from them when suffering for that crime." Inglis charges that the Congress "undervalued" American soldiers when discussing prisoner exchanges, refusing to exchange a British or German soldier one for one for Americans. He alleges that Congress would rather have the money sent for the support of British prisoners and have the prisoners as "pledges of security for their own precious persons" than to free Americans held prisoner.[66]

Another distinct disadvantage for the Americans was their poor relations with the Indians. Inglis accuses the Congress of "using every method in your power" to get various Indian tribes to fight against England, all the while complaining that England was using the Indians against them. Consequently, some tribes had been "perverted from loyalty, joined you [Americans], and have fought your battles." According to Inglis, Congress "did this, when government actually restrained the savages, and would not employ them." Now, however, "it is become absolutely necessary for government to employ the Indians; and employed they *will* be. You have imposed this disagreeable necessity on the Parent State." He says that enough Indians will be "brought on your frontiers" to occupy "all the forces you can muster." The result, warns Inglis, will be as horrific as Americans had feared: "You have cut off numbers of the Indians, you have destroyed their houses and settlements, because they would not take up the hatchet to support your rebellion. This will naturally stimulate them to revenge, and all the consequent horrors must be laid to your charge."[67]

Inglis points out one other serious disadvantage for the Americans: their dependence on help from European powers. Just after the announcement of the Declaration of Independence, Inglis suggests that it will not have its desired effect of drawing France and other European nations into alliance with America. On the contrary, says Inglis: "I think it infinitely more likely that it will produce a coalition or treaty between the several European nations, who have settlements in America, to guarantee and secure their respective settlements to each other; than that any of these nations will co-operate with our design, and thereby lend a hand to injure themselves." In other words, nations will work together to secure their own interests in a time of turmoil and dislocation. He also says that he has inside knowledge from a reliable source that France and Spain had already offered their assistance to Great Britain. Whether that is true or not, Inglis sees an alliance with France as an exceedingly dangerous venture: "Indeed were France ever so willing and able to assist us, the experiment would be imprudent in us, and hazardous to the highest degree. There is scarcely an instance recorded in history of Foreigners being called in to assist in domestic quarrels, that it did not prove ruinous to those that sought their aid." He then illustrates this point with two pages of historical examples.[68]

Contrary to Inglis's prediction and his source, France joined in an alliance with the Americans two years later. A year after that, Inglis still views the alliance as a bad thing for the American cause. First, he warns the Congress that, given her track record, France would break her treaty with America "if she could gain by it." He cautions that France entered the alliance "to serve her own ambitious purposes" and not "from affection to you or to the rights of mankind." Furthermore, by "duplicity, intrigue, perfidy and violence, France has gained more provinces in Europe than you had to bestow in America; and she gained them without a claim half so plausible as you gave her to the *Thirteen United States*." Inglis suggests that France will use the alliance to take over the colonies. Once French forces enter America, what is the guarantee that they will leave after the Revolution is won? Second, he advises the Congress not to expect Britain to be diverted by war with France into neglecting America. The British will keep their eye on the American prize. Third, he suggests that the French will not actually provide significant assistance to the Americans. Rather, the French alliance will "be of no advantage, but dangerous and disgraceful in the highest degree." In sum, says Inglis: "With all the infamy of a French faction, yet without French assistance, you must struggle against your 'gigantic adversary'; who, besides superior strength, has might and justice on his side, and the cause of liberty and the protestant religion to animate his exertions."[69] Inglis, like all of the Loyalist clergymen, expects a British victory in the war.

The Cost of Revolution

Another theme among the Loyalist ministers is the tremendous cost of the American Revolution. They measured this cost in terms of money, lives, property, and effects on souls. Writing in 1774 before the conflict began, Chandler compares the cost of simply protesting the actions of Parliament with the tax burden imposed by Parliament. He suggests that the "neglect of business" to engage in protest efforts has been "a greater expence to the *Americans* . . . than all the duties with which the parliament would probably charge us, would amount to in fifty years." He also warns that if the Americans cause trouble, then Parliament will take costly steps to ensure compliance and asks whether "an effectual support of the authority of parliament, . . . [can] be supposed to have so light an effect upon the property of *Americans*, as the small duty upon tea, if quietly submitted to, necessarily would have?" If Parliament must spend money to enforce its laws, then the cost would naturally be passed on to the colonists who made the added expense necessary. Also writing before the fighting started, Seabury looks ahead to the end of a war and the results of an inevitable British victory. When that happens, says Seabury, "we shall oblige Great-Britain to do the very thing that we are endeavouring . . . to *prevent*. We shall oblige her to raise a revenue upon us to support an army, to retain us in our dependence on her *imperial authority*."[70]

Charles Inglis spends quite a bit of ink on the cost of the Revolution—and he does so in the midst of the war. Consequently, his analysis is far less theoretical and is supported by experience and observation. In 1777, Inglis reports: "Dark and gloomy are the Scenes which surround us; and every benevolent Heart must be penetrated on considering the wide spread Ruin that overwhelms this Continent! . . . Who but must grieve still more at the complicated Distresses that are hereby brought on thousands of innocent Persons—whose Support, whose earthly Happiness and Comfort, are all swept away by the ruthless Hand of Rebellion!" His emphasis here is on the devastation and ruin of property. A few years later, in 1780, Inglis laments the effects of rebellion on the souls of men, what he calls "the horrid Train of Evils which follow Rebellion." These costs include deceit, violence, perjury, blood, distress, misery, and ruin. He says that "dark, malevolent

Passions of the Soul are roused and exerted; its mild and amiable affections are suppressed ... virtuous Principles are laid prostrate"; and that personal revenge, animosity, and rage reign in the souls of too many.[71]

In that same sermon, Inglis spotlights the human cost paid by the Loyalists:

> Thousands have perished by the Sword, and by the Calamities of War—thousands are driven from their once peaceful Abodes, stript [sic] of their Property, and exposed to Misery and Want, on Account of their Loyalty. The Land is polluted with innocent Blood—with the Blood of those who, from a Principle of Conscience, adhered to their rightful Sovereign; and rather than renounce Him, or bear Arms against Him, have submitted to Death.[72]

In addition to the suffering of the Loyalists, America itself has also paid a cost in the treatment of the Loyalists: the land is "polluted with innocent Blood." Inglis further points to what he believes will be a future price paid by America. He says: "They [the 'Leaders of Rebellion'] have leagued with the Popish, inveterate Enemies of our Nation, of our Religion and Liberties—they have virtually, and as far as in them lay, delivered this Country into the Hands of a despotic Power—a Power which has extinguished Liberty, and extirpated the Protestant Religion from all its Dominions."[73] That power is France, and he repeats his concern that, should the Americans actually win the war, they will lose the peace by losing their freedom to the French.

In one of his letters to John Jay, the president of the Congress, Inglis amplifies and develops the matter of the costs of the Revolution. He revisits the effects on lives, property, and morals; and he attempts to calculate the monetary cost in terms of economics and finances. In enumerating the "complicated miseries" caused by the Revolution, he includes

> discord, animosity and inhuman murders. Commerce is ruined, industry and useful arts are drooping, and nearly extinguished. Scenes of desolation—of the deepest distress are every where to be seen. Thousands who lived in ease and affluence are reduced to the lowest ebb of poverty; or banished from their once happy and peaceful habitations. The orphan's and the widow's tears are mingled with those of afflicted parents, for their respective relatives, cut off by the destroying sword. . . . Subject warring against fellow subject; . . .

parent and child, brother and brother stand forth to shed each other's blood.[74]

To be clear about who is to blame, Inglis declares to the head of the Congress: "These, Sir, are the fruits of your ambition! These the effects of your usurpation!" He then addresses "the malignant effects of your rebellion on the morals of the people—Your horrid prostitution of oaths—Compelling men to abjure their rightful Sovereign, and swear allegiance to you, contrary to the dictates of conscience, or else be deprived of all their property or hanged." He suggests that a "more effectual method perhaps could not be devised to extinguish all sense of duty and obligation, unhinge society, and make mankind a set of unprincipled villains."[75] According to Inglis, the American Revolution had been a disaster in many ways, including morally.

After reiterating the human and moral cost, Inglis engages in an interesting attempt to put a monetary price tag on the Revolution. He tries to reduce everything to numbers and calculate the total amount of money lost due to the war and the policies of the Congress. It should be noted that he made these calculations as of 1779. He begins with the number who have died or permanently left America; he puts this number at 70,000 and calculates the monetary loss to America as 4,900,000 pounds sterling. Another part of the human cost is the loss of immigration since the rebellion began, which he places at 16,000 potential inhabitants. This loss to America he sets at £1,120,000. Turning to the debt run up by the Congress, he estimates that they had spent $200 million ("for which you have mortgaged every estate in America")—roughly £45,000,000—and also borrowed £4,000,000 from France. He estimates that at least 5,500 houses had been destroyed, valued at £520,000. Other losses include "cattle and flocks" (£200,000); "injury to farms" (£150,000); and "negroes" lost (£25,000).[76]

In the last few pages of this accounting, Inglis abandons efforts to assign precise monetary values and instead makes summarizing statements. He reminds Jay: "By a decree of your Congress, all exports from the thirteen revolted colonies, were stopped in September 1775. . . . The exports for that period, should therefore be accounted as lost to America." Anticipating the argument that trade with France and the West Indies were exempted from the ban on exports, Inglis argues that trade with those two partners had been "very trifling" and mostly for "ammunition, arms, cannon and military stores, which are of no use to the farmers of America." Furthermore, the "few beneficial articles imported, such as cloathing [sic], sugars, &c. sold

... sometimes at *five hundred per cent.*—but oftenest at *five thousand per cent.*" Also lost were "the loss of shipping, of interest upon money, of the labour of those who were employed in your armies, and the decrease in value of lands, without any advances towards settling the western wilderness." In light of all of these things, Inglis concludes that the prohibition on exports had one of the most "extensive and pernicious" effects. Inglis ultimately computes the total loss for America of £66,503,960 plus £22,500,000 for "emissions of paper money," for a grand total of £89,003,960—all of this lost, he says, "For the sake of overturning the best of civil constitutions! For the sake of a nominal independency, which, if established, would be more destructive to this continent, for ages to come, than even the present rebellion has been! For sake of a ruinous alliance with France, the enemy of liberty and protestantism."[77]

France

The alliance with France was an important subject for the two Loyalist ministers who were able to write and publish after the alliance was made. Because "popery" and concerns about the expansion and toleration of Catholicism were among the expressed causes of the Revolution, and because France was a historic and perpetual enemy of England—and the American colonists were Englishmen—no one could have predicted such a development. Consequently, the earlier sermons and pamphlets did not address it. For Charles Inglis and John Joachim Zubly, however, it was a significant problem. It was almost inconceivable to Zubly, a Presbyterian Calvinist from Switzerland, that the American leadership would make an alliance with the imperialist Roman Catholic power. Zubly's criticism is equal parts denunciation of French diplomatic history and scathing criticism of those American leaders who trusted them in the face of that history. He refers to France as "a power the most remarkable for despotism and oppression of any in Europe," and he supplies a recent example of French duplicity in taking over an erstwhile ally. Referring to that example, Zubly sneers: "One would think this transaction, which happened while the American Congress was sitting, would not have encouraged them to fly to France; but so it is that they did, and on the very prince who thus treated the poor Corsicans they have bestowed the title of '*Protector of the Rights of Mankind,*' with the same propriety . . . that the Pope stiles a King of England the Defender of the Popish Faith."[78] In other words, the French king is as much a defender of human rights as the Protestant English king is Catholic.

Zubly is particularly upset with the agreement between the Americans and French not to make a peace without the other. He asks whether it is "a just and lawful plea against generous offers of peace, that they cannot be accepted because those to whom they were made called in a perfidious power [France] to support their opposition against their natural sovereign." He then suggests that the French will use this to their own advantage to refuse reasonable terms of peace, keep the war going, and achieve dominance over America. They have a history of breaking "every tie sacred among men, to reap an advantage from the rebellion" of their ally's subjects. Excoriating the American leadership for its stupidity or naivete, Zubly declares: "They have bargained and sold their country and dupes to France, and wish now, with the assistance of that arbitrary perfidious power, to seize, deliver, and make good the bargain." He indicts them for mortgaging their independence to France "and stupidly inviting that very power to foreclose every method of redemption."[79]

In his letters to John Jay, Inglis is also highly critical of the agreement not to make separate peace and says that the French prime minister "bullied" the Congress into making the deal. He too points to France's track record in international affairs and charges that France "is now playing the same game in America that she played a thousand times before in Europe." Because the Americans cannot make peace or even a truce "*without the formal consent of France,*" they are in "such a state of thraldom to France, what can remain of any value?" Inglis dwells on the glaring inconsistency of being unable to make a truce or peace with "their rightful sovereign" without the formal consent of the French king. "So that whatever overtures are made by Britain to the colonies, however beneficial or honourable to them, it matters not. As long as it suits the ambition, caprice, interest or policy of France, so long must the colonists wage war with their brethern [sic], and embrue [sic] their hands in kindred blood, even although the utter destruction of both should be the inevitable consequence!" Inglis's conclusion is that America has become a vassal of France. In response to the claim that France "is equally bound with the colonies," Inglis argues that France is not in a state of revolt, is not dependent on any other power, and has great resources, and that none of her subjects are "disaffected." He says that the only similarity between France and the Congress is despotism in governing—a bitter shot at Patriot governance.[80] His primary point in comparing the two is that France can afford to carry on this war indefinitely; America cannot.

Inglis follows with more reasons that the Americans cannot continue to fight for long. He says that they are in revolt, which "depresses your spirits"; the alliance with France shows dependence; "the wretched state of your paper currency" shows financial weakness; and "you cannot raise an army without *compelling* those to take arms who should cultivate the earth," which will result in famine. Building on the theme that France cannot be trusted, Inglis warns Jay: "Your weakness compelled you to fly for succour to France; and the longer the war continues, you must grow proportionably weaker, and more dependent on her; and this dependence will give her an intire [sic] ascendency [sic] and power over you." Because, Inglis explains, Congress has "contracted a large debt to France" and "MORTGAGED this country for that debt," it will be in France's interest to continue the war for as long as possible to increase the debt. In the end, the French king will be "Lord Paramount and Proprietor of North-America" and Americans will be vassals of France.[81]

Inglis also attacks the "palpable contradiction" and "inconsistency" of making such an alliance with France when an "alledged [sic] cause for your entering into this rebellion was the legal toleration of Popery in Canada." He questions the validity of that supposed cause because the Congress had offered "a compleat [sic] establishment" of Catholicism in Canada if they would join in the rebellion. Indeed, Inglis draws attention to the fact that in *Observations on the American Revolution*, sponsored by the Congress in 1779, the usual complaint about the British allowing popery in Canada is omitted. Drawing on Roman Catholic imagery, Inglis accuses Jay, as president, of "offering incense to, and throwing yourselves at the feet of, that insidious crown [France] which has extinguished liberty, and extirpated the protestant religion in all its territories" while "impiously plotting the ruin of your parent state, where more liberty exists than in any other state in christendom, and which is the principal support of the protestant religion!"[82]

In his open letter to the people of America, Inglis focuses on the potential danger of French influence and French control. He stresses the danger to American liberty and to Protestantism. He asks the people to consider that if the colonies are weak now and need French help, "what will the case be when they are still weaker and more exhausted than they are at present?" In a powerful emotional appeal, Inglis tells the people that the agreement with France means "that you and your brethren must continue butchering each other, till it suits the interest and policy of France to bid you stop." Turning to religion, Inglis calls the agreement "malignant" with regard to Protestantism and declares that "the door is thrown wide open to receive popery." The Patriots used the threat of popery to rouse support for the Revolution; Inglis now uses it to try to turn the people against the Revolution. Just because a Catholic state is an ally, Inglis asks, "is popery then changed? Is it purged from error and become less persecuting? No—it is now the very same as formerly." He suggests that all protestants should be "greatly and justly alarmed" at the accommodations being made for Catholicism. The Congress, he says, "will not permit a word to be said to the disadvantage of popery," and he relates anecdotes of New Englanders who used to be zealously anti-Catholic and who used to argue vociferously against Catholic doctrines, but who now say they see "*nothing amiss or erroneous in them.*"[83]

For his final proof of the encroachment of Catholicism under the Patriots, he quotes from a Philadelphia newspaper account of the third anniversary of independence: "President [Jay], and honourable Members of Congress attended divine worship in the forenoon" and at noon, "went, by invitation from the Honourable Minister of France, to the Roman Catholic chapel, where the great event was celebrated by a well adapted discourse pronounced by the Minister's Chaplain; and Mass and *Te Deum* solemnly sung." Inglis reminds his readers that "CHARLES I was called a *Papist* for permitting his Queen, who was bred a Roman Catholic, to attend mass: What are we to think of the American rulers, who not only permit their wives to attend mass, but attend it themselves in person! And offer up their *devout* orisons in the language, service and worship of Rome!"[84] Inglis expresses great concern that now that the French have their foot in the American door, both France and Roman Catholicism will have a profound influence in an independent United States of America.

Independence

As might be expected, nearly every Loyalist minister addressed the possibility and problems of American independence from Great Britain. Some of the discussion is argumentative and condescending. Inglis refers to "Independency, that Foible of weak Minds tinctured with local Pride," and Seabury uses sarcasm in referring to the "*grand* Congress" and "the piddling Committees" claiming "an absolute independency." Some of the discussion is couched in theoretical, almost wistful, terms. Zubly, for example, pleads: "Let *Britain* and *British America* ever be like one heart and one soul; he that would divide them, *anathema sit*, let him be held accursed by both." He says that the "idea of a separation between America and Great-Britain is big with so many and such horrid evils, that every friend to both must shudder at the thought." He urges "all wise men and all good men" to "speak, write and act against it." To his mind, anyone that supports such an idea "ought instantly to be suspected as a common enemy." Boucher appeals to Thomas Hobbes, a source not commonly cited in the Revolutionary period, to argue that every individual must express a desire to separate in order for such a separation to be justified; the majority cannot make that decision. Zubly likewise questions the authority of representatives to make such a decision for the people. He declares that "those Delegates who voted for independency, without express orders from their constituents, were traitors of their country," and he refers to the signers of the Declaration of Independence as "the blacklist of those who have been the bane of their country and disgrace of their species."[85]

It must be remembered that Zubly was an outspoken critic of Parliament's policies—so much so that he was chosen to be a member of the Second Continental Congress. He was a Whig until it came to the point of rebellion and independence. In his sermon to the delegates to Georgia's Second Provincial Congress, Zubly implores them: "Never let us loose [sic] out of sight that our interest lies in a perpetual connection with our mother country. Notwithstanding the present unwise and harsh measures, . . . let us convince our enemies that the struggles of America have not their rise in a desire of independency, but from a warm regard to our common constitution." Inglis urges remembrance of that constitution and obligations to it that were expressed right up to the signing of the Declaration. He reveals that several persons—"some of high rank"—expressed opposition to independence in 1776 and said they would take up arms against the Congress if they declared it. But they stuck with the Congress after independence was declared because they thought it would be "a breach of honour to desert the Congress." Inglis asks: "Could honour oblige these men to act against the conviction of their judgment, and violate the most sacred obligations? Was not their honour previously engaged to support the just rights of their Sovereign, and the interests of their country? . . . And was not their veracity, as well as duty engaged to oppose independency, which would prove ruinous to millions? Did not the *breach of honour* rather consist in the violation of these?"[86]

Most of the criticism of the prospect of independence centers on practical, material concerns. In his response to *Common Sense*, Inglis complains that Paine mentions evils that America will suffer from continued connection with England but "cautiously avoids any mention of the numberless evils and calamities which we must infallibly suffer by breaking it off." Inglis and the other Loyalist ministers fill that gap. As they see it, many detriments and dangers will come from outside—from other countries. Chandler expresses a common concern: "Should it be known abroad that *Great-Britain* had withdrawn her protection, and would no longer interest herself in our preservation and safety; within the compass of one year our sea-ports would be ravaged, and our vessels plundered or seized as soon as they left our harbours." The colonies would have to seek out the protection "of some maritime power" and would have to "pay dearly" for the protection of their ships and ports, and this would necessitate a "much heavier" tax burden than Parliament had imposed. In the absence of a protective British fleet, Inglis also expects a military threat from abroad: "A flourishing trade naturally increases wealth; and for this and other reasons, as naturally leads to war. ... The country that abounds in fertile fields and luxuriant pasturage—that produces the necessaries of life in abundance—that furnishes the various materials for industry and art, and the articles for an extensive commerce; such a country . . . is the most inviting to ambition, the most exposed to invasions; and such a country is North-America."[87]

If America declares independence, Inglis argues, "every avenue to an accommodation with Great-Britain would be closed; the sword only could then decide the quarrel." Any chance of settling things peacefully and avoiding full-scale war would be lost. Furthermore, the Americans had supporters arguing their case in the House of Commons, but that would be lost: "We should instantly lose all assistance from our friends in England. It would stop their mouths; for were they to say any thing in our favour, they would be deemed rebels, and treated accordingly." He contends that the only chance for European assistance is France, but he argues that it is unlikely that France would go to war with "the power which lately reduced her so low," especially "from a *disinterested* motive of aiding and protecting these Colonies." And, if France did come to the aid of America, it would only be because she "were sure of some extraordinary advantage by it, in having the colonies under her *immediate jurisdiction*." He argues that the other European states with colonies in North America or "adjacent islands" are "exceedingly jealous of those colonies," and the threat of them aspiring to independence would more likely induce them to join with England than with the Americans. In the event of a British loss of the thirteen colonies, Inglis also expects her to "parcel out this continent to the different European Powers"—Canada to

France, Florida to Spain, and "other states also might come in for a portion." He asks his readers to consider the effects of these changes—particularly having France on America's northern border.[88]

In addition to threats from abroad, Loyalist ministers argue that independence will likely bring very significant problems within America. Inglis estimates that it would cost "nearly *four Millions of Pounds Sterling*" each year in time of peace just to support the civil, naval, and military needs of the new country. "This, with the debts already contracted by the Congress, and the sinking their paper currency, would subject [Americans] to heavier taxes than are paid by any people in christendom." Inglis adds another problem: "All our property throughout the continent would be unhinged" because property rights were grounded in the British constitution and property was acquired under British rules and regulations. Boucher also sees problems regarding property under an independent American government. Assuming that an American government would be a democracy, he says it will "naturally aim at an equality of possessions." He explains: "Votes are easily collected, not only to equalize property, but to destroy all those artificial distinctions in society which are created by property. . . . The evil of levelling property goes yet infinitely farther. It destroys all the usual motives to exertion and industry; and, with them, a long train of concomitant virtues: above all, it destroys security, which forms one of the most endearing charms of the social state." In short, property inequality and class distinctions will be lost along with the motivation to excel and prosper. Inglis links the property issue with the question of liberty in general for those who had remained loyal to England. Independence would create a "horrid situation" for Loyalists who "must be compelled to renounce that allegiance [to the king], or abandon all their property in America!"[89] This, of course, is one of the few dire predictions about independence that actually came to fruition.

Before the beginning of the conflict, Seabury predicts that "tyranny and slavery" will result from rebellion and the move toward independence. He warns: "If we wantonly throw off that subordination to the British Parliament, which our present state requires, we shall inevitably fall under the domination of some foreign tyrant, or the more intolerable despotism of a few American demagogues." After several years of war and experience under the rule of Congress, Inglis suggests that the "more intolerable" of Seabury's expectations had unfortunately been realized. Inglis asks the people of America: "Supposing Britain and France were set aside, would the liberties of America be secure under the Congress? Would the Americans be a peaceful and happy people, and subject to few taxes?" His answer is no. He laments that the people no longer enjoy "liberties . . . such as you formerly enjoyed, and such as are the portion of British subjects." Rather, the "experience of three years has taught you how far these are attainable under a congressional government. You have been ruled with a rod of iron."[90] Tyranny from without or tyranny from within—according to the Loyalist ministers, the prospects for life in an independent America were grim.

The most commonly anticipated result of independence was warfare between the colonies. In the view of the Loyalist ministers, causes for conflict between colonies were abundant. Seabury declares that the consequences of an American victory and independence would be "horrid indeed." "We would presently turn our arms on one another . . . and destruction and carnage would dessolate [sic] the land." Why? Seabury sees at least two causes of inevitable conflict. First: "The interests, the commerce of the different provinces will interfere: disputes about boundaries and limits will arise. There will be no supreme power to interpose; but the sword and bayonet must decide the dispute." Second: "Probably it would cost the blood of a great part of the inhabitants to determine, what kind of government we should have—whether a Monarchy or a Republic." In both cases, the blame ultimately falls on New England. Seabury envisions the New England colonies forming a republic and, because they "have ever cast a wishful eye on the lands of [New York]," a "state of continual war with New-England, would be the inevitable fate of this province, till submission on our part, or conquest on their part, put a period to the dispute."[91] Seabury, a New York Anglican, assumes that New York and most of the middle and southern colonies would form monarchies, so wars such as this would determine boundaries and forms of government.

Boucher, a southern Anglican, and Chandler, a New York Anglican, agree with Seabury that the New England Congregationalists and Presbyterians will be the cause of civil wars in an independent America. These men were all leaders in the fight for an American Anglican bishop—a move vehemently and effectively opposed by New Englanders. They are all opponents of republicanism as well, and they believe that the New Englanders had planned all along to make America a republic. They are not neutral observers, and they earnestly believe that actions by the New Englanders before and during the conflict with England had demonstrated an unwillingness to compromise and a dangerous bent toward violence and aggression. Inglis, also a New York Anglican, does not specifically blame

New England, but he does list "Religious prejudices" among the causes of future wars between colonies.[92]

For Boucher, a mixture of southern Anglicans with New England Congregationalists in an independent America would be "a monstrous and an unnatural coalition," and he expects as soon to see "the wolf and the lamb to feed together, as Virginians to form a cordial union with the saints of New England." Writing to southern congressional delegates, Boucher says that conflict will be inevitable in an independent America because "your fellow-patriots from the North meditate a Reformation, as they call it, in Church as well as in State." "They must disregard their own principles, and be inconsistent with themselves, if they do not." In other words, the New Englanders will insist that all adhere to their theology and political views, as they had done in their own colonies. Although he does not name them, he says that "recent publications, patronized, if not written, by some leading men among them . . . prove that this is at the bottom, and the true and great object of all their present commotions." Not only is this a religious problem but it is also a political problem. Boucher refers to "the infuriate politics of the Republicans of the North" and reminds the southern delegates that "Republicanism will but ill accord with the genius of the people whom ye say ye represent." He then warns that independence will lead to "subjugating these Southern colonies to those of the North."[93] In terms of prospective peace or war, there is a sense in which it does not matter whether Boucher's or Seabury's assessment is correct or unfair; they reflect commonly held views that very well could lead to conflict between colonies.

Chandler shares the views of the others, but he is even more conspiratorial concerning the nefarious plans of the New England republicans. He agrees that "without the superintending authority of *Great-Britain* to restrain them, the colonies . . . [would] probably be soon at war among themselves; and . . . without the same authority to protect them, [would] probably soon become a prey to some foreign power." Because of "their jarring principles, and interests, and projects; we should soon see province waging war against province," and America would be left "open and exposed to the avarice and ambition of every maritime power in Europe or America." For Chandler, however, those devastating probabilities pale in comparison to "subjection to the authority of an American republic" under the leadership of "our future masters," the "republican zealots and bigots of New-England." He charges that their "tyrannical usurpation would be more oppressive, than the scorpion power of the most despotic Prince in Europe," and he engages in a lengthy discussion of persecution of other sects in New England. He concludes: "All these classes of people then, by promoting the present scheme for an independent government, are absurdly acting against their own interest and honour, and contributing to prepare yokes for their own necks."[94]

In 1775, Chandler writes: "It is the spirit of the present system, to depress the power of the crown, and to exalt the power of the people; and the design of it, to prepare the way for introducing and establishing an American Republic, or Aristocracy, or rather both; the former to the Eastward, and the latter to the Southward." As he sees it, "the New-England republican faction" had been plotting for many years to set up "a government of their own modelling, independent of Great Britain." In support of this claim, Chandler quotes extensively from the *American Whig* (April 11, 1768), from "*an agreement entered into by the inhabitants of Boston, on August 1, 1768; the declaration and resolves made by them in the September following*—The *Circular Letter* sent about the same time, from the *Selectmen* of Boston to the Selectmen of the *several towns*, within that province—and some other publications of that period." He also views the Suffolk Resolves as a partial fulfillment of this scheme. In light of this evidence, Chandler concludes that "it seems impossible for any judicious person to doubt, but that there is a set of people among us, disaffected to the constitutional supremacy of Great Britain over these Colonies, who have formed a scheme for establishing an independent government or empire in America; and that they have been regularly pursuing it for many years past." Those disaffected people reside in New England. Chandler contends that the First Continental Congress was "under the influence and direction of . . . the master builders" of this scheme and that explains the "ænigmatical proceedings of the Congress." There was no intention to reconcile with Great Britain, but rather to promote "the *glorious fabric* of an independent American republic."[95]

Inglis, like the others, sees "clashing interests, prejudices and principles" that "would burst out with destructive violence the moment that the claims and superintendence of Britain are entirely removed." He believes that "seeds of animosity and discord, of deadly feuds and bloody contests, are already sown," but unlike the others, he does not single out New England for blame. According to Inglis, a major problem would be land disputes—"mutual claims to certain districts"—fueled by ambitious claims to "the whole of the western unsettled lands." The province or provinces that possessed "so immense a territory" would create a "scene of bloody discord and desolation" until "a few provinces, or one sect had subjugated the rest." He further argues that with independence, "the circumstances that promoted our growth and oppulence [sic]—The protection of Britain, the mildness of our government, an exemption from taxes, the influx of Europeans, and a spirit of peaceful industry . . . would indubitably be reversed." Inglis concludes this part of the argument by reminding the people that "nothing but the power and interposition of Britain stands between you and the evils which I have now mentioned."[96]

Like the others, Inglis believes that "a republican form of government would neither suit the genius of the people, nor the extent of America." In support of this claim, he argues: "The Americans are properly Britons. They have the manners, habits, and ideas of Britons; and have been accustomed to a similar form of government. But Britons never could bear the extremes, either of monarchy or republicanism." Inglis runs through some British history in support of this claim and hails the superiority of a constitutional monarchy. In his letter to the people of America, Inglis celebrates the separation of powers in the British system and criticizes the Congress for its "absolute, paramount and unrestrained" power "without check or controul." He is concerned—especially given experience under the Congress—that a republic in an independent America would be too democratic: an "extreme" of republicanism that "necessarily . . . must lead to tyranny."[97] Ironically, given the future reality of the United States, the Americans are given a lecture about the glories of separation of powers and are scolded for violating that principle.

Inglis has another reason for pessimism concerning an independent American republic: "The republican form . . . is utterly unsuitable to such a wide extended continent as this"; "it is impossible for so extensive a country as America to remain under a republican form of government." This was, of course, the conventional wisdom of the day, and it remained so through the campaign of the Anti-Federalists at the end of the 1780s. Inglis explains that "America is too unwieldy for the feeble, dilatory administration of democracy." He argues that Rome fell into despotism when it became too large and that republics in Europe are viable because they are small.[98] No one in the mid-1770s knew that the United States would disprove conventional wisdom and turn an extended republic into an advantage.

Inglis takes the argument against independence one step farther. As he did regarding the Revolution, Inglis tries to determine the cost of independence. At the outset, he appeals to men of property, as those with much to lose, to pay particular attention to the cost. He begins his analysis with the confession that it "would be impossible to ascertain, with precision, the expence that would be necessary for the support of this New Republic. It would be very great undoubtedly—it would appear intolerable to the Americans, who have hitherto paid so few taxes." The latter comment sets the stage for harsh reality to crash in on those who have been arguably the least taxed people in the world, who have been making a largely theoretical and symbolic argument concerning taxes, and who have enjoyed the fruits of British protection for shillings on the pound. Inglis calculates a cost of £2,190,300 to build a navy less than half the size of the British navy to defend the trade and coast of America. He calculates the annual expense for keeping up this navy as £2,252,120 per year. Turning to ground forces, he estimates a need for £569,412 per year to keep up an army and cavalry. The total annual military expense, then, is £2,821,532 per year. Adding the civil expenses of a government, "which cost us nothing at present: The annual expence of America, when Independent, must greatly exceed THREE MILLIONS of pounds sterling—it will probably amount to three millions and an half . . . and yet many deluded people flatter themselves that they will pay no taxes, if we are once Independent!"[99]

That raises the crucial question of how an independent America will raise the needed money. Inglis speculates that Canada, Nova Scotia, and Florida would join, to make sixteen provinces. That would make the annual expense per province £189,500, or "833,333 Spanish milled dollars." He points out that Rhode Island is small, as is Delaware, and that Nova Scotia, Georgia, and Florida are "very young colonies." "None of these therefore could possibly contribute an equal share with the older and larger colonies; the expence of the latter must, of course, be proportionably greater, to make up the deficiency." Assuming a population of three million people, "each individual, man, woman, and child, black and white, would have *twenty shillings* sterling . . . to pay annually for defraying the public expence. Or, taking every seventh person for a Taxable, . . . then every Taxable in the colonies must pay £. 7 sterl. . . . *annually* [emphasis original] for the public expence, over and above what he has paid in times past. In case of war or any extraordinary emergency, those taxes must rise proportionably." The £2,373,000 needed to construct a navy and raise an army must be added to this annual expense. That, in addition to "sixteen millions of dollars, which I am informed the Honourable Congress has been obliged already to issue . . . and the prodigious sums of paper currency which the several colonies have struck, and must hereafter strike; will make a load of debt, that must prove ruinous to this continent."[100]

According to Inglis, total American exports in 1769 amounted to £500,000 less than the annual expense, so he declares: "What then must our situation be, or what the state of our trade, when oppressed with such a burthen of annual expence! When every article of commerce, every necessary of life, together with our lands, must be heavily taxed, to defray that expence!"[101] In short, by Charles Inglis's calculation, Americans could not afford independence.

Conclusion

In their attempts to convince fellow Americans that the American Revolution was both wrong and disastrously unwise, Loyalist clergymen heavily criticized a number of the actions that had been taken by the continental Congress and its agents. They relentlessly attacked the policy of nonimportation, nonexportation, and nonconsumption of British goods. The inherent justice and legality of the policy were challenged, as were the likelihood that it would achieve the desired results, the enforcement mechanisms and agents, and whether the results could possibly make up for the profound suffering it caused.

Speaking of suffering, the Loyalist ministers also chided the Patriots for their persecution of Loyalists and mocked them for their hypocrisy in denying rights to their political opponents while making high-toned demands for their own rights. Much of the Patriot argument was couched in the terms of natural or English rights, but they denied freedom of speech, freedom of the press, freedom of religion, and due process rights to the Loyalists. The Loyalist clergy were particularly acquainted with this problem, as they were particularly targeted for what they called persecution. Loyalist ministers were threatened, assaulted, proscribed, kidnapped, banished, and imprisoned; they had their homes ransacked and their property confiscated; they were even killed—all without due process of law and often without any pretense of a trial. Their churches were closed up and they were not allowed to speak publicly. Most importantly, they had committed no crime. They were not accused of espionage or sabotage; they were accused of praying for the king or of simply remaining loyal to the established government or of not being sufficiently supportive of the rebel cause.

Although the Loyalist writers were not always in agreement on everything, they all opposed the Revolution and engaged the logic of the Patriot justification for "resistance." Likewise, they all agreed that Great Britain would win the war and that the consequences of war for America would be devastating. Before the fighting began, they laid out the many advantages held by the British and the many obstacles and deficiencies that the rebels would have to overcome in such a conflict. After the war began, they regularly argued that the British could win at any time and gave excuses as to why they did not finish the colonists. Some of the clergymen took on the role of accountants and tried to calculate the cost of the revolution in terms of money, lives, and property, as well as the effects on societal and individual morals.

A special target of criticism was the Patriot alliance with France. Before the alliance was made, they argued that it was unlikely that France would come to their aid and that, if it did, it would backfire on the rebels and put America under the thumb of the French after the smoke cleared. Once the alliance with the Catholic French became reality, they taunted the Patriots for claiming concern about British support for popery as one of their justifications for the Revolution and suggested that Protestantism was now in jeopardy in America. They warned that inviting the French into America was much easier than getting them to leave after the war was over, and that America was likely to become a French vassal. They were particularly critical of the agreement between the revolutionaries and the French not to make peace with Britain without the other. According to the Loyalists, this agreement made America servile to French interests and ambitions. No matter what the British offered, the French could keep the conflict going until America and Great Britain were sufficiently weakened to suit their interest.

Finally, all of the writers among the Loyalist clergymen opposed American independence. Most of their concerns were practical and material. Americans would be threatened from abroad and on the border, the country would be too vast for republicanism to work, and the new focus on democratic impulses would jeopardize property rights. There would likely be conflict—even war—between the colonies (or states) because of land disputes, religious differences, and differences in forms of government. They were concerned about tyranny within: those who dominated the Continental Congress would dominate, and they had already shown themselves to be tyrants. It was unlikely that the new systems of government would include a separation of powers—the Congress did not. Ultimately, though, their criticisms and warnings focused on the exorbitant costs entailed in establishing, running, and defending the new country. Americans had shown no willingness to be taxed, and extensive taxation would be necessary. Furthermore, the prodigious amount of paper money infecting the colonial money supply appeared to be an insurmountable obstacle to financial health and stability in and of itself.

In short, the performance of the Patriot pseudoauthorities and the sheer realities of war, finance, alliance with Catholic France, and the costs of revolution followed by the costs of independence seemed to the Loyalist ministers to indicate without question that the Patriot cause was foolhardy and doomed to fail. Indeed, nearly every measurable indicator pointed to British victory and American humiliation. The indicators and the Loyalist clergymen were wrong.

Epilogue

> We surely have as good a right to preserve the
> union, even at the expense of some displeasure and
> some disadvantage to them, as they can have to
> dissolve it, to our ruin.
> —Jonathan Boucher

Most Americans would be very hard pressed to name a single person who remained loyal to England during the American Revolution. However, as a nineteenth-century biographer of Alexander Hamilton suggests: "If the well-meant exertions of this band of loyalists had succeeded in that which they proposed, and the relations of the Colonies with England been restored with honor and liberty, their names would have been cherished by grateful prosperity." Instead, as a twenty-first-century historian observes, "The character of the loyalists has endured deep scrutiny even as loyalist choices have been caricatured. The loyalists appear as hidebound conservatives or as political lackeys lacking ideological commitment, motivated by fear to maintain the status quo. When the loyalist choice has been acknowledged, the decision toward allegiance to the empire has been framed as an aberrant and individual one." This study has attempted to show that the Loyalists do not fit nicely into a simplistic category, were not ideologically shallow, and were not motivated by fear. They were, as the first quote indicates, well-meaning and seeking what they thought was best for their home: America. Even after being exiled, Samuel Curwen found himself defending America in England during the war and could write: "For my native country I feel a filial fondness . . . and to be restored to her embraces is the warmest of my desires." A biographer's observation concerning John Joachim Zubly applies generally to most Loyalists: he did not become a Loyalist because he was "an Anglophile or an obstructionist," but because "he loved America and so sought to avoid her destruction in a civil war."[1]

The decision by the Loyalists not to engage in rebellion is generally viewed today as "aberrant," but they simply saw it as the right thing to do and as a reflection of good character. To their mind, extraordinary actions were "the effect of some certain train of thinking" and were not well served by "the degeneracy of modern times." In modern times, "we rely solely on men's supposed interests and inclination, and conceive that they alone will lead to a right conduct." But interests and inclinations, which are particularly susceptible to passion, do not necessarily, or even usually, lead to right conduct. The Loyalists, however, believed in the importance of "right principles" and men "being trained to think, as well as to act, aright." In modern times, such precaution is passé, so untrained "rights of private judgment" take the place of principles, and the results are celebrated regardless of rectitude. Loyalists, trained in right principles, believed in and wrote much about duty—duty to the king, duty to the law, duty to posterity, and duty to God. In their view, all of those duties were violated in the Revolution. They "believed with total conviction that colonial resistance was morally wrong."[2]

Charles Inglis outlines three foundations for the duty to honor the king and government. The first appeals only to Christians and is self-explanatory: "The express Commands of God, of his inspired Prophets and Apostles." The other two have universal application and require some explication. The second foundation is "the Stability of Government," resulting in "the Peace of Societies" and "the Happiness of Individuals." Inglis explains that government is our only security against "Oppression, Injustice, Violence and Wickedness," but it cannot fulfill that function unless "those who rule, are honoured and obeyed." Failure to do so weakens the government and "prepares the Way for all those Disorders to rush in." The third foundation is the fact that "the greatest Evils which can befall Society, necessarily attend the Neglect or Breach" of this duty. In his explanation, Inglis particularly highlights the "Miseries and Calamities" of rebellion. He contends that great evils have often "arisen from seemingly small Beginnings" and that "this is often the Case of Rebellion." Inglis spends a couple of pages listing "the horrid Train of Evils which follow Rebellion" before concluding: "Add to all this, that when successful, it generally ends in Tyranny, and the most grievous Oppression." Late in the war, Inglis writes that he has "the satisfaction . . . of an approving conscience" and that he can "reflect with pleasure" that he had "discharged the duty of a good citizen and loyal subject," and that he had done "all in his power to avert the utter ruin of his country."³ That consoling sentiment was no doubt shared by all of the primary voices among the Loyalist clergy.

A nineteenth-century historian, writing fourteen years after the American Civil War, noted that Americans changed their view of loyalty during the Civil War. They learned that "'loyalty' was a virtue, that the supporters of 'the powers that be' were worthy of honor, and that 'rebels' and 'rebellion' were to be put down at any cost by the strong hand. A precisely similar view did very large masses of the people of the British Colonies take when the war of the American Revolution broke out."⁴ There are certainly significant parallels between British and Union claims of the national government's authority to legislate for all regions under their jurisdiction and between Patriot and Southern Confederate desires to reject all but local autonomy. Loyalists such as Inglis would no doubt appreciate the belated affirmation of their principles.

In contrast to the foundations of the duty to honor the government, Samuel Seabury charges that the "present Rebellion" is "founded in *Impiety, Ingratitude*, and *Falshood* [sic], and is supported by Injustice, Oppression, Cruelty and Tyranny." Chapter 2 explains in depth why the Loyalist clergymen saw the rebellion against England as impious. Chapters 3 through 6 lay out the evidence for their contention of falsehood on the part of the Patriots. The matter of ingratitude is discussed briefly in Chapter 5, but a statement on the cusp of war by Jonathan Boucher catalogs many reasons that Americans should have been grateful to England:

> From the Infancy of our Colonies, to this very Hour, we have grown up and flourished under the Mildness, and Wisdom of her excellent Laws; our Trade, our Possessions, our Persons have been constantly defended against the whole World, by the Fame of her Power, or by the Exertion of it. We have been very lately, rescued by her, from Enemies, who threatned [sic] us with Slavery, and Destruction, at the Expence of much Blood, and Treasure, and established after a long War, (waged on our Accounts, at our most earnest Prayers) in a State of Security, of which there is scarce an Example in History.

Boucher's statement reflects the close relationship between the colonies and their mother country as well as some of the benefits the colonists had received from her. "The adjective *unnatural*, used frequently by loyalists to describe the Revolution, reflected their belief that the colonies and Britain were naturally tied to each other by the bonds of culture, history, and mutual interest. Severing such a beneficial and deeply rooted link was contrary to the dictates of both reason and colonial self-interest."[5] To the Loyalists, the rebellion was impious and irrational, and lacked gratitude.

Why were they unable to win the battle of ideas? First, "except for the Anglican parsons, the principal Tories in the different provinces . . . did not even know each other," so it was difficult to mount an organized and coordinated campaign. The Loyalists "had no intercolonial organization to translate their ideas into actions" or to "execute alternative policies and counter Patriot coercion." Second, "Loyalists were writing about a vision or an ideal, about how the empire could or should operate in theory, but the practice, the reality unfolding before colonists' eyes, diverged markedly from the ideal." They thus had to "convince Americans that the empire could work to their advantage and fulfill all their expectations of it, even though it was obviously being mismanaged at that moment." Third, the Loyalist cause had to be carried by the clergy in sermons and pamphlets because the Loyalist press was not able to "enunciate a fully developed alternative ideology" or to refute the novel ideas of the Patriots.[6]

Still, especially in the middle colonies, the clergymen had a significant effect for as long as they were allowed to compete in the contest of ideas. There the writings of Seabury and Chandler "were widely read and well received." Seabury and Chandler urged New York to declare independence from America and to negotiate separately with Great Britain. A number of New York towns refused to cooperate with the demands of the Congress, and so many Loyalists showed up at the meeting to choose a committee in Oyster Bay that the meeting was declared to be illegal and adjourned. In towns and whole counties, majorities signed loyalty oaths. In its final session, after Seabury had met with "at least one third" of the members, the New York colonial assembly refused to approve the proceedings of the Congress, refused to appoint a delegation to the Congress, and "drew up its own petition of grievances to send to England"—in line with Seabury's and Chandler's recommendation. That petition was sent to the king and Parliament directly. Readers from Delaware to Maryland affirmed the effect of Chandler's pamphlets.[7]

Fourth, although the Loyalist "message was not aimed only at the educated or even literate segment of the population," the Patriots had better, more effective methods of communicating with and appealing to the common people—including "popular symbols, rituals, and mass rallies."

The fifth and ultimately decisive reason for the failure of the Loyalists' public opinion campaign was the aggressive and violent Patriot campaign to shut down access to Loyalist thought. With their enforcing committees and mobs denying ministers access to their pulpits, closing churches, destroying presses, and burning pamphlets, the Patriots silenced their opponents. The author of another study of Loyalist ideology concludes that "it was oppressive for the upholders of one view—the Patriots—to use their power to silence their opponents and thereby stifle the all-important debate about the future of their country."[8] Whether the Patriots could have won the battle of ideas against Loyalist thought in a fair contest in which both sides were allowed sustained opportunity to make their case is an interesting but unanswerable question.

Before and during the American Revolution, Loyalist clergymen made the case on several grounds for submission to and conciliation with the government of Great Britain, and against rebellion and American independence.[9] As ministers addressing a religious people, they scolded Patriot preachers for taking Scripture out of context, in particular for treating verses about spiritual liberty as if they referred to political liberty. They reminded their audiences of the clear and straightforward commands in Romans 13 and I Peter 2, and they supported their case against rebellion with Old Testament passages and the example of Jesus. In addition to being clergymen, the Loyalist ministers were highly educated observers of human nature, the law, and history. Confident that reason and the facts were on their side, they did not hesitate to engage in rational argument of a theoretical or practical nature—although they preferred concrete legal and historical arguments.

Although the Loyalist ministers preferred more empirical avenues, they did engage their readers with arguments concerning the nature of man and government in order to answer the key claims of their adversaries. They generally held a less optimistic view of human nature but emphasized the innate sociability of man. Connecting those ideas with the need for civil society, they believed in an organic, natural origin of human government rather than the mechanistic view of the modern political theorists such as Locke. Consequently, they defended monarchy and questioned notions of the natural equality of men and government by consent of the governed. Generally, the Loyalist ministers believed that the Bible taught the same views of the nature of man, government, and rebellion as did reason and nature.

In addressing the legal aspects of the dispute between the American colonists and the British government, the Loyalist ministers engaged in extensive analysis of the colonial charters and the relationship between colonies and their mother country. They found the Patriot position to be lacking any legal standing. Because the Patriots self-identified as British subjects even after the first battles were fought and appealed to their rights as Englishmen, the Loyalist apologists examined the British constitution and parliamentary authority under it to counter the Patriot arguments. The Continental Congress and its related committees and associations drew particular fire and ire from the ministers. According to their legal analysis, neither the Congress nor its enforcement arms had any legal validity, but amounted to mob rule. The fact that these Loyalists were not Tories in the English sense explains their emphasis on and promotion of the colonial assemblies in addition to the Crown and Parliament.

Because they were not uncritical apologists for England, they acknowledged errors made by the king and Parliament while at the same time affirming their motives as benign. From their perspective, the relationship between England and the American colonies was essentially that of parent and child. In addition, they maintained that because the Americans claimed their rights as Englishmen, they had an obligation to fulfill their duties as Englishmen. What had caused the familial crisis between parent and child? In their view, most of the conflict had been stirred up by troublemakers—rabble-rousers who had rebellion and independence in their minds from the beginning. The American people had been duped and led astray by clever and persistent propagandists. Largely because of the provocations promoted and carried out by the troublemakers, the Americans never made a good-faith effort at conciliation. The British had made numerous concessions; the Americans never made any. Particularly troubling to the Loyalist clergy were the tone used by American representatives, inattention to the conciliatory gestures made by Great Britain, and provocations passed by the Congress ostensibly representing the colonies as a whole.

Although the Loyalist ministers were upset about the very existence of the Congress and the method by which it came into existence and claimed authority, they became especially upset with the actions taken by the Congress and the committees spawned by it. In an interesting twist, they lectured the Americans about the need for separation of powers and checks and balances, using the British system as the model. They were pointed and relentless in their attacks on the congressional policies of nonimportation, nonexportation, and nonconsumption, charging the Patriots with foolishness in the idea and tyranny in the practice. The Loyalist ministers severely criticized the Patriots for denying both English and basic civil rights. The Patriots claimed tyranny on the part of the British, but the Loyalists pointed to real tyrannical actions by the Congress and committees. They charged the Patriots with rank hypocrisy for clamoring for rights and crying out for liberty while denying both to their political opponents. Due process of law, freedom of religion, freedom of speech, freedom of the press, and other rights were denied to their Loyalist political opponents. In short, the Loyalist ministers charged that the Americans behaved in hypocritical and "un-American" fashion.

Ultimately, of course, the dispute came down to whether to rebel against and go to war with England. The Loyalist ministers argued that this course of action would be morally and legally wrong on the one hand, and foolhardy and disastrous on the other. To them, it seemed blatantly obvious that the Americans could not win such a war against the strongest power on earth. In addition to the questions of right and wrong and potential for success, they warned about the cost of such a revolution and the cost of running an independent America if they happened to be victorious. With regard to the Revolution itself, they were exceedingly critical of the American alliance with France. Along with the hypocrisy of partnering with the papists after listing the threat of growing Catholic influence in America as one of the grievances against England, the Loyalists warned about the threat of French domination of America—that it was easier to invite their forces in than to get them to leave when the fight was over. Should independence be gained and the French induced to leave, how would Americans pay the expenses for an independent America? How would they defend themselves against foreign powers? How would they keep from fighting among themselves?

When they are discussed at all, the American Loyalists are often caricatured as wealthy, well-connected apologists for British tyranny who were unconcerned about Parliament's treatment of the colonies and who were motivated not by principle but by gain. As Chopra explains, however: "The loyal Americans were as passionate as their adversaries and resiliently defended their vision of liberty within the empire. A deep ideological commitment and a sentimental attachment to the empire determined the allegiance of this courageous minority. . . . They worried about an American future under the reign of power-hungry demagogues who conspired against the true freedoms of the British government."[10] They were just as concerned about liberty and arguably suffered greater violations of their liberty than did the Patriots.

Much of the battle of ideas in the American Revolutionary period was fought by clergymen in the pulpits of America, in published sermons, and in pamphlets. Along with their distinctive views of what the Bible teaches, pastors on both sides extended the argument well beyond the Bible and conventional religious instruction. Patriot preachers tapped into the theories of John Locke; Loyalist ministers delved into law, reason, and history. The decisive factor for the clergy, however, was arguably their respective views of Romans 13, I Peter 2, and other passages of Scripture. Were the instructions there to be taken literally or not? Lawrence Leder summarizes it very well:

> If government was God's ordinance to man, little more need be said. Disagreement with government became rebellion against authority and, in turn, opposition to God—an unthinkable situation. Only when the clergy accepted the idea that government originated not in a divine decree but by compact or agreement among the people could Americans explore possible limits upon political power. Having done that, they moved easily to the thesis that rulers were bound by law, and transgression of those limits released the people from further obedience.[11]

The Loyalist ministers took the passages literally—the prevailing view of the "Christian West" for more than 1,500 years.[12] Forced to choose between the teaching of philosophers and what they saw as the clear teaching of the apostles and the Holy Spirit, they chose the Bible. Consequently, they could not embrace notions of social contract, popular sovereignty, and resistance to authority. They consciously chose to defend God's ordinance and to reject a rebellion against authority that amounted to rebellion against God. Because God was against the American Revolution, so were they.

NOTES

Chapter 1. The Context for the Loyalist Argument

1. Philip Davidson, *Propaganda and the American Revolution, 1763–1783* (New York: Norton, 1973), 249, 258; Donald Barr Chidsey, *The Loyalists: The Story of Those Americans Who Fought against Independence* (New York: Crown, 1973), 84, 85.

2. See, e.g., chaps. 2 and 3 of Gregg L. Frazer, *The Religious Beliefs of America's Founders: Reason, Revelation, and Revolution* (Lawrence: University Press of Kansas, 2012); and James P. Byrd, *Sacred Scripture, Sacred War* (New York: Oxford University Press, 2013).

3. Chidsey, *Loyalists*, 3.

4. Holger Hoock, *Scars of Independence: America's Violent Birth* (New York: Crown, 2017), 29–30; Ruma Chopra, *Choosing Sides: Loyalists in Revolutionary America* (Lanham, MD: Rowman & Littlefield, 2013), 2; David J. Fowler, "Loyalty Is Now Bleeding in New Jersey," in *The Other Loyalists: Ordinary People, Royalism, and the Revolution in the Middle Colonies, 1763–1787*, ed. Joseph S. Tiedemann, Eugene R. Fingerhut, and Robert W. Venables (Albany: State University Press of New York, 2009), 50; Maya Jasanoff, *Liberty's Exiles: American Loyalists in the Revolutionary World* (New York: Knopf, 2012), 23, 24, 33.

5. Robert M. Calhoon, "Civil, Revolutionary, or Partisan," in *Tory Insurgents: The Loyalist Perception and Other Essays*, ed. Robert M. Calhoon, Timothy M. Barnes, and Robert S. Davis (Columbia: University of South Carolina Press, 2010), 204; Jonathan Boucher, *Reminiscences of an American Loyalist*, ed. Jonathan Bouchier [grandson] (Boston: Houghton Mifflin, 1925), 121; Clinton Rossiter, *The Political Thought of the American Revolution* (New York: Harcourt, Brace, & World, 1963), 55.

6. Edmund S. Morgan, *The Challenge of the American Revolution* (New York: Norton, 1976), 177; Patrick Griffin, *America's Revolution* (New York: Oxford University Press, 2013), 127; Chidsey, *Loyalists*, 4; Ruma Chopra, *Unnatural Rebellion: Loyalists in New York City during the Revolution* (Charlottesville: University of Virginia Press, 2011), 67; Chidsey, *Loyalists*, 7; Chopra, *Choosing Sides*, 2.

7. William H. Nelson, *The American Tory* (Boston: Beacon Press, 1964), 3; William Allen Benton, *Whig-Loyalism: An Aspect of Political Ideology in the American Revolutionary Era* (Madison, NJ: Fairleigh Dickinson University Press, 1969), 15; Morgan, *Challenge*, 177, 178.

8. Claude Halstead Van Tyne, *The Loyalists in the American Revolution* (Gloucester, MA: Peter Smith, 1959), 115; Nelson, *American Tory*, 90; Catherine S. Crary, ed., *The Price of Loyalty: Tory Writings from the Revolutionary Era* (New York: McGraw-Hill, 1973), 89; Robert M. Calhoon and Ruma Chopra, "Religion and the Loyalists," in *Faith and the Founders of the American Republic*, ed. Daniel L. Dreisbach and Mark David Hall (New York: Oxford University Press, 2014), 101; Chidsey, *Loyalists*, 85.

9. James B. Bell, *A War of Religion: Dissenters, Anglicans, and the American*

Revolution (New York: Palgrave Macmillan, 2008), 240.

10. Van Tyne, Loyalists, 112; Bell, War of Religion, 237; Chidsey, Loyalists, 5; Bell, War of Religion, 232; Crary, Price of Loyalty, 90; Chopra, Choosing Sides, 27; Bell, War of Religion, 227–228; Chopra, Choosing Sides, 27; Chidsey, Loyalists, 87.

11. Nelson, American Tory, 90; Janice Potter, The Liberty We Seek: Loyalist Ideology in Colonial New York and Massachusetts (Cambridge, MA: Harvard University Press, 1983), 12; Chidsey, Loyalists, 86, 85; Nelson, American Tory, 90; Fowler, "Loyalty Is Now Bleeding," 50; Griffin, America's Revolution, 141–142.

12. Nelson, American Tory, 91; Hoock, Scars of Independence, 30; Fowler, "Loyalty Is Now Bleeding," 49–50; Nelson, American Tory, 92, 91.

13. Griffin, America's Revolution, 127; Max Savelle, The Colonial Origins of American Thought (Princeton, NJ: D. Van Nostrand, 1964), 15, 16, 18, 17.

14. Nelson, American Tory, 187, 188.

15. Benjamin Rush, The Autobiography of Benjamin Rush, ed. George Corner (Princeton, NJ: Princeton University Press for the American Philosophical Society, 1948), 117–118, 118.

16. Boucher, Reminiscences, 95, 96.

17. Jonathan Sewall, letter to General Frederick Haldimand (May 30, 1775), in Colonies to Nation, 1763–1789, ed. Jack P. Greene (New York: Norton, 1975), 266–268; Van Tyne, Loyalists, 26.

18. Rush, Autobiography, 118.

19. Sewall, 268; T. H. Breen, American Insurgents, American Patriots (New York: Hill & Wang, 2010), 162; Jasanoff, Liberty's Exiles, 25; Griffin, America's Revolution, 141–142; Rush, Autobiography, 118–119; Van Tyne, Loyalists, 158–159; Rush, Autobiography, 119; Chopra, Choosing Sides, 3.

20. Bernard Bailyn, The Ideological Origins of the American Revolution (Cambridge, MA: Belknap Press of Harvard University Press, 1967), 47; Rossiter, Political Thought, 125, 48; Bailyn, Ideological Origins, 50.

21. Lawrence H. Leder, Liberty and Authority (Chicago: Quadrangle Books, 1968), 143; Savelle, Colonial Origins, 15, 16: Robert M. Calhoon, The Loyalists in Revolutionary America, 1760–1781 (New York: Harcourt Brace Jovanovich, 1973), 204; Rossiter, Political Thought, 75; Rivington's Gazette, January 12, 1782, in Van Tyne, Loyalists, 254.

22. See Frazer, Religious Beliefs of America's Founders, 85–105, for a discussion of Locke's influence on the Patriot preachers.

23. Savelle, Colonial Origins, 16. For a lengthy list and discussion of influential sources of Whig thought, see Bailyn, Ideological Origins, 22–54, and Rossiter, Political Thought, 64–75.

24. Van Tyne, Loyalists, 9.

25. Benjamin Franklin, letter to Thomas Cushing (June 4, 1773), in Franklin, The Complete Works of Benjamin Franklin, ed. John Bigelow (New York: G. P. Putnam's Sons, 1887), 5:147.

26. For a detailed discussion of the constitutionality of "no taxation without representation," see Gregg L. Frazer, "The American Revolution: Not a Just War," Journal of Military Ethics 14, no. 1 (2015): 39–45.

27. John Joachim Zubly, "The Law of Liberty" (Philadelphia, 1775), 28; Van Tyne, Loyalists, 9–10, 10.

28. For a detailed discussion of the types of taxes, see Rossiter, Political Thought, 23–28.

29. Van Tyne, Loyalists, 10.

30. Nelson, American Tory, 5, 7, 5.

31. Thomas Bradbury Chandler, quoted in John Wolfe Lydekker, *The Life and Letters of Charles Inglis* (London: Society for Promoting Christian Knowledge, 1936), 52; Thomas Bradbury Chandler, "What Think Ye of the Congress Now? Or, an Enquiry, How Far the Americans are Bound to Abide by, and Execute the Decisions of, the Late Congress?" (New York: James Rivington, 1775), 5, 15; Thomas Bradbury Chandler, "A Friendly Address to All Reasonable Americans, on the Subject of our Political Confusions" (New-York, 1774), 46, 47; Chandler, "What Think Ye," 15; Jonathan Boucher, "On the Character of Ahitophel" (1774), in *A View of the Causes and Consequences of the American Revolution* (New York: Russell & Russell, 1797), 417; Jonathan Boucher, letter to John James (December 9, 1765), in "Letters of Rev. Jonathan Boucher," *Maryland Historical Magazine* 7, no. 3 (September 1912): 295; Jonathan Boucher, letter to John James (March 9, 1767), in "Letters of Rev. Jonathan Boucher," *Maryland Historical Magazine* 7, no. 4 (December 1912): 344; Boucher, letter to John James (December 9, 1765), 295; Jonathan Boucher, letter to John James (July 25, 1769), in "Letters of Rev. Jonathan Boucher," *Maryland Historical Magazine* 8, no. 1 (March 1913): 44.

32. Hoock, *Scars of Independence*, 30.

33. Benton, *Whig-Loyalism*, 14, 16, 17.

34. John Joachim Zubly, *A Warm and Zealous Spirit*, ed. Randall M. Miller (Macon, GA: Mercer University Press, 1982), 6, 27, 26; Zubly, "Law of Liberty," 27. Randall M. Miller's transcriptions of John Joachim Zubly's "'Helvetius' Essays" are cited here for ease of access for the interested reader. The original newspaper essays are difficult to acquire on microform and are not paginated, making it extremely difficult to find specific quotes. Miller's transcriptions, though not inerrant, are accurate, and no errors affect meaning.

35. Zubly, *Warm and Zealous Spirit*, 21, 24, 25; Zubly, "Law of Liberty," 32; Bernard Bailyn and John B. Hench, eds., *The Press and the American Revolution* (Worcester, MA: American Antiquarian Society, 1980), 232; Van Tyne, *Loyalists*, 22; Griffin, *America's Revolution*, 128.

36. Lorenzo Sabine, *Biographical Sketches of Loyalists of the American Revolution* (Boston: Little, Brown, 1864), 1:528.

37. Van Tyne, *Loyalists*, 22.

38. Van Tyne, *Loyalists*, 24, 100, 42, 104; Rossiter, *Political Thought*, 136; Richard Mansfield quoted in Calhoon, *Loyalists*, 313.

39. Van Tyne, *Loyalists*, 92; Chidsey, *Loyalists*, 107, 106; Van Tyne, *Loyalists*, 73.

40. Chidsey, *Loyalists*, 3; Nelson, *American Tory*, v; Benton, *Whig-Loyalism*, 16; Chopra, *Choosing Sides*, 30.

41. Tiedemann and Fingerhut, introduction to Tiedemann, Fingerhut, and Venables, *Other Loyalists*, 1; Chidsey, *Loyalists*, 84.

42. Thomas N. Ingersoll, *The Loyalist Problem in Revolutionary New England* (Cambridge: Cambridge University Press, 2016), 23.

43. Ronald Hoffman and Peter J. Albert, eds., *Religion in a Revolutionary Age* (Charlottesville: University Press of Virginia, 1994), 190; Boyd Stanley Schlenther, "Religious Faith and Commercial Empire," in *The Oxford History of the British Empire: The Eighteenth Century*, ed. P. J. Marshall (New York: Oxford University Press, 1996), 131; Calhoon, *Loyalists*, 209; Nelson, *American Tory*, 13; Calhoon, *Loyalists*, 193.

44. Walter Bates, "The Narrative

of Walter Bates," in *Kingston and the Loyalists of the "Spring Fleet" of 1783*, ed. W. O. Raymond (1889; reprint, Woodstock, NB, Canada: Non-Entity Press, 1980), 7; Nelson, *American Tory*, 13; Charles Inglis, letter to the S.P.G. (May 6, 1782), in Lydekker, *Life and Letters of Charles Inglis*, 208.

45. Jonathan Mayhew, *Observations on the Charter and Conduct of the Society for the Propagation of the Gospel in Foreign Parts* (Boston: Richard and Samuel Draper, 1763), 155, 156; Ingersoll, *Loyalist Problem*, 257; Calhoon, *Loyalists*, 208; Bates, "Narrative," 9.

46. Ingersoll, *Loyalist Problem*, 131; Nancy L. Rhoden, *Revolutionary Anglicanism: The Colonial Church of England Clergy during the American Revolution* (Washington Square: New York University Press, 1999), 57; Samuel Auchmuty, Thomas B. Chandler, Myles Cooper, John Ogilvie, Richard Charlton, Samuel Seabury, Charles Inglis, and Abraham Beach, "An ADDRESS From the CLERGY of New-York and New-Jersey, to the EPISCOPALIANS in VIRGINIA; Occasioned by Some Late Transactions In That Colony Relative to an AMERICAN EPISCOPATE" (New-York: Hugh Gaine, 1771), 1, 9–10, 32.

47. Auchmuty et al., "ADDRESS From the Clergy," 33, 32, 48n; Lydekker, *Life and Letters of Charles Inglis*, 53–83; Lorenzo Sabine, *Biographical Sketches of Loyalists of the American Revolution* (1864; reprint, Port Washington, NY: Kennikat Press, 1966), 2:177; Auchmuty et al., "ADDRESS From the Clergy," 33; Jonathan Boucher, "On the American Episcopate" (1771), in *View of the Causes and Consequences*, 105.

48. Auchmuty et al., "ADDRESS From the Clergy," 50–51n, 55, 57; Thomas Gwatkin, "A LETTER to the CLERGY of New York and New Jersey, Occasioned by an ADDRESS to the Episcopalians in Virginia" (Williamsburg: Alex. Purdie and John Dixon, 1772), 8.

49. Boucher, "On the American Episcopate," 107, 137, 138.

50. Rhoden, *Revolutionary Anglicanism*, 58; Chidsey, *Loyalists*, 83; Van Tyne, *Loyalists*, 109; John Adams, *The Works of John Adams, Second President of the United States*, ed. Charles Francis Adams (Boston: Little, Brown, 1856), 10:288.

51. Nelson, *American Tory*, 17; Rhoden, *Revolutionary Anglicanism*, 62–63; Calhoon, *Loyalists*, 194, 215.

52. Nelson, *American Tory*, 17; Lydekker, *Life and Letters of Charles Inglis*, 71–72, 73; Nelson, *American Tory*, 15, 16, 73.

53. Calhoon, "Civil, Revolutionary, or Partisan," 204; Janice Potter-MacKinnon and Robert M. Calhoon, "The Character and Coherence of the Loyalist Press," in *Tory Insurgents: The Loyalist Perception and Other Essays*, ed. Robert M. Calhoon, Timothy M. Barnes, and Robert S. Davis (Columbia: University of South Carolina Press, 2010), 154; Jim Piecuch, *Three Peoples, One King: Loyalists, Indians, and Slaves in the Revolutionary South, 1775–1782* (Columbia: University of South Carolina Press, 2008), 5; Ingersoll, *Loyalist Problem*, 247–248, 251.

54. For the definitive study of what happened to Loyalists after the war, see Jasanoff, *Liberty's Exiles*.

55. Rhoden, *Revolutionary Anglicanism*, 103.

56. Hoock, *Scars of Independence*, 50, 51.

57. Mary Beth Norton, "Eighteenth-century Women in Peace and War: The Case of the Loyalists," *William and Mary Quarterly* 33 (1976): 398.

58. Van Tyne, Loyalists, 208–209.

59. Crary, Price of Loyalty, 88, 88n; Calhoon, Loyalists, 148.

60. John Wiswall, Wiswall Papers, Acadia University, Wolfville, Nova Scotia, qtd. in Crary, Price of Loyalty, 97–99; Samuel Peters, A General History of Connecticut, 2nd ed. (London: J. Bew, 1782), 416–419.

61. Van Tyne, Loyalists, 130–138; For a state-by-state analysis of the test laws, see Van Tyne, Loyalists, 318–326; Chidsey, Loyalists, 69–70; Van Tyne, Loyalists, 130.

62. For extensive coverage of violence on both sides, see Hoock, Scars of Independence.

63. Long-respected works on loyalism that detail the persecution of Loyalists include the following: Van Tyne, Loyalists, 60–86, 129–145, 190–285; Chidsey, Loyalists, 27–40, 62–70; Calhoon, Loyalists, 281–325, 397–414, 500–506; Crary, Price of Loyalty, 55–111, 201–239; Sabine, Biographical Sketches.

64. Piecuch, Three Peoples, 12, 331.

65. Piecuch, Three Peoples, 332.

66. These numbers were largely gleaned from Bell, War of Religion, 224–240, and Sabine, Biographical Sketches.

67. For an excellent brief discussion of the role of Quakers, see Mark A. Noll, Christians in the America Revolution (Grand Rapids, MI: Christian University Press, 1977), 123–147.

68. James S. M. Anderson, The History of the Church of England, in the Colonies and Foreign Dependencies of the British Empire (London: Rivingtons, 1845–1856), 3:254–255, 255; Calhoon, Loyalists, 220, 221.

69. Calhoon, Loyalists, 221–222, 222.

70. For a compelling discussion of this matter, see Anne Young Zimmer and Alfred H. Kelly, "Jonathan Boucher: Constitutional Conservative," Journal of American History 58, no. 4 (1972): 897–922.

71. Bell, War of Religion, 165, 166; S. Scott Rohrer, Jacob Green's Revolution: Radical Religion and Reform in a Revolutionary Age (University Park: Pennsylvania State University Press, 2014), 169; Bell, War of Religion, 168, 169; Jacob Green's Revolution, 258–260, 270.

72. For an interesting discussion of this question of authorship from which these quotes are taken, see Clarence Hayden Vance, "Myles Cooper," Columbia University Quarterly 22 (1930): 274–276.

73. Bell, War of Religion, 149, 150; Chopra, Unnatural Rebellion, 47, 81; Bell, War of Religion, 152; Chopra, Unnatural Rebellion, 47; Nelson, American Tory, 74; Bell, War of Religion, 154.

74. George Shea, The Life and Epoch of Alexander Hamilton: A Historical Study (Boston: Houghton, Osgood, 1879), 292n–293n, 292, 293; Nelson, American Tory, 75; Calhoon, Loyalists, 245; Nelson, American Tory, 74–75.

75. Bell, War of Religion, 162, 164, 165.

76. Zubly, Warm and Zealous Spirit, 7, 8, 9.

77. Zubly, Warm and Zealous Spirit, 15, 20, 21, 22, 23.

78. For a summary/synopsis of and commentary on major Loyalist themes, see Potter, Liberty We Seek.

79. Potter, Liberty We Seek, 10–11, 17, 148–149.

Chapter 2. Biblical Arguments

1. For extensive discussion of the content of Patriot preaching, see Byrd, Sacred Scripture, and chap. 3 of Frazer, Religious Beliefs.

2. Daniel L. Dreisbach, Reading the Bible with the Founding Fathers (New York:

Oxford University Press, 2017), 135, 112, 116–118, 112, 124, 115–135.

3. Byrd, *Sacred Scripture*, 116, 127.

4. Mark A. Noll, *In the Beginning Was the Word* (New York: Oxford University Press, 2016), 298, 301, 303, 300, 301, 303, 301, 302, 302–303, 303.

5. Dreisbach, *Reading the Bible*, 133.

6. Jonathan Boucher, "A Farewell Sermon" (1775), in *View of the Causes and Consequences*, 591, 592.

7. Jonathan Boucher, "On Fundamental Principles" (1773), in *View of the Causes and Consequences*, 300; Jonathan Boucher, "On Civil Liberty; Passive Obedience, and Non-Resistance" (1775), in *View of the Causes and Consequences*, 502.

8. Boucher, *Reminiscences*, 45.

9. Boucher, "On Civil Liberty," 504; 524–525.

10. Letter to Samuel Johnson (December 27, 1769), in Lydekker, *Life and Letters of Charles Inglis*, 86.

11. Letter to Samuel Johnson (December 4, 1770), in Lydekker, *Life and Letters of Charles Inglis*, 119.

12. Letter to Samuel Johnson (December 14, 1771), in Lydekker, *Life and Letters of Charles Inglis*, 142.

13. Inglis, letters to Johnson (April 30, 1771, and December 27, 1769), in Lydekker, *Life and Letters of Charles Inglis*, 128, 87.

14. Boucher, "On Civil Liberty," 497.

15. Boucher, "On Civil Liberty," 499.

16. Jonathan Boucher, "The Dispute Between the Israelites and the Two Tribes and an Half, Respecting Their Settlement Beyond Jordan" (1775), in *View of the Causes and Consequences*, 457.

17. Boucher, *Reminiscences*, 119.

18. Charles Inglis, "The Duty of Honouring the King, Explained and Recommended" (New York: Hugh Gaine, 1780), 27; Charles Inglis, "Letter VI to John Jay," in *Letters of Papinian: In Which the Conduct, Present State and Prospects, of the American Congress, Are Examined* (New York: Hugh Gaine, 1779), 78.

19. Letter to the Society for the Propagation of the Gospel (May 6, 1782), in Lydekker, *Life and Letters of Charles Inglis*, 208.

20. Inglis, letter to Richard Hind (October 31, 1776), in Lydekker, *Life and Letters of Charles Inglis*, 166.

21. Boucher, "Dispute Between the Israelites," 455; 451–452.

22. Boucher, "On Civil Liberty," 500.

23. Boucher, "Dispute Between the Israelites," 455–456.

24. Charles Inglis, "The Christian Soldier's Duty Briefly Delineated" (New York: H. Gaines, 1777), 17.

25. Boucher, "Dispute Between the Israelites," 485.

26. Boucher, "Dispute Between the Israelites," 453.

27. Boucher, "Dispute Between the Israelites," 486.

28. Boucher, "On Civil Liberty," 522.

29. Boucher, *Reminiscences*, 45–46.

30. Boucher, "Dispute Between the Israelites," 488.

31. Samuel Seabury, "A Discourse on II Tim. III. 16" (New-York: H. Gaine, 1777).

32. Seabury, "Discourse on II Tim. III. 16," 4, 5.

33. Seabury, "Discourse on II Tim. III. 16," 6–7.

34. Seabury, "Discourse on II Tim. III. 16," 10, 7n.

35. Seabury, "Discourse on II Tim. III. 16," 10, 11, 12, 14–15.

36. Boucher, "On Civil Liberty," 498.

37. Boucher, "Dispute Between the Israelites," 488.

38. Boucher, "Dispute Between the Israelites," 488–489.

39. Seabury, "Discourse on II Tim. III. 16," 15, 23.

40. See, e.g., George Micklejohn, "On the Important Duty of Subjection to the Civil Powers" (Newbern, NC: James Davis, 1768), 2; Chandler, "Friendly Address," 5; Inglis, "Duty of Honouring the King," 16, 27.

41. Zubly, "Essay Number 6" (September 28, 1780), in "'Helvetius' Essays," *Royal Georgia Gazette*, July 27–October 12, 1780, in Zubly, *Warm and Zealous Spirit*, 194.

42. Charles Turner, "1773 Election Sermon," in *They Preached Liberty*, ed. Franklin P. Cole (Indianapolis, IN: Liberty Press, 1977), 51.

43. Boucher, "On Civil Liberty," 505.

44. Zubly, "Law of Liberty," 7–8.

45. Boucher, "On the Character of Ahitophel," 411.

46. Micklejohn, "On the Important Duty," 1–2.

47. Micklejohn, "On the Important Duty," 3, 4.

48. Micklejohn, "On the Important Duty," 5.

49. Micklejohn, "On the Important Duty," 5, 6.

50. Micklejohn, "On the Important Duty," 6–7; 7.

51. Micklejohn, "On the Important Duty," 9–10.

52. Thomas Bradbury Chandler, "The American Querist: or, Some Questions Proposed Relative to the Present Disputes between Great Britain and Her American Colonies" (Boston: Mills & Hicks, 1774), 32.

53. See, e.g., Chandler, "Friendly Address," 5; Inglis, "Duty of Honouring the King," 11; Samuel Seabury, "St. Peter's Exhortation To fear GOD and honor the KING, Explained and inculcated" (New York: H. Gaine, 1777), 12; Myles Cooper, "The Patriots of North-America: a Sketch. With Explanatory Notes" (New York, 1775), 45.

54. Chandler, "Friendly Address," 5.

55. Cooper, "Patriots of North-America," 45.

56. Zubly, "Law of Liberty," 16.

57. Zubly, "Law of Liberty," 16.

58. Zubly, "Law of Liberty," 29.

59. Zubly, "Essay Number 2" (August 3, 1780), in "'Helvetius' Essays," 178.

60. Inglis, "Duty of Honouring the King," 9; Seabury, "St. Peter's Exhortation," 7.

61. Seabury, "St. Peter's Exhortation," 9, 5–6, 8; Inglis, "Duty of Honouring the King," 11.

62. Seabury, "St. Peter's Exhortation," 6, 8–9.

63. Inglis, "Duty of Honouring the King," 10–11.

64. Inglis, "Duty of Honouring the King," 11.

65. Seabury, "St. Peter's Exhortation," 12.

66. Inglis, "Duty of Honouring the King," 5; Seabury, "St. Peter's Exhortation," 15.

67. Inglis, "Duty of Honouring the King," 12.

68. Inglis, "Duty of Honouring the King," 13, 14.

69. Seabury, "St. Peter's Exhortation," 16.

70. William Hunt, *The History of England from the Accession of George III to the Close of Pitt's First Administration (1760–1801)* (London: Longmans, Green, 1905), 10:123.

71. Seabury, "St. Peter's Exhortation," 16.

72. Boucher, "On Civil Liberty," 560.
73. Boucher, "On Civil Liberty," 504.
74. Boucher, "On Civil Liberty," 504–505.
75. Boucher, "On Civil Liberty," 506.
76. Boucher, "On Civil Liberty," 507–508.
77. Boucher, "On Civil Liberty," 509.
78. John Joachim Zubly, "The Stamp-Act Repealed" (Savannah, GA: James Johnston, 1766), 24, 27, 29–30.
79. Zubly, "Law of Liberty," 7
80. Zubly, "Law of Liberty," 1, 5, 6, 8.
81. Zubly, "Law of Liberty," 7, 13, 14–15, 17.
82. Zubly, "Law of Liberty," 17.
83. Boucher, "Farewell Sermon," 590.
84. Boucher, "On Civil Liberty," 535.
85. Boucher, "On Civil Liberty," 536.
86. Boucher, "On Civil Liberty," 537–538
87. Boucher, "On Civil Liberty," 540.
88. Boucher, "On Civil Liberty."
89. Boucher, "On Civil Liberty."
90. Boucher, "On Civil Liberty," 542.
91. Boucher, "On Civil Liberty," 542–543.
92. Boucher, "On Civil Liberty," 543.
93. Micklejohn, "On the Important Duty," 6.
94. Micklejohn, "On the Important Duty," 13, 14.
95. Seabury, "St. Peter's Exhortation," 10; Inglis, "Duty of Honouring the King," 6, 17.
96. Chandler, "American Querist," 32; Samuel Seabury, "Discourse on Brotherly Love" (New-York: Hugh Gaine, 1777), 15–16.
97. Thomas Paine, "Common Sense," in *Common Sense, the Rights of Man, and other Essential Writings of Thomas Paine*, ed. Sidney Hook (New York: New American Library, 1969), 30.
98. Charles Inglis, "The True Interest of America Impartially Stated, in Certain Strictures on a Pamphlet Intitled Common Sense" (Philadelphia: James Humphreys Jr., 1776), 27, 28.
99. Inglis, "True Interest," 27, 28, 29, 30.
100. Inglis, "True Interest," 31–33.
101. Boucher, "On Civil Liberty," 532.
102. Boucher, "On Civil Liberty," 533.
103. See William Smith, "A Sermon on the Present Situation of American Affairs" (Philadelphia: James Humphreys Jr., 1775).
104. Boucher, "Dispute Between the Israelites," 470, 477.
105. Boucher, "Dispute Between the Israelites," 472, 477, 490, 491.
106. Jonathan Boucher, "On the Character of Absalom" (1774), in *View of the Causes and Consequences*, 394–395, 397.
107. The spelling of the name Ahitophel is now normalized as Ahithophel, but Boucher's spelling is consistent with the Hebrew.
108. Boucher, "On the Character of Ahitophel," 404–405, 419.
109. Boucher, "On the Character of Ahitophel," 421, 421–422, 423.
110. Boucher, "On the Character of Ahitophel," 421.
111. Boucher, "On the Character of Ahitophel," 426, 433; "Farewell Sermon," 589.
112. Micklejohn, "On the Important Duty," 1, 8, 9, 12.
113. Seabury, "St. Peter's Exhortation," 19, 8–9.
114. Inglis, "Christian Soldier's Duty," 17; "Duty of Honouring the King," 16; "Christian Soldier's Duty,"
115. Inglis, "True Interest," 31.
116. Boucher, "Dispute Between the Israelites," 472; "On Civil Liberty," 532n;

Jonathan Boucher, "A Letter From a Virginian, to the Members of the Congress" (1774), 8–9.

117. Boucher, "On Civil Liberty," 533.
118. Boucher, "On Civil Liberty," 546.
119. Boucher, "On Civil Liberty," 546, 555.
120. Boucher, "Dispute Between the Israelites," 481–482; "On Civil Liberty," 543, 559–560.
121. Boucher, "On Civil Liberty," 560.
122. Zubly, "Law of Liberty," 21; Zubly, "Essay Number 3" (August 31, 1780), in "'Helvetius' Essays," 183, 184.
123. Zubly, "Essay Number 6," 191, 195, 196.
124. John Sayre, "Letter to the Gentlemen of the Committee of the Town of Fairfield," in New-York Journal (1776?), 4; Jonathan Boucher, "On the Peace in 1763" (1763), in View of the Causes and Consequences, 45; Inglis, "Christian Soldier's Duty," 24; Inglis, "Duty of Honouring the King," 32; Zubly, "Stamp-Act Repealed," 27.
125. Samuel Andrews, "A Sermon Preached at Litchfield, in Connecticut, before a Voluntary Convention of the Clergy of the Church of England of Several Provinces in America" (1770), 8.
126. Samuel Andrews, "A Discourse, Shewing the Necessity of Joining Internal Repentance, with the External Profession of It" (New-Haven: Thomas and Samuel Green, 1775), 10–11, 11.
127. Andrews, "Discourse," 11–12, 12.
128. Andrews, "Discourse," 14.
129. Andrews, "Discourse," 14.
130. Andrews, "Discourse," 15.
131. Andrews, "Discourse," 15, 16.
132. Andrews, "Discourse," 16–17.
133. Andrews, "Discourse," 17.
134. Andrews, "Discourse," 18.
135. Boucher, "On Civil Liberty," 533–534.
136. Boucher, "On Civil Liberty," 534.

Chapter 3. Theoretical Arguments from the Nature of Government

1. Boucher, "On the American Episcopate," 100; "Letter From a Virginian," 6; "On the Character of Absalom," 392; "Letter From a Virginian," 7.
2. Charles Inglis, "Letter IX to the People of North America," in *Letters of Papinian*, 120, 124, 108, 109, 112.
3. Seabury, "Discourse on Brotherly Love," 8, 13, 10, 13–14, 12.
4. Seabury, "Discourse on Brotherly Love," 6, 7; Inglis, "True Interest," 11.
5. Inglis, "True Interest," 11, 12.
6. Boucher, "On Civil Liberty," 523, 521; "Dispute Between the Israelites," 463.
7. Boucher, "On Civil Liberty," 523, 526, 525, 528–529, 524, 525, 526–527; Boucher, "On the Character of Absalom," 391, 391–392.
8. Inglis, "True Interest," 17, 18, and see also 20; Charles Inglis, "Letter II to Henry Laurens," in *Letters of Papinian*, 25.
9. Inglis, "True Interest," 23, 24.
10. Boucher, "On Fundamental Principles," 313; "On Civil Liberty," 520–521, 514.
11. Boucher, "On Civil Liberty," 529n, 514–515, 520, 515; "On the Character of Absalom," 419.
12. Boucher, "On Civil Liberty," 514; e.g., Boucher, "On the Character of Absalom," 398; "On Civil Liberty," 523; "On Fundamental Principles," 300, 313, 322.
13. Boucher, "On the Character of Absalom," 391–392; "On Fundamental Principles," 306.
14. Boucher, "On Civil Liberty," 521n, 515.

15. Boucher, "On Civil Liberty," 515–516, 516.

16. Boucher, "On Civil Liberty," 516, 516–517.

17. Boucher, "On Civil Liberty," 517, 518.

18. Boucher, "On the Character of Absalom," 385, 386, 397–398.

19. Boucher, "On Fundamental Principles," 313; "On the Character of Absalom," 393.

20. Inglis, "Duty of Honouring the King," 27; Jonathan Boucher, "On the Strife Between Abram and Lot" (1774), in *View of the Causes and Consequences*, 366, 370.

21. Samuel Seabury, "The Congress Canvassed: or, An Examination into the Conduct of the Delegates, at Their Grand Convention" (New York: James Rivington, 1774), 20; Inglis, "Duty of Honouring the King," 12, 28, 12; Boucher, "Letter From a Virginian," 11–12; Boucher, "On Fundamental Principles," 310–311.

22. Boucher, "On Fundamental Principles," 312; Inglis, "Christian Soldier's Duty," 12–13; Inglis, "Duty of Honouring the King," 19.

23. Inglis, "Duty of Honouring the King," 19; Inglis, "Letter II to Henry Laurens," 22.

24. See, e.g., chap. 3 of Frazer, *Religious Beliefs*; Byrd, *Sacred Scripture*; Alice M. Baldwin, *The New England Clergy and the American Revolution* (New York: Frederick Ungar, 1958).

25. Inglis, "Letter IX to the People of North America," 116n.

26. Chandler, "Friendly Address," 5, 48n; Zubly, "Essay Number 1" (July 27, 1780), in "'Helvetius' Essays," 175; Inglis, "Duty of Honouring the King,"

22; Zubly, "Law of Liberty," 2; Boucher, "On Civil Liberty," 547.

27. Seabury, "St. Peter's Exhortation," 11.

28. Seabury, "St. Peter's Exhortation," 11.

29. William Falkner, *Christian Loyalty*, 2nd ed. (1684), 365, quoted in Boucher, "Dispute Between the Israelites," 483n.

30. Boucher, "Dispute Between the Israelites," 489.

31. Seabury, "St. Peter's Exhortation," 8; Boucher, "On Civil Liberty," 545, 545–546, 548; Boucher, "Dispute Between the Israelites," 468; Boucher, "On Civil Liberty," 543; Boucher, "On Fundamental Principles," 300, 301.

32. Charles Inglis, "Letter VII to John Jay," in *Letters of Papinian*, 85, 86, 87.

33. Boucher, "On Civil Liberty," 552, 552–553, 553.

34. Zubly, "Stamp-Act Repealed," 12; Zubly, "Essay Number 7" (October 12, 1780), in "'Helvetius' Essays," 196; Boucher, "On the Character of Ahitophel," in *View of the Causes and Consequences*, 422.

35. Zubly, "Essay Number 2," 178, 176; Inglis, "Duty of Honouring the King," 22, 23; Inglis, "Letter VII to John Jay," 86.

36. Inglis, "Duty of Honouring the King," 23; Chandler, "Friendly Address," 28.

37. Zubly, "Essay Number 7," 196; "Essay Number 1," 175; "Essay Number 2," 178

38. Boucher, "On the Character of Ahitophel," 423; "On Fundamental Principles," 322; "On the Character of Ahitophel," 418.

39. Inglis, "True Interest," 31;

Chandler, "Friendly Address," 48; Seabury, "Congress Canvassed," 22; Zubly, "Essay Number 2," 178.

40. Zubly, "Essay Number 2," 180–181; "Essay Number 3," 183.

41. Boucher, "Dispute Between the Israelites," 483, 484.

42. Boucher, "Dispute Between the Israelites," 485, 485–486.

43. Boucher, "Dispute Between the Israelites," 486; "Letter From a Virginian," 27–28.

44. Seabury, "Discourse on Brotherly Love," 8; Seabury, "St. Peter's Exhortation," 10; Zubly, "Law of Liberty," 26.

Chapter 4. Legal Arguments

1. Andrews, "Sermon Preached at Litchfield," 8, 8–9, 9.

2. Chandler, "American Querist," 10, 9, 11–14.

3. Samuel Seabury, "A View of the Controversy Between Great-Britain and her Colonies" (New-York: James Rivington, 1774), 12, 12–14, 14.

4. Chandler, "American Querist," 11, 12; Seabury, "View of the Controversy," 12–13.

5. Seabury, "View of the Controversy," 9.

6. Boucher, "Letter From a Virginian," 9, 10.

7. Boucher, "Letter From a Virginian," 11.

8. Charles Inglis, "Letter VIII to John Jay," in *Letters of Papinian*, 90n.

9. John Joachim Zubly, "An Humble Enquiry" (1769), 4; Boucher, "Letter From a Virginian," 25.

10. Chandler, "American Querist," 9, 10; Seabury, "View of the Controversy," 9, 10, 14.

11. Boucher, "On the Strife Between Abram and Lot," 360, 360–361.

12. Inglis, "Christian Soldier's Duty," 17, 18.

13. Seabury, "View of the Controversy," 9, 10.

14. Seabury, "View of the Controversy," 10, 11, 10; Chandler, "American Querist," 14; Zubly, "Humble Enquiry," 4.

15. Zubly, "Humble Enquiry," 5; "Law of Liberty," 28.

16. Seabury, "View of the Controversy," 10; Chandler, "American Querist," 23.

17. Seabury, "Congress Canvassed," 18.

18. Chandler, "American Querist," 16, 17, 18. Chandler says the congress took place in 1755, but it was 1754.

19. Boucher, "On the Strife Between Abram and Lot," 357, 372; "On Civil Liberty," 555, 559.

20. Boucher, "On Civil Liberty," 557, 558.

21. Samuel Seabury, "An Alarm to the Legislature of the Province of New-York" (New York: James Rivington, 1775), 5; Samuel Seabury, "Free Thoughts, on the Proceedings of the Continental Congress, Held at Philadelphia Sept. 5, 1774" (New York, 1774), 23–24; Seabury, "View of the Controversy," 17; Seabury, "Congress Canvassed," 8, 8–9.

22. Seabury, "Congress Canvassed," 9.

23. Seabury, "Congress Canvassed," 9; "Alarm to the Legislature," 4–5.

24. Boucher, "Letter From a Virginian," 4; "On the Strife Between Abram and Lot," 326; "Farewell Sermon," 563; "On the Strife Between Abram and Lot," 363, 354; "On the Character of Ahitophel," in *View of the Causes and Consequences*, 433.

25. Seabury, "Congress Canvassed," 10.
26. Seabury, "Congress Canvassed," 10, 11.
27. Seabury, "Alarm to the Legislature," 7, 8; "Congress Canvassed," 20; "View of the Controversy," 17.
28. Seabury, "View of the Controversy," 17; Seabury, "Alarm to the Legislature," 7, 8.
29. Seabury, "Congress Canvassed," 20.
30. Seabury, "Congress Canvassed," 20; "Alarm to the Legislature," 8; "Congress Canvassed," 20; "Alarm to the Legislature," 8.
31. Seabury, "Congress Canvassed," 24.
32. Seabury, "View of the Controversy," 16, 17.
33. Chandler, "Friendly Address," 46.
34. Chandler, "What Think Ye," 8–9, 9.
35. Chandler, "What Think Ye," 9, 10.
36. Chandler, "What Think Ye," 10, 10–11, 11.
37. Seabury, "View of the Controversy," 37.
38. Seabury, "Alarm to the Legislature," 5.
39. Seabury, "Alarm to the Legislature," 6; "Congress Canvassed," 13.
40. Seabury, "Alarm to the Legislature," 6, 7, 10.
41. Chandler, "American Querist," 3, 27.
42. Boucher, "On Fundamental Principles," 321; "On the Strife Between Abram and Lot," 361–362, 362; "On the Character of Ahitophel," 407, 407–408.
43. Boucher, "On the Character of Ahitophel," 408, 409.
44. Boucher, "On the Character of Ahitophel," 409, 409–410, 410.
45. Boucher, "Dispute Between the Israelites," in *View of the Causes and Consequences*, 483.
46. Seabury, "Congress Canvassed," 14; "Free Thoughts," 18.
47. Seabury, "Congress Canvassed," 14.
48. Seabury, "Congress Canvassed," 14–15.
49. Seabury, "Congress Canvassed," 15.
50. John Joachim Zubly, "To the Grand Jury of the County of Chatham, State of Georgia" (Savannah, GA: William Lancaster, 1777), 2.
51. Zubly, "To the Grand Jury," 1.
52. Seabury, "Alarm to the Legislature," 9.
53. Seabury, "Congress Canvassed," 15, 16, 16–17, 17.
54. Seabury, "Congress Canvassed," 18, 16, 23, 20, 23.
55. Inglis, "Letter VI to John Jay," iii, 61–62.
56. Inglis, "Letter VIII to John Jay," 105.
57. Seabury, "Congress Canvassed," 18; "Free Thoughts," 19; "Congress Canvassed," 9; "Alarm to the Legislature," 7, 12–13; "Free Thoughts," 19; "Alarm to the Legislature," 6.

Chapter 5. Rational Arguments Regarding the American Situation

1. Inglis, "Letter VIII to John Jay," 90n; Chandler, "What Think Ye," 48; Seabury, "View of the Controversy," 20; Boucher, "Farewell Sermon," 592; Zubly, "Stamp-Act Repealed," 23.
2. Boucher, "Dispute Between the Israelites," 475; Zubly, "Stamp-Act Repealed," 25; Inglis, "Letter IX to the People of North America," 129; Seabury, "View of the Controversy," 9.
3. Chandler, "American Querist," 6, 7; "Friendly Address," 35; "What Think Ye," 7–8.

4. Seabury, "St. Peter's Exhortation," 16; "Congress Canvassed," 26.

5. Chandler, "What Think Ye," 7; Chandler, "American Querist," 8; Zubly, "Humble Enquiry," 4.

6. Boucher, "Letter From a Virginian," 13; Chandler, "Friendly Address," 35; Inglis, "Letter VI to John Jay," 63; Chandler, "Friendly Address," 7.

7. Boucher, "On the Peace in 1763," 43, 44; Andrews, "Sermon Preached at Litchfield," 14; Inglis, "True Interest," 39, 39–40, 40.

8. Boucher, "Dispute Between the Israelites," 476; Seabury, "St. Peter's Exhortation," 10, 20; Inglis, "True Interest," 41.

9. Boucher, "On the Strife Between Abram and Lot," 374; Seabury, "View of the Controversy," 14–15.

10. Seabury, "View of the Controversy," 16, 15; Zubly, "Humble Enquiry," 20.

11. Boucher, "Dispute Between the Israelites," 475; Zubly, "Humble Enquiry," 13; Boucher, "On the Strife Between Abram and Lot," 339.

12. Boucher, "Letter From a Virginian," 26; Seabury, "St. Peter's Exhortation," 20.

13. Boucher, "Dispute Between the Israelites," 458, 472, 490.

14. Chandler, "Friendly Address," 3; Boucher, "Letter From a Virginian," 28.

15. Seabury, "St. Peter's Exhortation," 19–20; Boucher, "On the Character of Ahitophel," 427–428.

16. Inglis, "Letter VII to John Jay," 73–74, 74; Spurius Servilius quoted in Dionysius of Halicarnassus, *The Roman Antiquities of Dionysius Halicarnassensis*, trans. Edward Spelman (London, 1758), 9:4:61, in Boucher, "Dispute Between the Israelites," 492–493.

17. Micklejohn, "On the Important Duty," 10; Chandler, "Friendly Address," 7; Boucher, "On Civil Liberty," 555; Chandler, "Friendly Address," 24.

18. Chandler, "Friendly Address," 7; Boucher, "Letter From a Virginian," 20–21.

19. Chandler, "Friendly Address," 7, 9, 10.

20. Chandler, "Friendly Address," 10, 11, 11–12

21. Chandler, "What Think Ye," 13, 14; "American Querist," 24–25.

22. Andrews, "Sermon Preached at Litchfield," 9; Jonathan Boucher, letter to William Eden (January 7, 1776), in "Letters of Rev. Jonathan Boucher," *Maryland Historical Magazine* 8, no. 4 (December 1913): 341; Jonathan Boucher, letter to John James (November 16, 1773), in "Letters of Rev. Jonathan Boucher," *Maryland Historical Magazine* 8, no. 2 (June 1913): 184; Jonathan Boucher, letter to [William Knox] (November 27, 1775), in "Letters of Rev. Jonathan Boucher," *Maryland Historical Magazine* 8, no. 3 (September 1913): 254; Jonathan Boucher, letter to John James (April 6, 1776), in "Letters of Rev. Jonathan Boucher," *Maryland Historical Magazine* 8, no. 4 (December 1913): 352; Boucher, letter to [William Knox] (November 27, 1775), 248.

23. Inglis, "Letter VII to John Jay," 76.

24. Inglis, "Letter VII to John Jay," 76n; Boucher, letter to [William Knox] (November 27, 1775), 246; Inglis, "Letter VII to John Jay," 74.

25. See, e.g., Benton, *Whig-Loyalism*; and Zubly, *Warm and Zealous Spirit*.

26. Jonathan Boucher, letter to John James (December 9, 1765), in "Letters of Rev. Jonathan Boucher," *Maryland Historical Magazine* 7, no. 3 (September

1912): 295; Jonathan Boucher, letter to John James (March 9, 1767), in "Letters of Rev. Jonathan Boucher," *Maryland Historical Magazine* 7, no. 4 (December 1912): 344; Zubly, "Stamp-Act Repealed," 21, 24; Zubly, "Law of Liberty," 25; Inglis, "True Interest," 37; Chandler, "What Think Ye," 7, 44.

27. Boucher, letter to John James (December 9, 1765), 296, 295; Boucher, letter to John James (November 16, 1773), 183, 184; Boucher, letter to [William Knox] (November 27, 1775), 246–247; Boucher, letter to William Eden (January 7, 1776), 340.

28. Zubly, "Law of Liberty," 23, 25n; Boucher, "On the Strife Between Abram and Lot," 370, 371, 370.

29. Boucher, "On the Strife Between Abram and Lot," 372; Boucher, "On Fundamental Principles," 314–315, 315; Boucher, "On the Character of Ahitophel," 417.

30. Zubly, "Stamp-Act Repealed," 25, 22, Zubly, "Law of Liberty," 23.

31. Seabury, "St. Peter's Exhortation," 16, 17, 17–18.

32. Inglis, "Christian Soldier's Duty," 18n; Inglis, "Duty of Honouring the King," 29.

33. Boucher, "On Fundamental Principles," 306; Boucher, "On the Character of Ahitophel," 414; Boucher, "Letter From a Virginian," 8; Boucher, "On the Strife Between Abram and Lot," 356, 347; Boucher, "On the Character of Ahitophel," 417; Boucher, "On the Strife Between Abram and Lot," 341, 373; Boucher, "On the Character of Ahitophel," 417; Boucher, "On Civil Liberty," 554.

34. Boucher, "On the Character of Ahitophel," 416; Boucher, "On the Strife Between Abram and Lot," 335; Boucher, "On the Character of Absalom," 388; Boucher, "On the Strife Between Abram and Lot," 338, 335; Boucher, "On the Character of Absalom," 389, 390; Boucher, "On the Character of Ahitophel," 413, 414; Boucher, "On the Strife Between Abram and Lot," 337; Boucher, "Dispute Between the Israelites," 494; Boucher, "On the Character of Ahitophel," 417; Boucher, "On the Strife Between Abram and Lot," 338.

35. Boucher, "Letter From a Virginian," 7; Boucher, "Farewell Sermon," 571, 568–569; Boucher, "Letter From a Virginian," 6, 7; Boucher, "On the Strife Between Abram and Lot," 366n.

36. Seabury, "Congress Canvassed," 22; Seabury, "View of the Controversy," 19; Seabury, "Congress Canvassed," 22, 20.

37. Seabury, "Congress Canvassed," 12, 12–13.

38. Seabury, "Free Thoughts," 5.

39. Seabury, "View of the Controversy," 35; Seabury, "Congress Canvassed," 24; Seabury, "View of the Controversy," 22, 35.

40. Charles Inglis, "Letter III to Henry Laurens," in *Letters of Papinian*, 26–27; Charles Inglis, "Letter IV to John Jay," in *Letters of Papinian*, 38; Inglis, "Letter VI to John Jay," 68, 69, 71.

41. Inglis, "Christian Soldier's Duty," 13; Inglis, "Letter IX to the People of North America," 107–108, 109.

42. Inglis, "Letter IX to the People of North America," 108, 109; Inglis, "Christian Soldier's Duty," 22; Inglis, "Duty of Honouring the King," 25, 25n.

43. Inglis, "True Interest," 34.

44. Chandler, "Friendly Address," 29n–30n; Chandler, "American Querist," 27.

45. Chandler, "Friendly Address," 14, 15, 15–22, 22, 23.

46. Chandler, "Friendly Address," 31; Chandler, "American Querist," 26; Chandler, "Friendly Address," 47; Chandler, "What Think Ye," 13, 41; Chandler, "Friendly Address," 6.

47. Chandler, "American Querist," 30n; Chandler, "Friendly Address," 53, 54.

48. Chandler, "Friendly Address," 45; Chandler, "What Think Ye," 20.

49. Boucher, "On the Strife Between Abram and Lot," 341, 342, 345, 374, 375.

50. Seabury, "View of the Controversy," 5; Seabury, "Free Thoughts," 23; Seabury, "Congress Canvassed," 26; Seabury, "View of the Controversy," 33.

51. Inglis, "True Interest," 37–38, 36, 39, 43–44, 47.

52. These include an end to the "calamitous war"; peace restored; agriculture, commerce, and industry would flourish; "our trade would still have the protection of the greatest naval power in the world"; protection would be much cheaper than the cost of building our own navy; bounties for goods would be available; and immigrants will "flow in" and lands will rise in value. Inglis, "True Interest," 47–49.

53. Inglis, "True Interest," 47–49, 49.

54. Boucher, "Dispute Between the Israelites," 492; Boucher, "Letter From a Virginian," 13–14, 15.

55. Boucher, "On the Character of Ahitophel," 417–418; Boucher, "Dispute Between the Israelites," 493; Boucher, "On Civil Liberty," 559.

56. Seabury, "View of the Controversy," 20, 24, 23, 31, 32, 24.

57. Seabury, "View of the Controversy," 31; "Congress Canvassed," 5.

58. Seabury, "Congress Canvassed," 13, 17.

59. Inglis, "True Interest," 61–62, vii.

60. These include "the claim of parliamentary taxation be either explicitly relinquished; or else, such security given as the case will admit . . . that this claim shall not be exerted"; "such a freedom of trade as is consistent with the general welfare of the State"; and "many other particulars." Inglis, "True Interest," 62.

61. Inglis, "True Interest," 62.

62. Chandler, "Friendly Address," 5, 45; Chandler, "American Querist," 22, 7.

63. Chandler, "What Think Ye," 14, 15, 11, 15;.

64. Chandler, "Friendly Address," 45–46; Chandler, "What Think Ye," 47.

65. Chandler, "What Think Ye," 46, 47.

66. Boucher, "Dispute Between the Israelites," 479.

67. Charles Inglis, *Letters of Papinian*, iii; Charles Inglis, "Letter I to Henry Laurens," in *Letters of Papinian: In Which the Conduct, Present State and Prospects, of the American Congress, Are Examined* (New York: Hugh Gaine, 1779), 13; Inglis "Letter III to Henry Laurens," 26; Inglis, "Letter II to Henry Laurens," in *Letters of Papinian*, 21–22; Inglis, "Letter VII to John Jay," 74; Inglis, "Letter VI to John Jay," 63.

68. Zubly, "Essay Number 2," 177, 179, 177; Zubly, "Essay Number 3," 181, 182, 185.

69. Zubly, "Essay Number 4" [September 7, 1780], in Zubly, *Warm and Zealous Spirit*, 187, 190, 187; Zubly, "Essay Number 6," 193.

70. Seabury, "Alarm to the Legislature," 3–4.

71. Seabury, "Alarm to the Legislature," 11, 12.

72. Jonathan Boucher, letter to Rev. Dr. Smith, Provost of the College of Philadelphia (May 4, 1775), in "Letters of

Rev. Jonathan Boucher," *Maryland Historical Magazine* 8, no. 3 (September 1913): 239; Inglis, "Letter VI to John Jay," 64; Inglis, "Letter III to Henry Laurens," 33.

73. Chandler, "What Think Ye," 18, 6.

74. Chandler, "What Think Ye," 8; "Friendly Address," 31; "What Think Ye," 12, 13.

75. Chandler, "Friendly Address," 32–33; Chandler, "What Think Ye," 12, 21, 17, 32.

76. Chandler, "What Think Ye," 32, 6, 40.

77. Chandler, "What Think Ye," 6, 7, 13, 17, 18, 40.

78. Seabury, "View of the Controversy," 7; Seabury, "Congress Canvassed," 5; Seabury, "Free Thoughts," 3; Seabury, "View of the Controversy," 23.

79. Seabury, "Congress Canvassed," 13; Seabury, "View of the Controversy," 5; Seabury, "Congress Canvassed," 13.

80. Seabury, "Free Thoughts," 17, 18.

81. Seabury, "Free Thoughts," 18, 19.

82. Seabury, "Congress Canvassed," 18, 19.

83. Seabury, "Congress Canvassed," 16, 17, 19; "View of the Controversy," 17; "Congress Canvassed," 19–20, 20, 21.

84. Seabury, "View of the Controversy," 17, 8.

85. Seabury, "View of the Controversy," 5, 6.

86. Seabury, "View of the Controversy," 6.

87. Seabury, "Free Thoughts," 22.

88. Chandler, "What Think Ye," 42.

89. Seabury, "Congress Canvassed," 24; Seabury, "Free Thoughts," 22.

90. Chandler, "American Querist," 30; Chandler, "What Think Ye," 48.

Chapter 6. Rational Arguments Based on Colonial Actions

1. Boucher, "Letter From a Virginian," 17, 18.

2. Chandler, "Friendly Address," 42; Seabury, "Free Thoughts," 8; Seabury, "View of the Controversy," 28.

3. Boucher, "Letter From a Virginian," 19; Seabury, "Congress Canvassed," 21; Seabury, "Alarm to the Legislature," 6; Seabury, "View of the Controversy," 27; Seabury, "Free Thoughts," 17.

4. Boucher, "Letter From a Virginian," 20, 21.

5. Boucher, "Letter From a Virginian," 21.

6. Chandler, "Friendly Address," 37, 38; Chandler, "What Think Ye," 27.

7. Seabury, "Alarm to the Legislature," 6; Seabury, "Congress Canvassed," 18; Chandler, "What Think Ye," 41.

8. Seabury, "Free Thoughts," 9; Chandler, "Friendly Address," 38, 39, 41; Seabury, "Alarm to the Legislature," 6.

9. Seabury, "Free Thoughts," 6, 7; Seabury, "View of the Controversy," 30, 28, 29, 28, 29; Seabury, "Free Thoughts," 8, 14, 15.

10. Seabury, "Free Thoughts," 9, 10, 12, 13.

11. Seabury, "View of the Controversy," 25, 28; Seabury, "Free Thoughts," 13, 14, 6.

12. Seabury, "Free Thoughts," 9; Chandler, "What Think Ye," 28; Seabury, "View of the Controversy," 22; Chandler, "Friendly Address," 40; Seabury, "Free Thoughts," 9; Chandler, "Friendly Address," 41–42; Chandler, "What Think Ye," 41–42.

13. Seabury, "View of the Controversy," 25; Chandler, "What Think Ye,"

41; Seabury, "View of the Controversy," 24, 25.

14. Sayre, "Letter to the Gentlemen," 2.
15. Sayre, "Letter to the Gentlemen," 3.
16. Sayre, "Letter to the Gentlemen," 4.
17. Sayre, "Letter to the Gentlemen," 5, 6; Sabine, *Biographical Sketches*, 2:260.
18. Andrews, "Sermon Preached at Litchfield," 12, 13; Inglis, "Letter VI to John Jay," 67.
19. Jonathan Boucher, letter to Col. George Washington (Aug. 6, 1775), in Boucher, *Reminiscences*, 139, 140, 141.
20. Charles Inglis letter to Richard Hind (Oct. 31, 1776) in Lydekker, *Life and Letters of Charles Inglis*, 157; Samuel Seabury, "To the General Assembly of the Governor and Company of the Colony of Connecticut, now sitting in New Haven, in said Colony, by special Order of his Honor, the Governor" [December 20, 1775], in *Life and Correspondence of the Right Reverend Samuel Seabury, D.D.*, ed. E. Edwards Beardsley (Boston: Houghton, Mifflin, 1881), 39; Richard Mansfield letter to Samuel Peters (Jan. 12, 1776) in Crary, *Price of Loyalty*, 105; Daniel Leonard, "Massachusettensis" (Boston, 1776), 36; "Declaration of Dependence" [1781], in Chopra, *Choosing Sides*, 121.
21. Beardsley, *Life and Correspondence*, 27.
22. Boucher, *Reminiscences*, 130; Boucher, "Farewell Sermon," 563; Jonathan Boucher, letter to William Eden (January 7, 1776) in "Letters of Jonathan Boucher," *Maryland Historical Magazine* 8, no. 4 (December 1913): 341; Boucher, "Farewell Sermon," 587; Boucher, "On the Strife Between Abram and Lot," 366; Boucher, *Reminiscences*, 107; Seabury, "Alarm to the Legislature," 12.
23. Beardsley, *Life and Correspondence*, 35; Calhoon and Chopra, "Religion and the Loyalists," 101; Charles Inglis, July 24, 1777 letter to the S.P.G. in Lydekker, *Life and Letters of Charles Inglis*, 185.
24. Jonathan Boucher, letter to [William Knox] (November 27, 1775), in "Letters of Rev. Jonathan Boucher," *Maryland Historical Magazine* 8, no. 3 (September 1913): 254; Zubly, "Essay Number 1," 173; Inglis, "Letter II to Henry Laurens," in Inglis, *Letters of Papinian*.
25. Inglis, "Christian Soldier's Duty," 20; Seabury, "Alarm to the Legislature," 7.
26. Rhoden, *Revolutionary Anglicanism*, 103; Van Tyne, *Loyalists*, 240–241; Boucher, "On the Strife Between Abram and Lot," 365; Charles Inglis letter to Richard Hind (Oct. 31, 1776) in Lydekker, *Life and Letters of Charles Inglis*, 159.
27. Inglis, "Letter VI to John Jay," 69, 70, 71, 72.
28. Boucher, "On Civil Liberty," 502; Chandler, "What Think Ye," 34.
29. Inglis, "Letter VIII to John Jay," 105–106; Inglis, "Letter IX to the People of North America," 114; Charles Inglis letter to Richard Hind (October 31, 1776) in Lydekker, *Life and Letters of Charles Inglis*, 158.
30. Bell, *War of Religion*, 198; Rhoden, *Revolutionary Anglicanism*, 103; Charles Inglis letter VI to John Jay, 62; Zubly, "Essay Number 6," 192.
31. Zubly, "Essay Number 6," 195; MacKinnon and Calhoon, "Character and Coherence," 154.
32. Boucher, *Reminiscences*, 104, 105, 112, 74; Boucher, "Farewell Sermon," 562, 588.
33. Chandler, "Friendly Address," 49, 51.
34. Chandler, "Friendly Address," 51, 53. The last statement is a reference to I Kings 12:10.

35. Letter from "New-York Convention to the President of Congress" (July 11, 1776), in *American Archives: Consisting of a Collection of Authentic Records, State Papers, Debates and Letters and Other Notices of Publick Affairs . . .*, vol. 1, ser. 5 (Washington, DC: M. St. Claire Clarke and Peter Force, 1848), 1:202.

36. Inglis letter to Richard Hind (October 31, 1776) in Lydekker, *Life and Letters of Charles Inglis*, 160, 161.

37. Seabury, "To the General Assembly," 38.

38. Boucher, letter to Col. George Washington (August 6, 1775), in *Reminiscences*, 138; Chandler, "American Querist," 4.

39. Van Tyne, *Loyalists*, 199, 200–202, 200.

40. Chandler, "What Think Ye," 3, 4.

41. Chandler, "What Think Ye," 4; Charles Inglis's journal in Lydekker, *Life and Letters of Charles Inglis*, 152; Beardsley, *Life and Correspondence*, 29.

42. Van Tyne, *Loyalists*, 274; Inglis letter to Richard Hind (October 31, 1776) in Lydekker, *Life and Letters of Charles Inglis*, 166–167; Charles Inglis, S.P.G. Journal, 23:181 in Lydekker, *Life and Letters of Charles Inglis*, 212; Calhoon, *Loyalists*, 192; Seabury, "To the General Assembly," 38.

43. Calhoon and Chopra, "Religion and the Loyalists," 108.

44. Boucher, *Reminiscences*, 129–130.

45. Rossiter, *Political Thought*, 133, 134.

46. Charles Inglis letter to Richard Hind (October 31, 1776) in Lydekker, *Life and Letters of Charles Inglis*, 166; Zubly, *Warm and Zealous Spirit*, 22, 199.

47. Seabury, "To the General Assembly," 39–42.

48. Boucher, *Reminiscences*, 105, 106, 107, 108, 111–112.

49. Seabury, "Congress Canvassed," 26; Chandler, "What Think Ye," 5.

50. Boucher, "Farewell Sermon," 577; 577–578.

51. Jonathan Boucher, letter to Col. George Washington (August 6, 1775), in *Reminiscences*, 139; Seabury, "St. Peter's Exhortation," 18–19; Inglis, "Letter IX to the People of North America," 129.

52. Seabury, "St. Peter's Exhortation," 19.

53. Boucher, "On the Character of Ahitophel," in *View of the Causes and Consequences*, 421–422.

54. Boucher, "Dispute Between the Israelites," in *View of the Causes and Consequences*, 477, 457.

55. Zubly, "Essay Number 2," 176; Chandler, "Friendly Address," 47, 33, 48; Zubly, "Essay Number 2," 178; Zubly, "Essay Number 3," 183, 183–184.

56. Chandler, "What Think Ye," 21, 22–23, 23.

57. Chandler, "What Think Ye," 23, 25; Seabury, "View of the Controversy," 32, 33; Seabury, "St. Peter's Exhortation," 18; Zubly, "Essay Number 1," 173.

58. Chandler, "Friendly Address," 25, 36, 37.

59. Boucher, "On the Strife Between Abram and Lot," 370; Boucher, "Dispute Between the Israelites," 468, 468–469, 469; Boucher, "On the Character of Ahitophel," 407.

60. Chandler, "A Friendly Address," 47–48; Jonathan Boucher, letter to [William Knox] (November 27, 1775), in "Letters of Rev. Jonathan Boucher," *Maryland Historical Magazine* 8, no. 3 (September 1913): 248; Jonathan Boucher, letter to William Eden (January 7, 1776), in "Letters of Rev. Jonathan Boucher," *Maryland Historical Magazine*

8, no. 4 (December 1913): 342; Boucher, "Letter From a Virginian," 29.

61. Chandler, "What Think Ye," 21; Chandler, "Friendly Address," 26, 27.

62. Inglis, "True Interest," 51.

63. Inglis, "Letter IX to the People of North America," 125; Inglis, "Letter VIII to John Jay," 100; Inglis, "Letter IX to the People of North America," 125, 126.

64. Inglis, "Letter IV to John Jay," 46, 47; Jonathan Boucher, letter to John James (November 16, 1773), 352.

65. Seabury, "View of the Controversy," 32; Chandler, "What Think Ye," 26; Inglis, "Letter VIII to John Jay," 99, 100.

66. Inglis, "Letter VIII to John Jay," 100, 101, 102; "Letter IX to the People of North America," 126–127, 127, 128.

67. Inglis, "Letter VIII to John Jay," 102, 103.

68. Inglis, "True Interest," 66, 66–67.

69. Inglis, "Letter VIII to John Jay," 98, 99.

70. Chandler, "American Querist," 27, 25–26; Seabury, "Alarm to the Legislature," 11.

71. Charles Inglis, "A Sermon on Philip. III. 20, 21" (New York: H. Gaine, 1777), 16–17; Inglis, "Duty of Honouring the King," 23.

72. Inglis, "Duty of Honouring the King," 26.

73. Inglis, "Duty of Honouring the King," 26.

74. Inglis, "Letter VII to John Jay," 77.

75. Inglis, "Letter VII to John Jay," 77, 78.

76. Inglis, "Letter VII to John Jay," 79, 80, 81.

77. Inglis, "Letter VII to John Jay," 81, 82, 83, 84.

78. Zubly, "Essay Number 2," 179, 180.

79. Zubly, "Essay Number 3," 190, 192, 193.

80. Inglis, "Letter IV to John Jay," 41, 40, 42, 43–44, 44.

81. Inglis, "Letter IV to John Jay," 44, 45, 46.

82. Inglis, "Letter IV to John Jay," 42; "Letter VIII to John Jay," 89–89n; "Letter IV to John Jay," 43.

83. Inglis, "Letter IX to the People of North America," 113, 114, 115.

84. Inglis, "Letter IX to the People of North America," 117, 118.

85. Inglis, "Duty of Honouring the King," 25; Seabury, "View of the Controversy," 31–32; Zubly, "Stamp-Act Repealed," 23; Zubly, "Law of Liberty," 25n; Boucher, "On the Strife Between Abram and Lot," 361; Zubly, "Essay Number 3," 185.

86. Zubly, "Law of Liberty," 23; Inglis, "Letter IX to the People of North America," 111, 111–112.

87. Inglis, "True Interest," 38; Chandler, "A Friendly Address," 26; Chandler, "American Querist," 28; Inglis, "True Interest," 46.

88. Inglis, "True Interest," 50, 63, 63–64, 65, 51–52.

89. Inglis, "Letter IX to the People of North America," 122, 123; Inglis, "True Interest," 50; Boucher, "On the Strife Between Abram and Lot," 364; Inglis, "True Interest," 50.

90. Seabury, "View of the Controversy," 119.

91. Seabury, "Congress Canvassed," 25, 26, 25.

92. Inglis, "Letter IX to the People of North America," 123.

93. Jonathan Boucher, "To the Honble The Deputies in Congress from the Southern Provinces," in Reminiscences, 133, 135, 133, 134.

94. Chandler, "American Querist," 28; "Friendly Address," 26; "What Think Ye," 25; "Friendly Address," 49, 49–51, 49.

95. Chandler, "What Think Ye," 36, 37–38, 39–40, 40.

96. Inglis, "Letter IX to the People of North America," 123, 124, 123–124, 125.

97. Inglis, "True Interest," 52; "Letter IX to the People of North America," 120.

98. Inglis, "Letter IX to the People of North America," 124; "True Interest," 53.

99. Inglis, "True Interest," 53, 56–58, 58.

100. Inglis, "True Interest," 59, 59–60.

101. Inglis, "True Interest," 60.

Epilogue

1. Shea, *Life and Epoch of Alexander Hamilton*, 251; Chopra, *Choosing Sides*, 2; Samuel Curwen, letter to William Pynchon (January 10, 1780), in Samuel Curwen, *Journal and Letters of the Late Samuel Curwen*, ed. George Atkinson Ward (New York: C. S. Francis, 1842), 231; Zubly, *Warm and Zealous Spirit*, 24.

2. Boucher, "On Fundamental Principles," 302, 303, 303–304; Calhoon, *Loyalists*, 257.

3. Inglis, "Duty of Honouring the King," 15, 20, 21, 22, 23.

4. Edward Floyd de Lancey in Thomas Jones, *History of New York During the Revolutionary War*, 2 vols., ed. Edward Floyd de Lancey (New York: Trow's, 1879), 1:ix.

5. Seabury, "St. Peter's Exhortation," 20; Boucher, "Letter From a Virginian," 26; Bailyn and Hench, *The Press and the American Revolution*, 253.

6. Nelson, *American Tory*, 19; Potter, *Liberty We Seek*, 147–148, 146, 147; Bailyn and Hench, *The Press and the American Revolution*, 272.

7. Nelson, *American Tory*, 80, 81; Shea, *Life and Epoch of Alexander Hamilton*, 299; Nelson, *American Tory*, 82; Shea, *Life and Epoch of Alexander Hamilton*, 299; Nelson, *American Tory*, 83.

8. Potter, *Liberty We Seek*, 10, 149–150, 32.

9. For a more general and differently organized study of Loyalist ideology, see Potter, *Liberty We Seek*. Potter's work deals with Loyalist ideology in general under themes of her construction. The one missing element is the biblical argument made by the clergy. Potter has several references to Chandler, Inglis, and Seabury, but she mentions Boucher only once briefly and Zubly not at all.

10. Chopra, *Choosing Sides*, 2–3.

11. Leder, *Liberty and Authority*, 142.

12. Harry V. Jaffa, *A New Birth of Freedom* (Lanham, MD: Rowman & Littlefield, 2000), 135.

BIBLIOGRAPHY

Adams, John. *The Works of John Adams, Second President of the United States*. 10 vols. Edited by Charles Francis Adams. Boston: Little, Brown, 1850–1856.

Anderson, James S. M. *The History of the Church of England, in the Colonies and Foreign Dependencies of the British Empire*. 3 vols. London: Rivingtons, 1845–1856.

Andrews, Samuel. "A Discourse, Shewing the Necessity of Joining Internal Repentance, with the External Profession of It." New-Haven: Thomas and Samuel Green, 1775.

———. "A Sermon Preached at Litchfield, in Connecticut, before a Voluntary Convention of the Clergy of the Church of England of Several Provinces in America." 1770.

Auchmuty, Samuel, Thomas B. Chandler, Myles Cooper, John Ogilvie, Richard Charlton, Samuel Seabury, Charles Inglis, and Abraham Beach. "An ADDRESS From the CLERGY of New-York and New-Jersey, to the EPISCOPALIANS in VIRGINIA; Occasioned by Some Late Transactions In That Colony Relative to an AMERICAN EPISCOPATE." New-York: Hugh Gaine, 1771.

Bailyn, Bernard. *The Ideological Origins of the American Revolution*. Cambridge, MA: Belknap Press of Harvard University Press, 1967.

———, and John B. Hench, eds. *The Press and the American Revolution*. Worcester, MA: American Antiquarian Society, 1980.

Baldwin, Alice M. *The New England Clergy and the American Revolution*. New York: Frederick Ungar, 1958.

Bates, Walter. "The Narrative of Walter Bates." In *Kingston and the Loyalists of the "Spring Fleet" of 1783*, edited by W. O. Raymond. 1889; reprint, Woodstock, NB, Canada: Non-Entity Press, 1980.

Beardsley, E. Edwards, ed. *Life and Correspondence of the Right Reverend Samuel Seabury, D.D.* Boston: Houghton, Mifflin, 1881.

Bell, James B. *A War of Religion: Dissenters, Anglicans, and the American Revolution*. New York: Palgrave Macmillan, 2008.

Benton, William Allen. *Whig-Loyalism: An Aspect of Political Ideology in the American Revolutionary Era*. Madison, NJ: Fairleigh Dickinson University Press, 1969.

Boucher, Jonathan. "A Farewell Sermon" (1775). In Boucher, *View of the Causes and Consequences*.

———. "A Letter From a Virginian, to the Members of the Congress." 1774.

———. *A View of the Causes and Consequences of the American Revolution*. New York: Russell & Russell, 1797.

———. "The Dispute Between the Israelites and the Two Tribes and an Half, Respecting Their Settlement Beyond Jordan" (1775). In Boucher, *View of the Causes and Consequences*.

———. "Letters of Rev. Jonathan Boucher." *Maryland Historical Magazine* 7, no. 1 (March 1912), through 8, no. 4 (December 1913).

———. "On the American Episcopate" (1771). In Boucher, *View of the Causes and Consequences.*

———. "On the Character of Absalom" (1774). In Boucher, *View of the Causes and Consequences.*

———. "On the Character of Ahitophel" (1774). In Boucher, *View of the Causes and Consequences.*

———. "On Civil Liberty; Passive Obedience, and Non-Resistance" (1775). In Boucher, *View of the Causes and Consequences.*

———. "On Fundamental Principles" (1773). In Boucher, *View of the Causes and Consequences.*

———. "On the Peace in 1763" (1763). In Boucher, *View of the Causes and Consequences.*

———. "On the Strife Between Abram and Lot" (1774). In Boucher, *View of the Causes and Consequences.*

———. *Reminiscences of an American Loyalist.* Edited by Jonathan Bouchier [grandson]. Boston: Houghton Mifflin, 1925.

———. "To the Honble The Deputies in Congress from the Southern Provinces." In *Reminiscences of an American Loyalist.* Edited by Jonathan Bouchier [grandson]. Boston: Houghton Mifflin, 1925.

Breen, T. H. *American Insurgents, American Patriots.* New York: Hill & Wang, 2010.

Byrd, James P. *Sacred Scripture, Sacred War.* New York: Oxford University Press, 2013.

Calhoon, Robert M. "Civil, Revolutionary, or Partisan." In *Tory Insurgents: The Loyalist Perception and Other Essays*, edited by Robert M. Calhoon, Timothy M. Barnes, and Robert S. Davis. Columbia: University of South Carolina Press, 2010.

———. *The Loyalists in Revolutionary America 1760–1781.* New York: Harcourt Brace Jovanovich, 1973.

———, and Ruma Chopra. "Religion and the Loyalists." In *Faith and the Founders of the American Republic*, edited by Daniel L. Dreisbach and Mark David Hall. New York: Oxford University Press, 2014.

Chandler, Thomas Bradbury. "A Friendly Address to All Reasonable Americans, on the Subject of our Political Confusions." New-York, 1774.

———. "The American Querist: or, Some Questions Proposed Relative to the Present Disputes between Great Britain and Her American Colonies." Boston: Mills & Hicks, 1774.

———. "What Think Ye of the Congress Now? Or, an Enquiry, How Far the Americans are Bound to Abide by, and Execute the Decisions of, the Late Congress?" New York: James Rivington, 1775.

Chidsey, Donald Barr. *The Loyalists: The Story of Those Americans Who Fought against Independence.* New York: Crown, 1973.

Chopra, Ruma. *Choosing Sides: Loyalists in Revolutionary America.* Lanham, MD: Rowman & Littlefield, 2013.

———. *Unnatural Rebellion: Loyalists in New York City during the Revolution.* Charlottesville: University of Virginia Press, 2011.

Cooper, Myles. "The Patriots of North-America: a Sketch. With Explanatory Notes." New-York, 1775.

Crary, Catherine S., ed. *The Price of Loyalty: Tory Writings from the Revolutionary Era.* New York: McGraw-Hill, 1973.

Curwen, Samuel. *Journal and Letters of the Late Samuel Curwen.* Edited by George Atkinson Ward. New York: C. S. Francis, 1842.

Davidson, Philip. *Propaganda and the American Revolution, 1763–1783.* New York: Norton, 1973.

"Declaration of Dependence" (1781). In Ruma Chopra, *Choosing Sides: Loyalists in Revolutionary America.* Lanham, MD: Rowman & Littlefield, 2013.

Dreisbach, Daniel L. *Reading the Bible with the Founding Fathers.* New York: Oxford University Press, 2017.

Fowler, David J. "Loyalty Is Now Bleeding in New Jersey." In *The Other Loyalists: Ordinary People, Royalism, and the Revolution in the Middle Colonies, 1763–1787*, edited by Joseph S. Tiedemann, Eugene R. Fingerhut, and Robert W. Venables. Albany: State University Press of New York, 2009.

Franklin, Benjamin. *The Complete Works of Benjamin Franklin.* 10 vols. Edited by John Bigelow. New York: G. P. Putnam's Sons, 1887–1888.

Frazer, Gregg L. "The American Revolution: Not a Just War." *Journal of Military Ethics* 14, no. 1 (2015): 39–45.

———. *The Religious Beliefs of America's Founders: Reason, Revelation, and Revolution.* Lawrence: University Press of Kansas, 2012.

Greene, Jack P., ed. *Colonies to Nation, 1763–1789.* New York: Norton, 1975.

Griffin, Patrick. *America's Revolution.* New York: Oxford University Press, 2013.

Gwatkin, Thomas. "A LETTER to the CLERGY of New York and New Jersey, Occasioned by an ADDRESS to the Episcopalians in Virginia." Williamsburg: Alex. Purdie and John Dixon, 1772.

Hoffman, Ronald, and Peter J. Albert, eds. *Religion in a Revolutionary Age.* Charlottesville: University Press of Virginia, 1994.

Hoock, Holger. *Scars of Independence: America's Violent Birth.* New York: Crown, 2017.

Hunt, William. *The History of England from the Accession of George III to the Close of Pitt's First Administration (1760–1801).* London: Longmans, Green, 1905.

Ingersoll, Thomas N. *The Loyalist Problem in Revolutionary New England.* Cambridge: Cambridge University Press, 2016.

Inglis, Charles. "A Sermon on Philip. III. 20, 21." New-York: H. Gaine, 1777.

———. "Letter I to Henry Laurens." In Inglis, *Letters of Papinian.*

———. *Letters of Papinian: In Which the Conduct, Present State and Prospects, of the American Congress, Are Examined.* New York: Hugh Gaine, 1779.

———. "Letter II to Henry Laurens." In Inglis, *Letters of Papinian.*

———. "Letter III to Henry Laurens." In Inglis, *Letters of Papinian.*

———. "Letter IV to John Jay." In Inglis, *Letters of Papinian.*

———. "Letter VI to John Jay." In Inglis, *Letters of Papinian.*

———. "Letter VII to John Jay." In Inglis, *Letters of Papinian.*
———. "Letter VIII to John Jay." In Inglis, *Letters of Papinian.*
———. "Letter IX to the People of North America." In Inglis, *Letters of Papinian.*
———. "The Christian Soldier's Duty Briefly Delineated." New-York: H. Gaines, 1777.
———. "The Duty of Honouring the King, Explained and Recommended." New York: Hugh Gaine, 1780.
———. "The True Interest of America Impartially Stated, in Certain Strictures on a Pamphlet Intitled Common Sense." Philadelphia: James Humphreys Jr., 1776.
Jaffa, Harry V. *A New Birth of Freedom.* Lanham, MD: Rowman & Littlefield, 2000.
Jasanoff, Maya. *Liberty's Exiles: American Loyalists in the Revolutionary World.* New York: Knopf, 2012.
Jones, Thomas. *History of New York During the Revolutionary War.* 2 vols. Edited by Edward Floyd de Lancey. New York: Trow's, 1879.
Leder, Lawrence H. *Liberty and Authority.* Chicago: Quadrangle Books, 1968.
Leonard, Daniel. "Massachusettensis." Boston, 1776.
Letter from "New-York Convention to the President of Congress" (July 11, 1776). In *American Archives: Consisting of a Collection of Authentic Records, State Papers, Debates and Letters and Other Notices of Publick Affairs . . .*, vol. 1, ser. 5. Washington, DC: M. St. Claire Clarke and Peter Force, 1848.
Lydekker, John Wolfe. *The Life and Letters of Charles Inglis.* London: Society for Promoting Christian Knowledge, 1936.
Mayhew, Jonathan. *Observations on the Charter and Conduct of the Society for the Propagation of the Gospel in Foreign Parts.* Boston: Richard and Samuel Draper, 1763.
Micklejohn, George. "On the Important Duty of Subjection to the Civil Powers." Newbern, NC: James Davis, 1768.
Morgan, Edmund S. *The Challenge of the American Revolution.* New York: Norton, 1976.
Nelson, William H. *The American Tory.* Boston: Beacon Press, 1964.
Noll, Mark A. *Christians in the America Revolution.* Grand Rapids, MI: Christian University Press, 1977.
———. *In the Beginning Was the Word.* New York: Oxford University Press, 2016.
Norton, Mary Beth. "Eighteenth-century Women in Peace and War: The Case of the Loyalists," *William and Mary Quarterly* 33 (1976): 398.
Paine, Thomas. "Common Sense." In *Common Sense, the Rights of Man, and Other Essential Writings of Thomas Paine.* Edited by Sidney Hook. New York: New American Library, 1969.
Peters, Samuel. *A General History of Connecticut.* 2nd ed. London: J. Bew, 1782.
Piecuch, Jim. *Three Peoples, One King: Loyalists, Indians, and Slaves in the Revolutionary South, 1775–1782.* Columbia: University of South Carolina Press, 2008.
Potter, Janice. *The Liberty We Seek: Loyalist Ideology in Colonial New York and Massachusetts.* Cambridge, MA: Harvard University Press, 1983.
Potter-MacKinnon, Janice, and Robert M. Calhoon. "The Character and Coherence of the Loyalist Press." In *Tory Insurgents: The Loyalist Perception and Other Essays,*

edited by Robert M. Calhoon, Timothy M. Barnes, and Robert S. Davis. Columbia: University of South Carolina Press, 2010.

Rhoden, Nancy L. *Revolutionary Anglicanism: The Colonial Church of England Clergy during the American Revolution*. Washington Square: New York University Press, 1999.

Rohrer, S. Scott. *Jacob Green's Revolution: Radical Religion and Reform in a Revolutionary Age*. University Park: Pennsylvania State University Press, 2014.

Rossiter, Clinton. *The Political Thought of the American Revolution*. New York: Harcourt, Brace, & World, 1963.

Rush, Benjamin. *The Autobiography of Benjamin Rush*. Edited by George Corner. Princeton, NJ: Princeton University Press for the American Philosophical Society, 1948.

Sabine, Lorenzo. *Biographical Sketches of Loyalists of the American Revolution*. Vol. 1. Boston: Little, Brown, 1864.

———. *Biographical Sketches of Loyalists of the American Revolution*. Vol. 2. Boston: Little, Brown, 1864; reprint, Port Washington, NY: Kennikat Press, 1966.

Savelle, Max. *The Colonial Origins of American Thought*. Princeton, NJ: D. Van Nostrand, 1964.

Sayre, John. "Letter to the Gentlemen of the Committee of the Town of Fairfield." In *New-York Journal* [1776?].

Schlenther, Boyd Stanley. "Religious Faith and Commercial Empire." In *The Oxford History of the British Empire: The Eighteenth Century*. Edited by P. J. Marshall. New York: Oxford University Press, 1996.

Seabury, Samuel. "A Discourse on II Tim. III. 16." New-York: H. Gaine, 1777.

———. "An Alarm to the Legislature of the Province of New-York." New-York: James Rivington, 1775.

———. "A View of the Controversy Between Great-Britain and her Colonies." New-York: James Rivington, 1774.

———. "Discourse on Brotherly Love." New-York: Hugh Gaine, 1777.

———. "Free Thoughts, on the Proceedings of the Continental Congress, Held at Philadelphia Sept. 5, 1774." New York, 1774.

———. "St. Peter's Exhortation To fear GOD and honor the KING, Explained and inculcated." New-York: H. Gaine, 1777.

———. "The Congress Canvassed: or, An Examination into the Conduct of the Delegates, at Their Grand Convention." New York: James Rivington, 1774.

———. "To the General Assembly of the Governor and Company of the Colony of Connecticut, now sitting in New Haven, in said Colony, by special Order of his Honor, the Governor" [December 20, 1775]. In *Life and Correspondence of the Right Reverend Samuel Seabury, D.D.*, edited by E. Edwards Beardsley. Boston: Houghton, Mifflin, 1881.

Shea, George. *The Life and Epoch of Alexander Hamilton: A Historical Study*. Boston: Houghton, Osgood, 1879.

Smith, William. "A Sermon on the Present Situation of American Affairs." Philadelphia: James Humphreys Jr., 1775.

Tiedemann, Joseph S., Eugene R. Fingerhut, and Robert W. Venables, eds. *The Other Loyalists: Ordinary People, Royalism, and the Revolution in the Middle Colonies, 1763–1787*. Albany: State University Press of New York, 2009.

Turner, Charles. "1773 Election Sermon." In *They Preached Liberty*, edited by Franklin P. Cole. Indianapolis, IN: Liberty Press, 1977.

Vance, Clarence Hayden. "Myles Cooper." *Columbia University Quarterly* 22 (1930): 274–276.

Van Tyne, Claude Halstead. *The Loyalists in the American Revolution*. Gloucester, MA: Peter Smith, 1959.

Zimmer, Anne Young, and Alfred H. Kelly. "Jonathan Boucher: Constitutional Conservative." *Journal of American History* 58, no. 4 (1972): 897–922.

Zubly, John Joachim. "An Humble Enquiry." 1769.

———. "Essay Number 1" [July 27, 1780]. In Zubly, *Warm and Zealous Spirit*.

———. "Essay Number 2" [August 3, 1780]. In Zubly, *Warm and Zealous Spirit*.

———. "Essay Number 3" [August 31, 1780]. In Zubly, *Warm and Zealous Spirit*.

———. "Essay Number 4" [September 7, 1780]. In Zubly, *Warm and Zealous Spirit*.

———. "Essay Number 6" [September 28, 1780]. In Zubly, *Warm and Zealous Spirit*.

———. "Essay Number 7" [October 12, 1780]. In Zubly, *Warm and Zealous Spirit*.

———. "'Helvetius' Essays." *Royal Georgia Gazette*, July 27–October 12, 1780. In *A Warm and Zealous Spirit*. Edited by Randall M. Miller. Macon, GA: Mercer University Press, 1982.

———. "The Law of Liberty." Philadelphia, 1775.

———. "The Stamp-Act Repealed." Savannah, GA: James Johnston, 1766.

———. "To the Grand Jury of the County of Chatham, State of Georgia." Savannah, GA: William Lancaster, 1777.

INDEX

Adams, John
    on Bishop Controversy, 23–24
    delegate from Congress to Parliament, 160
    on due process of law, 196
    on support for rebellion, 3
Adams, Samuel, 18, 48
Addison, Joseph, on rebellion, 91, 93
American independence, 190–191, 215–224
American Revolutionary War, 204–212
Andrews, Samuel
    on colonial charters, 99–100
    on dissenting ministers, 138–139
    on gratitude to England, 131
    on hypocrisy of Patriots, 181
    on rebellion, 75–76
    on sins of Americans, 73–76
    on slavery, 74
    on treatment of Loyalists, 75–76
Anglicans. See *Church of England*
associations, continental, 117–122, 126, 165–166, 179–180, 185, 232

Baptists, 6, 19, 28, 191
Bishop Controversy, 19–25, 30, 189, 219
Boston Tea Party, 13, 67, 147, 150, 151
Boucher, Jonathan, 1, 29–30, 31, 57, 78, 94, 104, 122, 227
    on American independence, 216, 218–220
    on American Revolutionary War, 204, 205, 206
    on Bishop Controversy, 22–24
    on causes of the American Revolution, 139–140
    on colonial relationship with Great Britain, 101–104, 128, 130–136, 140, 229–230
    on committees, 118–120
    on conciliation with Great Britain, 67, 153–155, 159
    on consent of the governed, 83–86
    on due process of law, 198
    on equality of man, 82–83
    on errors by Great Britain, 14, 58, 107–108, 140–143
    on First Continental Congress, 108, 110, 162
    on I Peter 2, 54–55
    on hermeneutics, 38–44
    on human nature, 78–79, 90
    on Jesus, 58–60, 70–71
    on John Locke, 43, 63–64, 69, 77, 85–86, 91–92, 94, 96
    on liberty, 44, 55–56, 58
    on need for civil government, 80–82
    on nonimportation/nonexportation/nonconsumption, 172–174
    on Parliament, 101–102, 130
    on persecution of Loyalists, 181–187, 190, 192–193, 196, 198–199
    on preaching, 39–44
    on rebellion, 63–67, 69–71, 77, 86–92, 94, 96–97, 201, 203–204
    on republicanism, 65, 66, 69, 139
    on Romans 13, 48, 77
    on sin, 73
    on support for the American Revolution, 3
    on taxation, 102–103, 136

Boucher, Jonathan, *continued*
    on troublemakers inciting rebellion, 86, 145–146, 148, 159
    on Whig and Tory motivations, 9

Catholicism
    and alliance with France, 212, 214–215, 225, 233
    Bishop Controversy, 21
    cause of American Revolution, 25, 152, 189, 225, 233
    Whig or Tory?, 5–6
Chandler, Thomas Bradbury, 29, 30–31, 172
    on American independence, 190–191, 217, 219–221
    on American Revolutionary War, 205–206, 209
    on Bishop Controversy, 22, 24
    on colonial relationship with Great Britain, 100–101, 103, 128–131
    on committees, 117–118
    on conciliation with Great Britain, 157–158, 161, 163, 169
    on errors by Great Britain, 14, 141
    on First Continental Congress, 113–115, 162–164, 169–170
    influence of, 29, 230
    on John Locke, 137–138
    on nonimportation/nonexportation/nonconsumption, 173–175
    on Parliament, 105–107, 134–138
    on persecution of Loyalists, 187, 193–194, 198
    on propaganda, 151–152
    on rebellion, 62, 88, 93, 95, 201–203
    on Romans 13, 48
    on taxation, 134–138
    on troublemakers inciting rebellion, 150–153
Church of England, 30, 31, 40, 188, 191, 219, 220, 230
    Bishop Controversy, 19–24, 189, 219
    persecution of, 24, 26, 184–185, 191–192
    Whig or Tory?, 5–6, 8, 28–29, 88, 130, 185
Common Sense, 31, 62, 81, 82, 131, 150, 194, 195, 216
Conciliatory Resolution of 1775, 159
Congregationalists, 28–29
    on Bishop Controversy, 19–24
    as oppressors of religious minorities, 191, 219
    Whig or Tory?, 5–6, 16
Cooper, Myles, 24, 31
    on rebellion, 48–49, 51

days of prayer and fasting, 26–27, 73–76, 192, 197

Episcopalians. *See* Church of England

First Continental Congress, 108–117, 122–125, 162–170, 183–185
Franklin, Benjamin
    delegate from Congress to Parliament, 160
    on taxation, 13

George III, 143–144
Glorious Revolution, 11, 12
    and justification for rebellion, 68, 94–96

hermeneutics
    Loyalist, 36, 38–45, 48–49, 56
    Patriot, 36–38, 48–49
hypocrisy of Patriots, 25, 27–28, 74, 159, 168, 180–200, 224, 233

Inglis, Charles, 29, 30, 31
    on alliance with France, 208–209, 212–215
    on American independence, 215–219, 221–224
    on American Revolutionary War, 205–212

on Bishop Controversy, 20, 22, 24
on Catholicism, 214–215
on causes of the American
    Revolution, 139–140
on colonial relationship with Great
    Britain, 102, 128, 130–132, 135,
    139–140, 154–157, 159–160
on committees, 124
on conciliation with Great Britain,
    154
on due process of law, 196
on errors by Great Britain, 140–141
on First Continental Congress, 124,
    162
on I Peter 2, 51–53
on hermeneutics, 39
on human nature, 79–80
on Jesus, 61
on King George, 144
on monarchy, 62–63, 81–82
on need for civil government, 79–80
on Parliament, 104, 128, 130
on persecution of Loyalists, 124,
    181–182, 184–188, 192, 194–195,
    199
on preaching, 20, 39–40
on propaganda, 150
on rebellion, 68–69, 87–89, 91,
    93–95, 228–229
on republicanism, 68, 139, 159, 222
on sin, 73
on troublemakers inciting rebellion,
    86, 148–150

Jews, 5, 6, 55, 59

Lawn Sleeves Controversy. *See* Bishop
    Controversy
Locke, John, 231
    on consent, 85
    Loyalist criticism of, 43, 63–64, 69,
        77, 85–86, 91–92, 94, 96, 137–138
    source of Patriot thought, 2, 12, 43,
        63–64, 69, 234

Machiavelli, Niccolo, 124, 186
Mansfield, Richard
    on persecution of Loyalists, 182
    on Whigs and Tories, 17
Mayhew, Jonathan, 20, 23
    on rebellion, 12, 43, 50
Micklejohn, George
    on example of Jesus, 46–47, 60–61
    on rebellion, 36, 67–68, 135
    on Romans 13, 45–48

nonimportation/nonexportation/
    nonconsumption, 115–116,
    147–148, 172–180, 232

Old Testament, 34, 39, 44–45, 58, 59,
    61–67, 69, 72, 74, 77, 134, 142,
    153–154, 201, 231

Paine, Thomas, 31, 131, 154, 194, 195,
    216
    on monarchy, 62–63, 81–82
    as propagandist, 32, 150
persecution of Loyalists, 25–28, 34, 122,
    124, 180–200, 224
    assault, 25, 27, 166, 181, 184, 186, 192
    death, 25–28, 119, 181, 188, 210, 211
    due process of law denied, 25, 28,
        121, 181, 196–198, 224, 233
    exile/banishment, 26, 28, 33, 53,
        121–122, 181, 185–188, 197, 200,
        210, 211, 224, 227
    freedom of press denied, 28, 34,
        108, 117–118, 122, 162, 181, 183,
        189–190, 192–196, 224, 231, 233
    freedom of religion denied, 28, 34,
        99, 108, 117, 122, 181, 189–192,
        193, 196, 199–200, 224, 231, 233
    freedom of speech denied, 25, 28, 34,
        108, 117–118, 122, 181, 183, 187,
        189–196, 198–200, 224, 231, 233
    imprisonment, 25–28, 32, 119, 122,
        181, 183, 187–188, 197, 200, 224

persecution of Loyalists, *continued*
ostracism, 11, 28
property confiscation, 11, 25, 28, 33, 117, 121, 122, 123, 124, 181, 185, 186, 187, 197, 210, 211, 224
proscription, 28, 119, 184, 186, 202, 224
tarring and feathering, 10, 28, 124, 166, 187, 195, 196
threats, 9, 11, 17, 25, 26, 28, 173, 184, 185, 188, 189, 190, 192, 195, 224
Presbyterians, 5, 6, 8, 28, 29
Bishop Controversy, 19, 20, 22–24
cause of American Revolution, 88, 139, 163
as oppressors of religious minorities, 191, 198, 219
propaganda, 2, 9, 18, 19, 24, 32, 34, 146, 149–152, 203, 232

Quakers, 6, 28, 29, 191

republicanism/republicans, 112, 222, 225
cause of American Revolution, 139, 148–151, 163–164, 219, 221
ideology, 25, 37, 65–66, 68–69, 159
propaganda, 9, 148–151
tyranny of, 168, 190–191, 220, 222, 225
Rush, Benjamin
on types of Whigs and Tories, 10
on Whig and Tory motivations, 8–9

Sayre, John
on continental association, 178–180
persecuted, 180
on sins of Americans, 73
Seabury, Samuel, 29, 31–32, 127
on American independence, 215, 218–220
on American Revolutionary War, 206, 209
on Bishop Controversy, 24
on colonial relationship with Great Britain, 100–101, 103–104, 128–130, 132–133, 135
on committees, 120–122, 124–125, 166–167, 169, 183–185
on conciliation with Great Britain, 154–156, 161
on continental associations, 120–121
on due process of law, 121, 197–198
on First Continental Congress, 108–113, 115–117, 122–123, 125, 162, 164–169, 183–185
on I Peter 2, 51–54
on hermeneutics, 41–43
on human nature, 79
influence of, 230
on Jesus, 61
on King George, 143–144
on need for civil government, 79
on nonimportation/nonexportation/nonconsumption, 173–177
on Parliament, 100–101, 103–105, 129–130
on persecution of Loyalists, 122, 182, 192, 194–195, 197–200
on propaganda, 148
on rebellion, 62, 68, 87, 89, 90, 95, 97, 203, 229
on taxation without representation, 105–106, 166
on troublemakers inciting rebellion, 147–148
Seven Years' War, 14, 131, 205
Sewall, Jonathan, on Whig and Tory motivations, 9–10
slavery/slaves, 4, 29, 56–58, 74, 167–168, 179, 204, 218
Society for the Propagation of the Gospel (SPG), 5, 19, 21, 24, 31, 195
Sons of Liberty, 10, 18, 30, 117–118, 147, 150–151, 194
Stamp Act, 14, 56, 58, 100, 140, 152, 155, 157, 171
Suffolk Resolves, 116, 147, 156, 163, 202–203

taxation, 1, 12–14, 23–24, 25, 26, 47, 60, 99–103, 105–107, 114–115, 118, 125–126, 132–133, 135–138, 140–141, 149, 157–158, 160, 162, 166, 174, 178, 185, 205, 206, 209, 217–219, 222–224, 226
test acts, 27
Tillotson, John, on rebellion, 97
Tories, 17–18, 24, 140, 144, 182, 230, 232
    criticism of British policies, 14–15
    identification, 2–5, 7–11
    ideology, 7–8, 13–16
    Whig treatment of, 124

Washington, George
    friendship with Jonathan Boucher, 29, 30, 181–182
    and persecution of Loyalists, 26, 181–182, 192–193
Whig-Loyalists, 15–16, 140, 201
Whigs, 14–15, 17–18, 28, 66, 103, 191, 195
    identification, 2–11
    ideology, 7–8, 11–13, 58, 91, 106, 111, 182, 199
    Loyalist treatment of, 182

Zubly as, 15, 33, 49, 50, 56–58, 71, 73, 102, 105, 160, 216
Wiswall, John, 27

Zubly, John Joachim, 29, 32–33, 98, 99, 127, 170, 227
    on alliance with France, 212–213
    on American independence, 215–216
    on colonial relationship with Great Britain, 102, 128, 130, 133
    on committees, 121–122
    on conciliation with Great Britain, 160–161
    on due process of law, 121–122, 197
    on errors by Great Britain, 140–141
    on King George, 143
    on liberty, 44, 56–58
    on Parliament, 105
    on persecution of Loyalists, 184, 185, 188, 196–197
    on rebellion, 49–51, 58, 71–72, 88–89, 92–96, 202, 203
    on Romans 13, 49–51
    on sin, 72, 73
    on taxation without representation, 13, 105
    Whig-Loyalist, 15–16, 140

www.ingramcontent.com/pod-product-compliance
Lightning Source LLC
Chambersburg PA
CBHW070756230426
43665CB00017B/2389